CLOSING HELL'S GATES

CLOSING HELL'S GATES

the death of a convict station

HAMISH MAXWELL-STEWART

ALLEN&UNWIN

First published in 2008

Allen & Unwin
83 Alexander Street
Crows Nest NSW 2065
Australia
Phone: (61 2) 8425 0100
Fax: (61 2) 9906 2218
Email: info@allenandunwin.com
Web: www.allenandunwin.com

National Library of Australia
Cataloguing-in-Publication entry:

Maxwell-Stewart, Hamish.
    Closing hell's gates: the death of a convict station.

    ISBN: 978 1 74175 149 9 (pbk.)

    Convicts—Tasmania—Sarah Island—History.
    Prisons—Tasmania—Sarah Island—History.
    Penal colonies—Tasmania—Sarah Island—History.
    Penal colonies—Tasmania—Macquarie Harbour—History.
    Sarah Island (Tas.)—History—1803–1851.
    Macquarie Harbour (Tas.)—History.
    Macquarie Harbour Penal Settlement.

994.66

Cover and internal design by Kirby Stalgis
Index by Russell Brooks
Maps on pages viii and ix by Simon Barnard
Set in 10/13.5 pt Adobe Caslon Pro by Bookhouse, Sydney
Printed in Australia by McPherson's Printing Group

10 9 8 7 6 5 4 3 2 1

For Clare

A ship negotiating the passage through Hell's Gates into Macquarie Harbour, with James Lucas and his crew in the foreground. (Artist unknown)

Contents

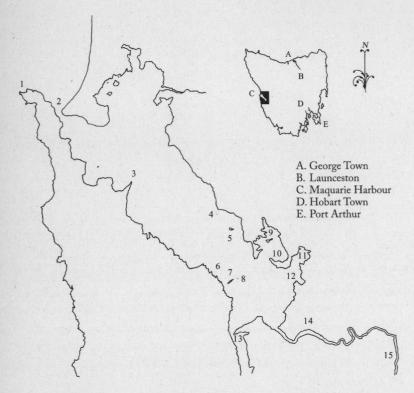

MACQUARIE

c.1822–33

HARBOUR

N

A. George Town
B. Launceston
C. Maquarie Harbour
D. Hobart Town
E. Port Arthur

1. Pilot Station	6. Brickmakers' Bay	11. Kelly's Basin
2. Hell's Gates	7. Settlement Island	12. Charcoal Burners' Bluff
3. Liberty Point	8. Small Island	13. Birch's Inlet
4. Coal Head	9. Soldiers' Island	14. Gordon River
5. Phillip's Island	10. Farm Cove	15. Lime Kiln Reach

SETTLEMENT
c. 1828
ISLAND

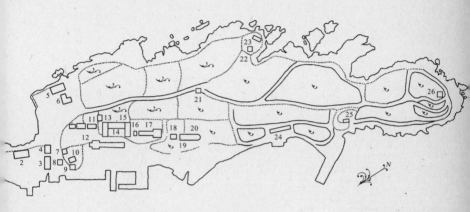

1. Sawpits
2. Shipwright
3. Boat crew hut
4. Blacksmith
5. New penitentiary
6. Old penitentiary
7. Cook house

8. School house
9. Carpenter
10. Shoemaker
11. Warton's and
   Douglas's quarters
12. Commissariat and
   engineer store

13. Bakehouse
14. Tannery
15. Gaol
16. Guard house
17. Barracks
18. Chaplain's house
19. Surgeon's quarters

20. Commandant's quarters
21. Lookout house
22. Mortuary
23. Hospital
24. New Sawpits
25. Gardener's hut
26. Flagstaff

Gardens ~   Plots ~   Fences ·············   Paths ====

Where men are bound both hand and foot
Fast to the fatal wood,
From mangled flesh that's basely cut
Runs streams of British blood.

John Thompson, aged 22,
prisoner, Macquarie Harbour penal station

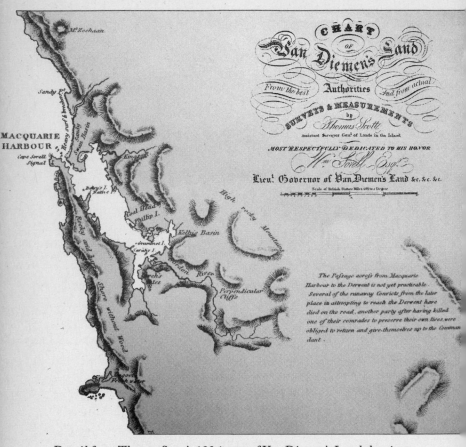

Detail from Thomas Scott's 1824 map of Van Diemen's Land showing the uncharted wilderness that surrounded Macquarie Harbour.

1

'Pluto's land'

At the farthest corner of an island, at the very end of the world, lies a windswept shore that was once home to some of history's most isolated outcasts. Cut off by mountain ranges it served as a place of exile within a land of exile, a prison within a prison. Some of those who were sent there talked as though they had slipped below the crust of the earth to dwell in some terrible netherworld. They called this place 'Pluto's land', after the kingdom of the Roman god who ruled over the dead. Others knew the area as Macquarie Harbour, a vast body of water that interrupted the western coast of Van Diemen's Land. Although it may not technically have been an underworld, it was universally regarded as a sink—the rubbish pit of the British Empire.

From 1787 onwards the British transported convicted prisoners to Australia. They were sent first to New South Wales, but after the discovery that Van Diemen's Land was separated from the mainland by Bass Strait, increasing numbers of convicts were despatched there too. Although the first detachments were sent to secure the territory as a British possession, they later became the labour force that powered the process of colonisation. Between 1803 and 1853 around 73,500 were landed in Van Diemen's Land. They cleared timber, built houses, bridges, roads and wharves, and prepared the way for wider settlement. The work to which they were put ensured that their new environs would be far from gaol-like. Most of the convicts were not locked up at night and during the day almost all of them were set to work unencumbered by leg irons or other physical restraints. Those who encountered official wrath, however, could be transported for a second time. They were shipped to one of several penal stations of which Macquarie Harbour was perhaps the most notorious.

According to the nineteenth-century historian, John West, this far-flung region was a place 'sacred to the genius of torture', separated from the rest of the world by 'impenetrable forests, skirted with an impervious thicket'. It was the lowest reach of the British penal system, a forlorn outpost where 'every object wore the air of rigour, ferocity and sadness'. Writing nearly two decades after the Macquarie Harbour penal station had been abandoned, it was for West a place 'associated exclusively with remembrance of inexpressible depravity, degradation and woe', a nightmarish world where 'man lost the aspect, and the heart of man!'

Given the difficulties of getting to Macquarie Harbour it is incredible that any convicts were shipped there. It was a remote spot, beyond the pale of colonial society. A bleak anchorage located at the back of a wind-blasted, rain-soaked shore. But between January 1822 and December 1833 some 1136 male and sixteen female prisoners were battened down below decks and shipped to this isolated station. In August 1828, at the height of the settlement, 386 prisoners were secured there on two small islands surrounded by an expanse of water, which in turn was ringed by mountain ranges. The convicts themselves immortalised the terror of the place in 'The Cyprus Brig', a ballad considered to be so subversive that it was said to have been suppressed:

> *When we landed in this colony to different masters went,*
> *For little trifling offences boys to Hobart Town gaol were sent,*
> *Now the second sentence we received and ordered for to be,*
> *Sent to Macquarie Harbour, that place of tyranny.*

Despite its size, Macquarie Harbour had at first escaped European attention. Flinders sailed clean past the narrow entrance in 1798. Driven by high winds, he had left a warning of the dangers of that gale-ravaged coast for the benefit of future mariners. In his journal he wrote it is 'as dreary and as inhospitable a shore as has yet been discovered; and the great swell sufficiently announces, that the consequence of coming near it...with a south westerly gale and a dull sailing vessel would be to be wrecked upon it'.

James Kelly encountered better weather during his circumnavigation of Van Diemen's Land in a five-oared whaleboat. After feasting on wild swan, turned into a three-decker 'sea pie', he pulled into the heads on 28 December 1815 and spent the next three days exploring the huge expanse of water. On his return to Hobart Town, Kelly provided the merchant T. W. Birch with some samples of timber. Birch, who had sponsored the expedition, was more than pleased with what he saw.

In order to understand why Macquarie Harbour was established as a penal station it is necessary to see the world through pre-industrial eyes. The settlement was the product of an age obsessed with timber. Late-eighteenth and early-nineteenth century Britons admired landscapes of trees because it was from their trunks and boughs that ships were wrought. Oak trees possessed of great curved limbs, or compass timber, from which the frames and knees of vessels could be fashioned, were described as the sinews of the nation. People drank toasts to them in creamware mugs emblazoned with patriotic verses like: 'May England's oak produce the bark to tan the hide of Bonaparte'. A single 74-gun ship could consume over 3000 mature trees, and so nurturing the nation's stock of timber was serious business. It is said that Admiral Collingwood carried a pocket full of acorns while on shore leave, which he would liberally distribute through the estates of his hosts. The ships that made colonisation possible—those that carried commodities like sugar, calico, tea and convicts—were made from oak.

It was thus inevitable that when Europeans surveyed Australian shores they searched for oak substitutes. In 1804, the crew of the whaler *Alexander* found pine logs stranded on bars at the mouth of the Huon River. Although it was clear that they had been in the water for many years, they showed little signs of rot. For men with nautical eyes it must have been an electric discovery. As the surveyor general John Oxley wrote: 'This wood is of a fine white yellow, close grained, extremely light, and of a strong aromatic smell, and, when bit, conveys a hot pungent taste not unlike cloves. This hot quality of the wood preserves it free from worms and all other insects.' As Kelly reported to Birch, the banks of the rivers and streams that flowed into Macquarie Harbour were full of Huon pine; it was not long before plans for future expeditions were put in place. In June 1816 the brig *Sophia* returned with the first commercially cut cargo of the stuff, which was soon selling in Hobart Town for the exorbitant price of sixpence a foot. The captain of the *Sophia* also reported that he had seen an immense stratum of coal exposed to a level of six feet at the base of a head on the northern shore of Macquarie Harbour.

Clearly Macquarie Harbour had advantages in natural resources. But its remoteness gave it an additional appeal—it was a perfect location to send dangerous recidivists. As early as 1818, Governor Macquarie had drawn up plans to turn the harbour that Kelly had named in his honour into a penal station, a place where absconders, thieves, forgers and other undesirables could be exiled to work cutting timber and mining coal until they had atoned for their crimes and indiscretions. As Macquarie confidently proclaimed, 'escape from thence would be next to impossible'. He concluded that, as a place where the 'worst description of convicts' could be safely banished to labour for the public good, 'I am inclined to think it would answer remarkably well'. Still, it was not until a further three years had elapsed that the plan was put into action. The difficulties of navigating the bar at the mouth of the harbour caused significant delays.

He instructed Lieutenant Governor William Sorell to construct a vessel of 60 to 70 tons, small enough to cross the bar at the mouth of the harbour, but of sufficient size to run supplies to a future settlement. In view of these plans, all other schemes to open up Macquarie Harbour to commercial exploitation were put on hold. When a pair of surveyors applied for permission to construct a water-powered timber mill there the application was turned down. Instead, one of them was hired to undertake a survey of Macquarie Harbour to assess its suitability as a place of punishment. Two further surveys were commissioned before the plan was finally sanctioned.

On 12 December 1821 the *Sophia* and the colonial brig *Prince Leopold* departed from the Derwent. On board was the Hobart Town harbour master, James Kelly—the man who had first navigated a whaleboat through the heads at Macquarie

Harbour—and the deputy surveyor, G. W. Evans. It was their task to advise on navigation, to place marker buoys and to locate the best sources of timber and coal.

The settlement was to be commanded by Lieutenant John Cuthbertson of the 48th Regiment, a Peninsular War veteran who would also serve as magistrate. The immediate health of the small party was placed in the hands of Assistant Colonial Surgeon James Spence, a graduate of Edinburgh University, while James Lucas who had been born on Norfolk Island was appointed as pilot. The remainder of the military detachment consisted of Sergeant Waddy, an ardent Methodist who was placed in charge of the stores, and sixteen rank and file of the 48th Regiment.

The task of constructing and maintaining the new settlement would fall on 23 public works prisoners who had volunteered for the job on the promise that they would receive suitable indulgences for their services. The brute work of cutting timber and coal, hauling stone and collecting shells for lime would fall to the first contingent of secondarily transported convicts. Described as bad and incorrigible characters, there were 52 of them in all, 44 men and eight women.

On 30 December 1821 the *Sophia* arrived at the roadstead outside of the heads. The bulk of her stores were unloaded so she could slide safely over the bar unencumbered. Four days later she arrived at a little island fifteen miles inside the bar—the place that Evans had selected as the most suitable site for the future settlement. While it had been officially named Sarah Island after the wife of T. W. Birch, the financier of Kelly's first expedition to the harbour, for the life of the station it was generally known as Settlement or Headquarters Island.

Cuthbertson reported that in a few days all the stores were safely landed, notwithstanding the 'tempestuous and rainy weather'. Those who hoped that the bad weather was a phenomenon that would soon pass were to be severely disappointed—tempestuous and rainy conditions proved to be characteristic of this part of the coast.

Cuthbertson's immediate concern, however, was the fate of the *Prince Leopold*. The two vessels had parted company on 17 December and she had not been sighted since. In fact the *Prince Leopold* had overshot the harbour mouth and, rather than turn back in the bad weather, she ran for the northern settlement at George Town on the Tamar River. During the course of the voyage a seaman named Richard Rose was killed when he slipped from the foretop sailyard and fell on the anchor stock. The vessel, too, felt the full impact of the weather—her main boom was carried clean away, the mainsail split in two and the bulwark and one of her boats were stoved in by the force of the sea. It was an eventful first passage and the battered vessel did not arrive at Macquarie Harbour until 17 February 1822. There were to be many such voyages in the years to come.

In the meantime, Evans busied himself surveying the surrounding country. He reported that the hills were 'closely covered with heavy timber, and almost impenetrable vines and brush-wood'. In words that would have pleased Lieutenant Governor Sorell and Governor Macquarie, he described how 'the persons sent thither can have no communication with the eastern side of the island, for so completely shut in is this part by the surrounding rugged, closely wooded, and altogether impracticable country, that escape by land is next to impossible'. It was an observation that was about to be sorely tested.

Convict gang boats returning across Macquarie Harbour with a raft of pine logs in tow. On the left is Small Island, with the notoriously draughty barracks over which the surf often broke with 'great violence'. (Thomas Lempriere)

2

Voyage through the gates of hell

The voyage to Macquarie Harbour was an oceanic rite of passage. To be transported for a second time was to be slipped once more over the horizon. All but one of Australia's penal stations were constructed on coasts (the exception was Wellington Valley in New South Wales). This time, however, the journey would take the convict beyond the boundary of society. The most senior member of the colonial administration ever to visit Macquarie Harbour during the life of the settlement was the colonial surveyor. No lieutenant governor ever saw its shores, nor did the colonial surgeon, or superintendent of convicts, or any architect.

It was, for the vast bulk of 'respectable' society, a place of mystery. Indeed, such was the extent to which it was terra incognita that elaborate drawings of the settlement had to be prepared for trials held in Hobart Town. They were necessary in order to inform the court of the geography of a landscape that its judge and jury would never see for themselves. As each secondarily convicted man and woman passed through the small hatchway in the deck they descended into a shadowy realm.

As the experience of the *Prince Leopold* had shown, a voyage to Macquarie Harbour was not a matter to be taken lightly. Average sailing time for a colonial vessel departing from Hobart Town was 27 days—nearly a month at sea to make a trip of less than 200 miles. By contrast, the return passage, in which the vessel had the weather in its favour, took on average just four days. Vessels sailing to Macquarie Harbour frequently had to shelter from bad weather in a series of bays and inlets before beating up the west coast with its dangerous lee shore.

The government brig *Cyprus* made many eventful trips to this remote posting. She may have been a pretty looking ship with a carved bust of a Highlander for a figurehead, imitation cabin windows and a yellow streak of paint on each side, but prettiness was no insurance against bad weather. She was ill-maintained as well and twice caught fire on the passage to Macquarie Harbour, a consequence of her cooking apparatus being 'broke and wore out'. The constant troubles with the galley stove meant that those on board were sometimes 'obliged to go without victuals daily'.

In November 1826 the *Cyprus* encountered such severe winds at the mouth of the Derwent after leaving Hobart Town that the master, Mr Kinghorn, decided to take her round by the east coast. She finally reached her destination after 53 days at sea, having lost an anchor at Kent's Bay off Cape Barren Island. Even inside the bar at Macquarie Harbour she was not safe. In a thunderstorm the brig was hit by lightning which 'shivered the top mast to pieces'. During another trip in July 1829, the *Cyprus* hit a heavy gale in Recherche Bay and once more lost her anchors and cables on a shoal as well as damaging her windlass. On this occasion she was forced to return to Hobart Town to be refitted.

Other supply vessels were often delayed by bad weather and there were constant concerns that overdue ships had been wrecked. As many testified, the experience of sailing to this remote penal outpost could be truly terrifying.

For the convicts, battened down in the dark with nothing to sit on but heaving ballast and covered in spew and bilge water, the experience must have transcended terror. Their voyage to Macquarie Harbour started when they were removed from the gaol in Hobart Town and marched to the wharf in irons. Their legs encumbered by iron basils closed tight with rivets, each prisoner's step was restrained by the two feet of chain that linked the fetters on their legs. The only way to move was to lift the links off the ground—a task commonly achieved by attaching a scrap of rope or cord to the central ring of the chain. As the line of prisoners progressed the sound of their irons clanking in unison rang through the streets. It was a common refrain in Hobart Town—a cacophony that heralded the approach of the damned.

Once loaded onto a colonial transport, they were mustered on deck in two ranks and inspected, usually by a non-commissioned officer of the detachment that would guard them during the voyage. It was his duty to check that 'they were as clean as circumstances would permit' and that their irons were in order. Each prisoner was paraded in front of the senior official on board while their names were called and then one by one they were fed through a hatchway into the ship's prison. While this ritual took place the military detachment stood by with bayonets fixed. The routine was designed as much for psychological effect as for reasons of security.

The space that the prisoner descended into was a small section of the brig divided by bulwarks from the rest of the hold and the forecastle where the military detachment were quartered. The convicts were kept in irons for the whole of the voyage. The space in which they were confined was not high enough for them to stand upright, but they could stretch out on the deck of the hold, if there was one, huddled in the one blanket doled out to every prisoner. It would be small comfort on that terrible passage.

As each brig and schooner ploughed into the trough of a wave before riding up and rolling off the crest of the next, the prisoners in the hold rolled with the vessel in their pitch-dark hell. In rough weather they were slammed from side-to-side amid the stench of vomit and the contents of the 'nuisance tub'. On some vessels the hold was not decked and the prisoners were forced to lie on ballast. In many cases they were half naked, having traded their clothes for tobacco and other small luxuries in Hobart Town gaol.

Sometimes the space in which they lay was further cramped by stores that were placed in the ship's prison since no room could be found for them elsewhere. A supply of 98 sheets of tin tied up in bale wrapping was conveyed to the settlement like this in the *Cyprus*. During the voyage the prisoners urinated on it and it became so thoroughly soaked that the sheets rusted and over half had to be condemned. In May 1823, six prisoners were charged with stealing vinegar from the stores on board the *Waterloo*—their desperate attempt to wipe out the memory of the passage by getting drunk. Five of them were given 25 lashes.

The *Waterloo* appears to have been particularly prone to on-board thefts. In October 1826, William Murray and Charles Newman, two absconders from Maria Island, were sentenced to be flogged for pilfering trousers from a bale of clothing which had been part of the cargo, probably as they lacked suitable clothes of their own. Two days later, Murray was sentenced to a further 60 lashes and to serve in chains in the gaol gang for stealing pork—presumably from a cask that they had broken open. Three other prisoners were sentenced to 48 lashes and hard labour for the same offence.

When conditions permitted the convicts were allowed up on deck to jangle their irons in the space before the windlass as they breathed in fresh air under the watch of the detachment. During the entire passage a soldier stood constant guard over the prison hatchway. In calmer weather two further sentries were placed on deck, 'the one on one side returning with his face toward the prison, at the time the other was going in the opposite direction'.

Perhaps it was fitting that the last leg of that terrible voyage would take the convict through the gates of hell itself. The west coast of Van Diemen's Land had one of the worst lee shores in the world with a prevailing wind that bore down (frequently with a savage intensity) on a jagged shoreline. The waves that slammed into that coast had started their journey more than halfway round the globe off the shores of South America. Unobstructed over such a vast oceanic distance the swell could build to frightening proportions.

The heads of Macquarie Harbour were both narrow and, at one and a half fathoms, or nine feet, dangerously shallow. The channel could only be negotiated at high tide for at other times a current of six or seven knots rushed through. A pilot was needed to steer each vessel into the relative safety of the harbour.

The first glimpse of Macquarie Harbour penal station was of the pilot's house and the cluster of buildings where his boat crew and a small military detachment were quartered. Along the shore, pigs roamed between the bleached bones of slaughtered whales. At the back of the weatherboard houses beds for growing potatoes stretched up the slope of the hill. Fertilised with rotting kelp, they must have given the place an Atlantic look, as though it really belonged on the shores of Donegal or the edge of some Hebridean island.

The heads at Macquarie Harbour were originally named Hell's Gates, not because they marked the entrance to the penal hell beyond, but because they were a navigational hazard of infernal dimensions. It was the pilot's job to thread each colonial vessel across the shallow bar and through the narrow channel scoured by surging tidal currents. If the weather was rough the supply vessels had to wait outside of the bar for calmer conditions, attached to a mooring. Two anchors of between 1500 and 2000 pounds in weight had been commissioned for the purpose in the King's Yard in Sydney. They were attached to fifteen fathoms of strong chain that in turn were linked to a bridle ring. A further twelve fathoms of good fourteen inch 'European' cable was required to secure the ring to a buoy. Without this mooring there could be no hope of maintaining the penal station. It permitted a vessel to ride out the worst that the southern ocean could throw at it. When the weather subsided and the tide was right the pilot was conveyed out to the waiting ship.

For much of the life of the settlement, the pilot was a man named James Lucas, who had been born on Norfolk Island in 1792. The son of Lieutenant James Hunt Lucas of the New South Wales Corps and the convict Sarah Greggs, he had already served in the Royal Navy—first in the *Buffalo* and then for two years as second and chief officer on the brig *Kangaroo* and for four years in His Majesty's brig *Elk*. As he later wrote, the hardships of shipboard life had made him 'familiar' with the dangers of the job, and dangers there certainly were. As Lucas himself wrote to the colonial secretary, 'I am at all times exposed to numerous accidents and on many occasions I have narrowly escaped with my life'. He suffered a particularly serious injury in May 1828 when he was sucked under a boat in heavy seas, while unsuccessfully attempting to rescue a sailor who had been knocked overboard while lowering the topgallant yard in a gale. Four years earlier he had been lucky to survive when the pilot's boat was upset at the heads, an accident in which four of his boat crew had drowned. Such were the perils of life on a coast where the sea on a calm day had a swell as great as that on the east coast of Van Diemen's Land in a gale.

The men who manned the whaleboat that brought Lucas out to the waiting brig—and shared with him the daily dangers—were all secondarily transported convicts. Many were sailors with experience that spanned the breadth of the Atlantic. Thomas Day, for example, had been born a slave in Spanish Town, Jamaica, but had contrived to forge a certificate of freedom and escape to sea. Others who were colonially born had been brought up with boats, since the areas first colonised by Europeans were invariably close to estuaries, and water remained for long the principal means of communication. As he too was a 'native', Lucas had taken it upon himself to watch over the handful of 'currency lads', as the native born were commonly termed, and many of the colonial youth who found their way to Macquarie Harbour ended up in his boat.

John Popjoy, a transported seaman from London who served as Lucas's coxswain, placed his faith in a more divine protector. He was tattooed on his upper right arm with the talismanic verse:

Rocks, hills and sands,
and barren lands,
kind fortune set me free,
from roaring guns and women's tongues,
O Lord deliver me.

For additional insurance he had caused the words: 'From rocks and shoals and every hill, may God protect the sailor still' to be added below the elbow. Surmounting these was a picture of a sailor, a woman, an anchor and a crucifix, the last two being the signs of hope and salvation. As a device it failed to protect him. He was drowned in December 1833 when the ship he was on was blown onto a sandbank near Boulogne in the English Channel.

According to the Quaker missionaries Backhouse and Walker, who visited the Australian colonies in the early 1830s, the prisoners who passed through the heads into Macquarie Harbour despaired of salvation or hope. They reported that convicts 'recklessly' asserted that Hell's Gates was so named as 'all who entered in hither, were doomed to eternal perdition'. It was perhaps an inevitable presumption—nomenclature informed the traveller, both bond and free, that to pass through the entrance to Macquarie Harbour was to enter an earthly hell, an allusion reinforced by the topography of the place.

The colonial historian, John West, borrowed the 'awful colouring of Milton's *Paradise Lost*' to describe the region:

Rocks, caves, lakes, fens, bogs, dens, and shades of death,
Where all life dies, death lives, and nature breeds
Perverse all monstrous, all prodigious things.
Abominable, UNUTTERABLE!

The landscape that enclosed Macquarie Harbour defied the surveyor. Protected by folded mountain ranges, fast flowing rivers, high rainfall and large areas of temperate rainforest, it was difficult to map and thus knowledge about it could not be captured in black and white. The chart drawn up by Thomas Scott, the assistant surveyor general, and engraved in Edinburgh in 1824, depicts Macquarie Harbour as a body of water surrounded by a void. In places around the edges of the harbour there are occasional annotations: 'Rocky and barren shore without wood', 'Perpendicular cliffs', 'High rocky mountains'—words that confirm that, as far as colonial men of power were concerned, the land was a wilderness.

Naming is one of the great symbolic acts of the colonist. Through naming, landscapes are converted into the cultural and literal property of the coloniser. Survey maps were powerful as they could capture a place on paper and remove it to a 'centre of calculation' where ownership could be legally confirmed. The country that surrounded Macquarie Harbour resisted this process. The boundaries of the penal station were restricted to the waterways that could be charted by vessels and a number of islands and other areas that had been cleared of timber by convict labour.

The limits of the settlement can be traced in the names imposed on the landscape. On the south side of Macquarie Harbour a series of small streams bear the names of Lucas the pilot, Schofield the Wesleyan catechist and the commandants Butler, Baylee, Briggs and Cuthbertson. On the other side of the mouth of the Gordon River there is a bay named after Commandant Wright and, flowing into the lower reaches of the river itself, are tributaries named after the assistant colonial surgeons Barnes and Spence. Further up beyond Limestone Reach there is another rivulet named after Kinghorn, master of the brigs *Cypress* and *Waterloo*, and a little after that an island which sits midstream in the river that bears the name of Commandant Butler. The furthest extremity of the penal station is marked by a waterfall named after the commissariat officer Thomas Lempriere. Beyond this point the Gordon River ceases to be navigable with ease and, cartographically speaking, the country faded into the great blanks of Scott's map.

This does not mean that it was country unknown to all. When James Kelly had 'discovered' Macquarie Harbour the country on the south side of the heads had been ablaze and he had heard 'a large number of natives shouting and making a great noise, as if they were hunting kangaroo'. So worried had he and his party been about the possibility of attack from the Mimegin people who inhabited the area that they had camped out on an island. If there was an Aboriginal presence in the northern reaches of the harbour then Europeans failed to report it.

It is possible that the Mimegin rarely journeyed into the country on the north side, although they certainly possessed the means to do so. They regularly crossed the neck of Macquarie Harbour on catamarans, as did the peoples further north who moved on annual migrations as far south as Port Davey. It seems likely that the Mimegin visited Birch's Inlet in winter to collect eggs. The first Europeans to penetrate into the harbour reported vast flocks of swans there. The country from Birch's River to the coast was less thickly timbered and may have been cleared with firesticks to create hunting grounds similar to those that Kelly observed near the heads.

Most of the year, however, the Mimegin lived close to the coast where crustaceans and shellfish were abundant. The surface waters of Macquarie Harbour have a low salt content and few marine shellfish are to be found along its shores. There is a species of mussel that infests the rocks in some areas, but it is too small to be of any practical use as a food source. Any convict contemplating absconding would encounter the same problem. Compared to the ocean coasts, the shores of Macquarie Harbour presented lean pickings—they were a natural culinary wilderness.

In biblical terms, the counterpoint of Eden is the 'wilderness', a place to which those who had encountered God's displeasure were banished. Macquarie Harbour must have felt like such a place, especially when the convicts who had been exiled to that wilderness were sometimes literally called upon to haul themselves into their own place of penal servitude. When the winds failed, colonial vessels were 'warped' or 'kedged' through the heads, a process that involved loading an anchor into a boat and rowing it some distance ahead of the vessel where it was dumped overboard. The prisoners were then ordered to man the capstan, winding the anchor cable so that the brig was slowly winched until it came to rest over the anchorage point and the whole process could be started again.

On such calm days the waters of Macquarie Harbour could appear to be made of glass. Stained by tannins leeched out of button grass, the harbour was the colour of tea and in still conditions its surface perfectly reflected the trees, hills and mountains that bounded its edges. As a body of water it was vast—twice as big as Sydney Harbour, or Port Jackson as it was then known.

The first view that the brig had of the two small islands that lay at the heart of the settlement came when it rounded Liberty Point. In this there was an irony. Like Hell's Gates, Liberty Point originally got its name for reasons that had nothing to do with the penal station. James Kelly, the first person to attempt to chart Macquarie Harbour, had brought with him some black swans that he had captured further south at Port Davey. Seeing that there were plenty of swans in the harbour, he set four of the birds he had previously taken captive free, naming the adjacent headland in honour of the occasion. Once the penal station had been established, the name of this point of land took on a new meaning. It marked the route to freedom, the first landmark that each colonial vessel passed on its return passage to Hobart Town.

The main settlement at Macquarie Harbour was located on Sarah Island. To the north was a much smaller outcrop of rock which Kelly had named Grummet, probably after the ring used to fasten the edge of a sail to its stay. The name was inspired by the prominent cave that interrupted the eastern face of the island. The allusion, however, may have masked a more earthy pun. Grummet was also nineteenth-century slang for female genitalia. During the era of the penal station, however, both of these names were rarely used. Sarah Island, as mentioned previously, was instead referred to as Headquarters or Settlement Island—names which were useful in that they underscored the extent of the penal establishment which stretched from the pilot station beyond the heads, to various outstations on the shores of the harbour and the lime burners' and timber cutters' camps far up the Gordon River. For its part, Grummet was more commonly known as Small Island, a name that graphically conveyed the extent to which it was dwarfed by the vast expanse of water surrounding it.

From afar, Settlement Island presented quite a spectacle. The timber on the slopes had been cleared shortly after the station had been founded to make way for vegetable gardens. This had exposed the island to the full force of the winds that whipped down the length of the harbour. Cuthbertson had ordered fences to be erected to break the passage of the gales but, as Lieutenant Wright his successor complained, these were blown down 'almost daily'. Over the next five years an ever more elaborate network of defences was constructed, which included a 26-foot-high, two-foot-thick barrier at the back of the shipyard. This wooden palisade was buttressed by substantial logs that jutted out into the land and sea like a malevolent crown of thorns. From a distance, the effect must have been daunting. When first glimpsed from Liberty Point, nine miles up the harbour, the settlement presented 'the appearance of a walled castle, the Small Island looking like a detached fort'. At points the effect was accentuated by fake crenellations and the turret-like protuberance of the new penitentiary.

But even before these structures were added, the island must have looked like a windswept fortress guarding the upper reaches of the harbour. The analogy is appropriate since these wooden walls did not just battle the wind, they extended inward criss-crossing the settlement and enclosing the entire island. They cut off the area in which the officers resided from the bakehouse and tannery. They separated the stores and boat pond from the penitentiary where the prisoners slept, and their stout stockading ringed the lumberyard and gaol. They stamped the mark of property and power over the surface of the island in a manner that would have been impressive if it had not been so compre-hensively overshadowed by the scale of the wild untrammelled commons that surrounded this small fortified penal outpost.

When a brig finally arrived after its long passage the retransported were disembarked at Settlement Island where the irons were struck off their feet. Suddenly unencumbered, and without the rolling motion of the sea beneath them, it must have appeared as if they were drunk. When there was spare slop clothing in the store ('slops' being the term used to describe what passed for a government uniform) new articles were issued and the prisoners' old clothes burnt, infused as they were with the stench of the floating prison to which they had been confined.

According to official returns, each prisoner was entitled to two issues of clothing a year. In summer they were kitted out in a frock (a loose overall with sleeves such as those worn by farm workers) and trousers made of duck, a stiff and durable form of canvas, and a cotton shirt and a pair of shoes. While they were allowed four pairs of shoes a year, their clothing had to last until winter, when they were supplied with a jacket and trousers made of wool and a fresh shirt. This would have meant that each man had no spare set of clothes. The records do not specify the articles of clothing issued to the female convicts at Macquarie Harbour, but these probably differed little from those issued elsewhere in the colony: a jacket, skirt, shifts and a calico cap were standard, although some prisoners also received an apron and handkerchiefs to wear round their necks.

As early as February 1823 the settlement surgeon had reported that a supply of good 'necessaries' would ward off dysentery and rheumatism. He recommended that upon arrival every prisoner should be allocated his winter and summer allowance, which would have provided each man with two sets of clothing. In addition, he argued for the provision of a neckcloth, a cap to ward off the rain and a blanket and palliasse, a form of thin straw-filled mattress. Spare clothes may have been issued as a reward to some prisoners, but as others were forced to sleep in wet gear it is apparent that this was never applied as a general rule.

The slops issued to the prisoners were of different colours. Some were yellow, others grey, brown and blue. It was usual for trousers and jackets of different colours to be supplied to the same man—the choice being dependent on what was in the store at the time. At other stations it was common practice to mark each article of clothing with the insignia of the station to which the convict had been consigned. Thus prisoners stationed in the prison barracks in Hobart Town could be distinguished by the prominent P.B. stencilled in paint on the knees of their trousers and the backs of their jackets. At Macquarie Harbour there was no need to take such measures. It was obvious which station each prisoner belonged to, the nearest other being the government timber felling and sawing establishment at Birch's Bay in the D'Entrecasteaux Channel south of Hobart Town. Items of clothing were marked, however, with the initials B.O. (which stood for Board of Ordnance) and a broad arrow to distinguish them as government property. Other than that their slops were anything but uniform.

Once equipped, new prisoners were ranked up and given a long lecture by the commandant during which the settlement rules, and the consequences of breaking them, were spelled out. After this they were shipped across the short expanse of water to the Small Island where all new arrivals, excepting those who were aged or infirm or had arrived with special recommendations, were housed for a probationary period.

This barren skerry was by all accounts a cramped and miserable place. It had originally been the site of the settlement hospital—it was widely held in the early nineteenth century that stagnant air was the source of much ill health and that it was important to house the sick in places exposed to purifying draughts. Since the hospital was largely staffed by female prisoners, they too had originally been barracked on Small Island. Exposed to the elements and difficult to access, the hospital was soon moved to a new site behind the windbreak fence on the western side of Settlement Island.

The old rudimentary building constructed of green timber in which the sick had originally been housed was converted into a penitentiary. Accessed by a steep roadway that curved up the southern side of the rock, it contained four rooms. The furthest two, surrounded on three sides by steep cliffs, were dormitories where the men were locked up at night. Adjoining these, and guarding the approach, were the constables' quarters and a kitchen staffed by two cooks. Each room was equipped with a fireplace and a small window that looked out on the leeward side of the island. To place openings in the other wall would have been totally impractical as it would have let in the very worst of the weather. As things were, the barracks was notoriously draughty and during storms, 'the surf often broke over it with great violence'. Newly arrived convicts shared their quarters with a number of old hands who had been placed in leg irons and barracked on Small Island as punishment. As a result the rooms of the Small Island penitentiary were often so crowded that the men could not sleep on their backs, but had to huddle together side on to each other.

Many of the prisoners in chains at Macquarie Harbour were double-ironed—two sets of three-pound leg irons were riveted to their ankles. These could not be removed without striking the rivet head off. For this reason prisoners were issued with trousers that buttoned up and down the sides—since this was the only way that they could undress. The prisoners in the chain gang slept, ate and worked in irons for the period that they had been sentenced to wear them. Thus encumbered they were imprisoned by simple physics as escape by swimming was impossible. It was as effective a system of incarceration as could have been devised within the limitations of the available technology.

There was no water on the island, apart from that which could be collected in rain barrels or butts, and this supply had to be augmented with water brought over from the mainland in casks. Firewood also had to be supplied on a daily basis—although this, like the timbers used to construct the barracks, was selected from wood that would not float in order to thwart the machinations of would-be raft-makers. After a failed attempt in early 1827 to construct a raft from two water butts and a night tub, these too were removed. A large water cask was instead cemented with masonry into the rock in such a fashion that any attempt to remove it would result in it falling to pieces. The night vessels were replaced with iron tar barrels that had been cut in half.

The cookhouse was staffed by a man named James Cock. He had served in the armed forces and for his pains had lost his right leg below the knee. It was commonplace for cooks on board ships to be 'dismasted' men, since there were few other jobs that they could perform; thus it was that deformity proved a blessing for Cock. He had nearly swung from the Hobart Town gallows after he had been sentenced to death in the supreme court for forging a promissory note and 'uttering and publishing' it as true. Transported to Macquarie Harbour instead, he had been placed in the cookhouse since he was unfit for heavier duties.

For a long time, Cock's assistant was Felix Patehouse. Originally born in Malta, Patehouse had been sentenced to life transportation by a Court Martial in Messina in 1818 for desertion. Once in Australia he had kept on running and, like so many other absconders, got caught and ended up being sent to Macquarie Harbour.

Each morning before they proceeded to their daily labours, the prisoners on Small Island were served a breakfast of about a pint and a half of 'skilly'. The settlement commissariat officer described this as 'a kind of hasty pudding composed of flour, water and salt'. Patehouse was twice punished for concealing oatmeal on Small Island—he once tried to stash 15 quarts or 30 pints of the stuff—and it seems that oatmeal was substituted for flour on at least some occasions. Described by Commandant Wright as a great rascal, the Maltese cook dished this hot, but otherwise unappetising slop out to each mess with wrists tattooed with bracelets and arms bedecked with angels and crucifixes.

After breakfast had been served, Cock and Patehouse lit a signal fire. This was the sign for the gang boat to come over and ferry the men to the main settlement for morning muster. From among the ganged convicts one was selected on rotation to stay and act as 'delegate'. This was considered to be a great privilege and was counted as a day of rest. The role of the delegate was to help collect the rations delivered from the commissariat store, to transport the wood and water delivered by boat up the steep roadway to the barracks, and to stack and light the fires in preparation for the evening meal. For his pains he got a share of the slush skimmed from the top of the meat boiler—a benefit that had long been established as the cook's perk.

There was no jetty on Small Island, and the prisoners had to wade through the water in order to clamber on board the 12-ton launch sent over each morning to collect them. When the sea ran heavy the launch would be compelled to hold fast offshore and those who could not swim, or who were wearing irons, were hauled on board with a rope. It could be a dangerous operation. On one occasion a launch was lost when it struck a rock on the return trip, a misfortune that the commandant blamed on the crew being 'fresh water sailors'.

While the Small Island prisoners were loaded on board, a light whaleboat with three soldiers and a handpicked crew kept watch at 'a pistol shot' distance. Every soldier at Macquarie Harbour was equipped with a pouch made from kangaroo skin that contained ten cartridges. They were instructed to carry these at all times and, in addition, their weapons had to be constantly loaded. As a result, the rate at which charges were expended was prodigious.

Every time a flintlock was loaded the cartridge was effectively destroyed. The whole process of clearing a Brown Bess musket was an elaborate operation. Each corporal was equipped with a tool called a worm—a type of corkscrew that could be threaded onto the end of a ramrod. By this means the remains of the paper cartridge that had been rammed down the muzzle of the weapon to provide compression, and the lead ball, could be extracted. The remaining powder could be cleared by pulling the trigger and igniting the charge in the pan. Black powder is highly hydroscopic, and given the wet conditions at Macquarie Harbour, weapons must have been constantly loaded and unloaded to check that they remained effective. While the men from Small Island waited in wet clothes huddled under the cover of the sawpits for the sound of the morning bell, the soldiers of the detachment fired the charges in their weapons in the barrack yard so that no prisoner could be in any doubt that the muskets with which they were guarded were loaded and dangerous.

Every prisoner had to attend morning muster. Ranked up in front of the superintendent of convicts, each man had to answer as his name was called out, on pain of punishment. When they had all been accounted for, the men were divided up into gangs and those who were detailed to work on the mainland were marched to the pier where they were 'rigidly' searched by the constables who seized anything that could assist an absconder. Thus, John Riley was sentenced to five days solitary confinement after he was caught trying to take two loaves of bread with him in a gang boat destined for Kelly's Basin. This, however, was a relatively light punishment. James Robinson was sentenced to a hundred lashes and to labour in irons for six months when he was caught with cooking fat in his possession. Jonathon Smith was also sentenced to irons and awarded 50 lashes for attempting to smuggle a biscuit into a gang boat. Sea biscuits were a particular concern since they were designed to be portable and did not spoil easily. Commandant Butler was to later write to the colonial secretary, pointing out the 'evil' of supplying an item so 'highly dangerous to the security of the prisoners'.

Other prisoners were flogged for smuggling knives and fishing hooks. The latter were particularly frowned upon since they enabled a prisoner to subsist while on the run. Several of the streams that entered Macquarie Harbour were populated with 'mountain trout'—a small spotted fish that grew to several inches in length. The fish was named *Galaxias truttaceus* in 1816 by Cuvier—the French comparative anatomist who was famously said to be able to deduce the shape of a whole animal from an examination of a single bone—and it could be caught using simple equipment. Commandant Butler discovered to his displeasure that a detachment of soldiers based at the King River had hooked several dozen using bent pins attached to lines fashioned out of strips of bark. This is why, as one convict reported, the constables would seize so much as a pin, or a needle, 'or 6 inches of thread' and throw them into the sea.

The boats took the gangs in several different directions. Some proceeded to Kelly's Basin, Birch's Inlet or the Gordon River to collect timber. Others crossed over to the north shore of the harbour to Farm Cove or to Phillip's Island to clear ground to grow potatoes and wheat. Others proceeded to Brickmakers' Bay, Charcoal Burners' Bluff or Limekiln Reach. Although the gangs rowed themselves to work in launches and longboats, some were rigged with masts and square sails that provided assistance when the winds were favourable. Because of the direction of the prevailing winds this tended to be on the outward voyage rather than on the run home.

Coal was initially mined from an exposed seam on the northern shore of the harbour. The operation was soon abandoned, possibly because of the poor quality of the coal recovered, although Lieutenant Governor Sorell blamed the failure on the lack of scientific expertise and lamented the fact that he could not send a qualified mineralogist to the place. There were other failures.

At Brickmakers' Bay, an adit or shaft was driven into the cliff face for some seventeen yards. Hacked out by convicts wielding picks in pursuit of an iron-rich seam of sandstone, the fruits of their labours were smelted on the beach immediately outside the mine. It was a process that required considerable heat and as a result the sands of the beach were fused together. Bellows were employed to get the rock to melting point, upon which the liberated iron sank to the bottom of the furnace. The waste slag was then raked off the top and scattered on the beach.

It was an incredible amount of effort to expend—a reminder of the value of iron in a colony dependent upon imports from the other side of the world. Indeed, several convicts at Macquarie Harbour were transported there for stealing objects made of iron. They included the blacksmith Thomas Warwick, who was convicted in the Hobart Town Supreme Court for making away with eighteen bars valued at £6—three times more than the 40 shillings threshold required to make the offence capital. In this sense he got off lightly when he was sentenced to serve seven years in a penal station. The metallurgical experiment on the beach, however, was at best painfully inefficient—at least some of the waste slag having as much iron in it as the sandstone body from which it had been smelted.

Greater success was met in the area above the adit where clay was mined to manufacture bricks. A large seam of the stuff was cut back in terraces, the exposed area being drained by means of a channel cut down to the beach. The brickmakers used moulds to turn out thousands of raw bricks. They produced 84,000 in 1827 alone. These were stacked in clamps in the bush—long lines of soft clay blocks supported one upon the other, the weight of the bricks above pushing the pliable clay into the gaps below until each was marked with a seam. While the clamps dried they were protected by the cover of a large shed that kept out the worst of the elements. Many were marked with the thumbprints of the brickmakers—marks that were preserved for posterity when the clamps were fired. Thus the bricks from which the solitary cells and other structures in the settlement were built carried the thumbprint signatures of the prisoners they were designed to incarcerate.

Large amounts of timber were needed to fire each clamp and the surrounding slopes were cleared for some considerable distance. In its natural state the bush was so thick in this quarter that a man would have been hard pressed to see beyond ten yards. But when Constable Richardson walked up a hill by the brick shed he saw two runaway convicts from the crest. It was an indication of just how much timber was felled to fire the clamps. It took hours of heavy labour to clear the thick scrub, remove the overburden and cut out the wet heavy clay—all of this was done by ganged convicts. After the fired clamp had cooled down the enforced labour had to transport tens of thousands of bricks to Settlement Island in oared barges.

Other materials were needed in order to aid the daily functioning of the settlement. Before iron can be given an edge it needs to be infused with carbon. This was necessary in order to make sturdy pins that could be sunk into the keel of a ship, or to forge pick heads sharp enough to dress a block of sandstone. To do this, charcoal was required. In the British Isles coppiced oak was grown specifically for this process. At Macquarie Harbour, as in so many other things, the charcoal burners' trade had to be adapted to make use of unfamiliar timbers. Among those selected to oversee the process was Thomas Walker, an apprentice gunsmith from Gloucestershire who was later to participate in a spectacular escape by boat from Port Arthur penal station. It was his job to ensure that the six- to eight-foot pyramid of tree limbs of the right width was perfectly covered with wet sand apart from the small aperture in the top through which the pile could be ignited. Once kindled the burn had to be constantly tended so that sods and more wet sand could be applied wherever smoke was seen to issue from the stack. If the fire was not continually smothered in this manner, the burn would not be sufficiently controlled to reduce the timber to charcoal.

As well as charcoal, the penal station required large amounts of lime to spread on agricultural land and for use in making mortar. Originally, the raw material was plundered from the Aboriginal shell middens that were prolific along parts of the coast. Lime contaminated with sea salt, however, makes a poor mortar and when limestone cliffs were discovered a considerable distance up the Gordon River the lime burning operation was shifted there. By February 1824 a kiln capable of turning out 130 bushels every four days had been established. As at Charcoal Burners' Bluff, the remoteness of the location and the nature of the operation—which required round the clock supervision—meant that there was no option but to quarter a small party of convicts at the site.

Limekiln Reach was some 21 miles from Settlement Island, and the men who manned the kiln were regularly posted to this isolated outstation for periods of three to four months. A camp for two soldiers to guard supplies was established in the bush on the opposite bank of the river, an expensive but necessary measure in order to avoid the tedium of a daily 42-mile rationing run. In June 1824 the three convicts camped out in the damp hut beside the Gordon were Thomas Crawley, a stonecutter from County Cork, Richard Morris, a farming man from Barrow in Shropshire, and John Newton, a horse dealer from Hull. Every afternoon at three o'clock one of the soldiers was instructed to row across the river with the daily rations for the gang, while the other stayed behind in charge of the arms and provisions.

It was a necessary precaution. Both Crawley and Newton had been sent to Macquarie Harbour for absconding. For some inexplicable reason, on the evening of 2 June 1824 both soldiers crossed the river together leaving their firearms behind. The three prisoners immediately seized the boat, marooning their erstwhile guards, and rowed across the river to plunder the soldiers' encampment. They then set off up the Gordon equipped with muskets, ammunition and several days' supply of provisions. Their boat was afterwards found moored to a stump about twelve miles upstream with the words 'to be sold' written on the stern with a chunk of lime.

In 1827 alone, 2345 bushels of lime, or just over 73 imperial tons, were manufactured, all of which had to be shipped out. In the first quarter of 1832, when the penal station at Macquarie Harbour was being wound down, over nine tons of charcoal were also produced. These were considerable weights, which had to be loaded onto boats and rowed from one location to another by the labour of ganged convicts.

As well as its use in building, lime was required to prepare the acidic soils of the harbour for agriculture. Along with seaweed it was turned into the prepared ground at the rate of 137 bushels per acre. At first the settlement tried to grow wheat in Farm Cove and, in expectation of success, a series of hand mills was ordered from Hobart Town. The wheat crop, however, failed to ripen due to a combination of the inclement weather and the 'foulness and general bad quality of the land'. The place was so infertile that the land appeared 'just as if the tide had fresh gone out'—it was a barren, rocky, acidic place where the cultivation of cereals was next to impossible. As a substitute, Commandant Wright switched his attention to the cultivation of potatoes. This was a particularly valuable crop since it was an effective antiscorbutic, and the regular supply of potatoes undoubtedly helped to reduce the rate of scurvy.

Potato fields posed other problems however. Since they were difficult to guard at night, they were regularly plundered and many convicts were punished after being found with this article in their possession. William Budd, for example, who had been sent to Macquarie Harbour for the rest of his sentence for 'attempting an unnatural offence with a sow', was once awarded 75 lashes for having plundered potatoes concealed in his hat. It was a particular concern that the cultivation of extensive potato beds on the mainland would provide succour to convict runaways. In order to prevent this, the farm was located on a peninsula that stuck out into the harbour. It was connected to the mainland by an isthmus about 130 yards wide. The plan was to construct a fence with a guardhouse to prevent all unregulated land access, but all this came to naught. In all, 97 acres were twice turned with hand hoes but the soil still proved to be too wet. Deep drainage ditches were then cut and bushel after bushel of lime was mixed with the earth. Yet, despite the months of ganged labour spent clearing, fertilising and draining the land, the potatoes rotted in the ground.

The attempt to farm Phillip's Island which lay about two miles eastward proved more successful. The soil there was described as a kind of 'peaty loam'. After the land was cleared and prepared with lime, eight acres were sown with potato seeds. By the late 1820s these grounds were producing nearly 40 tons annually and proved more productive than the gardens on Sarah Island. On the basis of this success, one of the officers applied for permission to grow a small patch of wheat to try to preserve the seed stock. To the amazement of all this also flourished, producing stalks 'upwards of six feet in height' with ears that 'were full and productive'. Commandant Briggs even used the straw from this experimental crop to fashion hats for his boat crew.

To capitalise on all the work that had been done clearing the land at Farm Cove it was turned over to a piggery. The pigs were at first fed on condemned stores—meat that had gone bad because the brine had leaked out of the cask, and peas and bran declared unfit for human consumption. They could also forage for themselves, particularly for orchis tubers, a member of the orchid family that flourished on the north shore of the harbour. There were problems though, when the piggery expanded, and the amount of available forage declined. In October and November 1829 alone, ten pigs died from starvation. Once more the solution was found at Phillip's Island. A further fifteen acres was cleared, broken up and turned over to be cropped with turnips. After these had been dug out the pigs were left to forage over the fields, which helped to further fertilise the soil.

In contrast to its foreboding surroundings, Phillip's Island was considered a picturesque place. In outline it was wedge shaped, presenting 'an abrupt bank about fifty feet high' to the sea. As the crest of the island was never cleared of trees, the canopy acted as a natural windbreak. It was the more gradual slopes that faced towards the mainland that were cultivated. A steep path led up through the gardens 'planted on each side with native shrubs and rendered firm' by the trunks of trees and ferns laid down corduroy style. The gardeners' whitewashed huts, which were situated near the summit of the island, rapidly became overgrown with Macquarie Harbour vine—'a luxuriant climber' that bore small bitter fruit.

It was a favourite resort of the settlement officers who wandered among the tree ferns (noted for their incredible size) and collected drinking water from springs that were clearer than the tannin-stained streams that flowed off the hills surrounding the harbour. Thomas Lempriere, the commissariat officer, made three small ink-wash sketches of the place—one of these even has the commandant's boat crew in the foreground, replete with their pitch-sealed straw boaters. In another he drew a crude likeness of the overseer, Patrick Kirwin, raking the potato beds—his three charges are depicted in the distance hoeing the ground. Kirwin claimed to have been a commissioned officer in the 67th Regiment and to have served a total of thirteen years in the army. At the time he was arraigned before the supreme court in Launceston for receiving a stolen gold ring, he was a serving sergeant in the Buffs, or the 3rd East Kent Regiment. Found guilty, he was sentenced to death, but this was subsequently commuted to fourteen years transportation and he was shipped to Macquarie Harbour.

Commandant Butler thought it was 'a dreadful thing to see a man of his good feeling and conduct exposed to association with the convicts of this settlement', although he reported with some satisfaction that 'so marked is the distinction' between Kirwin and the other prisoners 'that they invariably address him as "Mr"'. It was for this reason that he was posted to Phillip's Island, where he could be spared the indignity of having to rub shoulders with the general mass of prisoners. His presence gave the place an added attraction for the settlement officers. They could wander about its pleasant slopes, and practise their sketching while stopping to talk to 'Mr' Kirwin—a suitable object of charity.

Lempriere also sketched the view across the cleared peninsula at Farm Cove towards Soldiers' Island. His pale washes captured something of the enormous scale of the task undertaken by the ganged prisoners who had cleared the land of dense forest, broken up the waterlogged soil, and heaved the bushels of lime—each weighing 70 pounds—from the gang boats to the acres of potato furrows that had been carved into the land. Without their labours

View of part of the 97 acres at Farm Cove cleared of timber and twice turned over with the hoe for naught. (Thomas Lempiere)

there would have been no view—all would have been obscured by trees—and it was from this onerous duty that 'Mr' Kirwin had been spared by his class.

The principal task undertaken by the ganged convicts was rolling timber. Armed with cant hooks and handspikes they shifted logs sometimes weighing as much as twelve and a half tons. These leviathans of the forest were lopped of their branches and cut to suitable lengths before being manoeuvred onto roads fashioned from the debris of the felling operation. The latter were a kind of rough and ready version of the slips, or skids used in the launching of ships. Where the ground was swampy, branches and small trees were laid across the roadway. Two long straight logs were then fixed at right angles with a gap of about five yards between them. By means of these roads, felled trees were levered down to the water's edge, where in groups of 30 or so they were formed into rafts by means of chains.

Often the cut timber had to be moved over considerable distances. As Commandant Wright wrote to the lieutenant governor: 'A strong gang was required for this duty as many of the trees were felled at a great distance from water in thick brush and swampy ground.' Mechanical aids were also used. A list of settlement stores includes 'a bush block' and 40 fathoms of rope. The use of blocks and tackles lessened the burden of labour and increased the efficiency of the gang. Nevertheless, the Quaker missionary George Washington Walker concluded, 'From the nature of the ground, as well as having to work so much in the water, the labour in which the men are thus engaged is of a most arduous and disagreeable kind'. The Wesleyan missionary, the Reverend William Schofield, described a gang that he had gone to preach to at Kelly's Basin as wet 'up to their knees & so dirty that several of them went into the water upon their arrival to wash themselves'. They were, he thought, in a miserable state—although he suspected that many wished to make their circumstances appear as bad as possible in the hope that he might intervene on their behalf.

What individual convicts lacked in strength was compensated for by use of numbers. As Wright wrote to the colonial secretary: 'A strong gang has been constantly employed in rolling logs to the water's edge for the purpose of rafting'. The efficiency of a gang depended upon the degree to which it could be co-ordinated—or, perhaps more appropriately, driven—by its overseer. He dictated the pace of work, decided when the gang required resting, organised tasks so as to minimise accidents, and reported those whom he thought should be brought before the commandant to stand trial.

Overseers were selected not on the basis of their conduct record, but because they could get the job done. Charles Bradshaw petitioned the lieutenant governor asking to be removed from Macquarie Harbour as his life was in danger due to the services he had rendered to the government in his duties as overseer; his plea was rejected on grounds of character—he had been sentenced to death in the Hobart Town Supreme Court for robbery and had formerly kept a brothel and run a sly grogshop. Other overseers clearly had particular talents for the job. Many were tall men. Benjamin Sharman and George Craggs were both six feet one inch tall and would have towered over their charges who were on average just short of five feet five inches. Some were picked for the task on account of their former station in life. John Anderson, for example, had been a mate on a slave ship. As one convict claimed, 'iniquity was carrying on to a Great length it was a common thing for an Overseer to knock a man down with a handspike and beat him with his stick when he was down take him to the office when they came home and get him 50 Lashes for Insolence and neglect of work'.

As the gangs were not permitted to carry food with them to the mainland—a measure considered essential to prevent escapes—they had to row 'from 10 to 14 Miles daily in a boisterous Harbour' and complete their tasks with nothing to sustain them other than the pint and a half of skilly that they had received for breakfast. It was a hard thing to work all day without anything to eat; but worse was to follow. Once the rafts of cut logs had been completed they were towed to Settlement Island by a team of launches. Thus the return trip was far worse than the outward journey, especially as it was completed against the prevailing wind. Just keeping the rafts together was a task in itself. The settlement blacksmiths had to be employed to add eighteen fathoms to the 'strong chain' that was sent down to assist in the operation.

Sometimes the raft met with bad weather and the chains gave way. As Lempriere recalled: 'Such accidents always gave much trouble and indeed it seldom happened that the whole number of the logs were recovered.' In late January 1824 a raft of logs broke up while it was being towed to the heads for collection by one of the supply vessels. In the end the gang was forced to go ashore on the beach at the mouth of the King River and roll each log that had broken free above the high tide mark to prevent it being washed away. A few days later another gang had to return to roll every log back into the waters of the harbour and once more raft them together. After that time-consuming mishap it was decided to stockpile timber at Settlement Island, rather than risk the long exposed journey to the pilot station. A breakwater was constructed which stuck out into the harbour like a large arm. Logs were collected in the calmer water on the lee side of this structure and from here they were rolled to the sawpits.

Even in the best of weather the tasks that the gangs were ordered to complete were arduous in the extreme. In bad conditions they fell beyond the capacity of human endurance. Thus it was that in 'wet and stormy Weather' the prisoners were employed on Settlement Island 'grubbing Roots of Trees and preparing the Ground for Vegetables', erecting fences or spreading lime on the ground in an attempt to improve the fertility of the soil. To row against the wind would have proved impossibly futile. As the chain gang consisted largely of absconders, and because the irons on their feet would have made work in the scrub of the mainland unproductively slow, they were permanently employed on Settlement Island. It often fell to them to work up to their waists in water disassembling the timber rafts that had been towed to the safety of the breakwater. Each log had to be rolled up the beach and hoisted onto the stockpiles that could reach a height of 30 feet.

The day's work completed, the newly arrived prisoners who were still undergoing probation were conveyed back to Small Island together with those in the chain gang. There they were discharged in their wet clothes and set about drying themselves as best they could. The two rooms of the penitentiary where the prisoners were housed were equipped with fireplaces. 'Once on shore', in Lempriere's words, 'affairs wore a more agreeable aspect and a comfortable warm meal greeted their craving appetites, whilst a blazing fire invited them to dry their clothes and warm their shivering limbs'.

The description was, to say the least, disingenuous. In February 1829, when there were 71 convicts in the two rooms of the penitentiary, each man had a space of less than six feet five inches square. The building was hopelessly crowded, and particularly in winter it was 'bleak and exposed' despite the luxury of an evening fire. As one of the convicts who experienced it concluded: 'It was a most wretched place'—a miserable draughty barracks that contained 'a more starved ragged wretched looking crew' than can be imagined. The only way off the island was through the largesse of the commandant, for it was he who decided who should be quartered in the comparative comfort of the barracks on Settlement Island or condemned to the sodden squalor on Small Island where the 'out and outers' dwelled.

*Sergeant Patrick Kirwin, the 'gentleman' overseer of Phillip's Island.
He was transported to Macquarie Harbour for knowingly receiving a
stolen gold ring. (Thomas Lempriere)*

3

The 'crimes' of the damned

It is easy to assume that the convicts secondarily transported to Macquarie Harbour were serious malefactors who had perpetrated crimes of the deepest dye. It would be convenient if this were so, for the weight of punishment that fell upon the backs and limbs of the prisoners sent there could be justified by the need to exact suitable retribution.

There certainly were convicts at Macquarie Harbour who had been sent there for violent transgressions. William Roadknight, for instance, had received a seven-year sentence for maliciously firing a gun at Thomas Thorpe and wounding him just below the knee. Roadknight, a free settler of some standing, claimed he had mistaken the man for a bushranger. As Thorpe was fishing in the River Derwent at the time, the explanation was far from convincing. William Stewart was transported to the penal station following a bushranging outbreak during which he had repeatedly fired shots through the double weatherboarding of his master's house.

Other convicts found themselves at the settlement for assaults committed for more pecuniary reasons. John Begley was exiled there for the rest of his sentence for beating and attempting to rob the Reverend William Marsden. Marsden possessed a fierce reputation as a disciplinarian (he was known as the 'flogging parson') and it is perhaps no surprise that Begley was also ordered to receive 100 lashes for the offence. William Blunt and Joseph Saunders were flogged and transported to Macquarie Harbour when they were found guilty of breaking and entering a house at New Town and violently beating William Baker and his wife. Public houses were common places for assaults. While drinking in Easton's bar Richard Perrhyn flew into a rage, drew a knife and attempted to stab his wife. He then beat a police constable who came to her aid. Such cases, however, formed the exception rather than the general rule.

In all, only three per cent of convicts transported to Macquarie Harbour were sent there for crimes that explicitly involved violence (about the same number who were banished there for acts of mutiny and insubordination). Of these, none was convicted of murder, although one, James Buckley, was retransported for manslaughter. There was a simple reason for this. Few murderers were reprieved from the gallows in the early-nineteenth century. While graphically violent offences were committed at the settlement, there is little in the records of the men sent there to suggest that they were disproportionately composed of deranged psychopaths predisposed to acts of murder, cannibalism and mutilation.

The truth was that prisoners were sent to Macquarie Harbour for all sorts of reasons. Some were secondarily transported for great crimes—spectacular robberies that had been conceived over many months. Perhaps the most audacious was planned to coincide with the anniversary of the battle of Waterloo. At about ten past six on 18 June 1827 the sentries on duty outside the Colonial Treasury in Hobart Town were relieved and Private Thomas McGuire of the 40th Regiment took up his station at the front of the building and Private Patrick Rice at the rear. McGuire had not been there long when James Davis, a convict, walked up to him and after a brief chat, presented the sentry with a pint of brandy and persuaded him to take his prize round to the rear of the building. There, he and Rice employed a bayonet to knock the head off the bottle. They drank the contents accompanied by the regimental band that was playing at the ball held at the barracks to commemorate the anniversary of Wellington's victory.

Now that the front door of the treasury was temporarily unguarded, James Thomas and Charles James crossed the street and used a key to open the front door. The making of the precious key had been a delicate operation. Charles James, a blacksmith who worked for Harris, the brass founder in Macquarie Street, had been supplied with impressions marked in soap by Matthew Pennell, a convict employed as a messenger at the treasury. At night in his lodgings in Melville Street, James would fashion the key with a file. By day Pennell would wax it before trying it in the lock of the treasury door. Any impediment would leave an impression in the wax to guide James' nocturnal filing. The same process was repeated for the key to the door of the colonial treasurer's office and to the strong box screwed to the floor behind the treasurer's desk.

Once inside the building, Thomas and James moved on to tackle the door to the treasurer's office. The warning bell at the back of the door had already been disabled by the ever-helpful Pennell, so the two men were able to gain access to the inner sanctum of the treasury without difficulty. The lock of the strong box similarly yielded to the turn of a fake key. It was at this point that Thomas and James encountered a problem. The weight of their haul, which largely consisted of rupees, Spanish dollars and silver coin, was too much for them to carry.

They were forced to go to the premises of Harris, the brass founder, and throw stones at the window to attract the attention of his assigned servant George Ralph. It was now two in the morning and, with the assistance of Ralph, the precious booty was spirited away through the silent streets of Hobart Town. At seven the next morning a triumphant Thomas came to the lumber yard to do up the government horses. There he met James Davis and broke the news of his success. Having completed their morning duties they went to the house of Harry Webb to celebrate with James and Ralph over a draught of hot ginger beer.

The robbery was discovered when a £20 cheque was found lying on the treasury floor. As Thomas and James had locked the chest and doors upon their retreat from the building, it appeared at first that the robbery had been committed by phantoms. On closer examination, however, it was discovered that the inside bolt of the back door had been left undone and the seal on the strong box had been broken. The two sentries immediately fell under suspicion and were taken into custody. As it was evident that the burglars must have had intimate knowledge of the locks, the public works blacksmith who had fitted them was also arrested. The government advertised a reward of £50 for information and a promise of a free pardon to any prisoner who was prepared to break ranks.

In the event, the inducement of a reward was hardly necessary as alcohol and loose talk proved the burglars' undoing. On the Wednesday of the following week they retired to a public house owned by James's brother where they feasted on a supper paid for with a score of silver shillings which they had earmarked for post-robbery expenses. Thomas was in a celebratory mood and shouted food and drink for his friends. Later he boasted about his involvement in the raid on the treasury in Bernard Walford's public house over a pint of porter and a half pint of rum. He repeated the claim in the Waterloo, a public bar that lay just across the road from the site of the robbery, where he announced that the thieves would never be discovered.

All that week Thomas continued his celebration, attending dances at Walford's and Brownlow's public houses. The supper at Jack James's house, however, proved to be Thomas's last moment of triumph. After he and his fellow conspirators had finished dining they were all arrested.

At the subsequent trial no evidence was proffered by the Crown against James Davis—a reward for providing damning testimony against his co-conspirators. Nevertheless, the Crown case collapsed when the solicitor general failed to turn up in court and the judge was faced with no option but to instruct the jury to return a verdict of not guilty. Thomas and James had to be rearrested and charged with stealing ten one-pound notes, ten five-pound notes and three twenty-pound notes, the property of Jocelyn Thomas, the colonial treasurer. They were sentenced to seven years transportation along with Thomas McGuire, the sentry who had been bribed with a pint of brandy, and Matthew Pennell, the messenger who had so helpfully disabled the rudimentary alarm bell.

In all, 44 per cent of the prisoners who served time at the settlement were sent there for theft of some description. In the case of thirteen per cent of these the offence was aggravated in that it had either been committed in a dwelling house, or involved breaking and entering. The list of items stolen was extensive. It included kangaroo skins, cocoa, 400 panes of window glass, a Waterloo medal, a glazier's diamond, a keg of butter, 40 cheeses, a thermometer, 338 yards of printed cotton, two axle trees, 114 gallons of rum, eighteen yards of ribbon, twenty gallons of turpentine, 30 pigs, 40 gallons of porter, a roasting jack and chain, 3080 bricks, a bullet mould and boats and vessels of all descriptions.

Others were sent to the penal station, as the words of the ballad 'The Cyprus Brig' would have it, for 'trifling offences'. John Mawer was sentenced to seven years transportation in the Hobart Town Supreme Court for stealing a loaf of bread valued at five pence. The brothers Michael and Philip Flannagan were ordered to receive 50 lashes and be transported to Macquarie Harbour for the remainder of their sentence for stealing two canvas sacks. As they had originally been sentenced by a court in Down Patrick to life, this left them with few grounds for optimism. They were among the first prisoners to abscond from the settlement, slipping into the rainforest and button grass plains of western Van Diemen's Land, never to be seen again.

John Wood, a cooper's apprentice who had been fond of playing bagatelle before he was lagged to Van Diemen's Land, was sentenced to serve seven years at Macquarie Harbour for stealing five bars of soap. Samuel Jones, who had sold apples on the streets of London prior to embarking on a new career as a convict in the Antipodes, was sentenced to Macquarie Harbour for two years for receiving some sheets of paper to the value of twopence. In fact, many of the convicts responsible for the most shocking acts of violence committed at the penal station were sent there for relatively trivial matters. Samuel Higgins, who cut John Onely's throat in a quarrel over the slush from the meat boiler, had been given three years for stealing a pint of wine. Edward Broughton, who barbarously murdered three of his fellow Macquarie Harbour absconders, roasting and consuming their remains, was sent to the settlement for seven years for stealing a blanket. Somehow this initial sentence was subsequently construed by Bell's *Weekly Dispatch* as an 'outrage'—the assumption being that a man who would kill and eat his fellow absconders had always been disposed to violent acts.

Indeed the majority of prisoners at Macquarie Harbour were tried by lesser, as opposed to higher, courts. Of the 245 convicts there in January 1825, for example, 72 per cent had been sent there on the orders of a magistrates' bench—a court that was not empowered to try cases of a serious criminal nature. Of the remainder, only 19 per cent had been sentenced in the supreme court while nine per cent had been sent under no court order at all.

Nearly one in three prisoners at the settlement had been sent there for absconding and as such their only offence was that they had tried to regain their liberty. They included John Mayo who would later break open James Bailey Jones's skull with repeated blows from an axe. Mayo was sent to Macquarie Harbour for three years 'for making away with his parti-coloured clothing'. These were the yellow and black government slops that he was in fact wearing when he made his escape from the Number 1 chain gang in Hobart Town.

Other prisoners were sent to Macquarie Harbour as an example. James Reid and William Holt were shipmates—they had been transported together on board the *Medina*. When the two men ran from the Number 1 chain gang they were apprehended at Salt Pan Plains by a mounted orderly. As punishment, Reid was sentenced to receive 100 lashes and Holt 50. The triangles were set up in the very place where the chain gang was at work and the men were flogged right there, in front 'not only of the gang, but the whole neighbourhood'. As they were being taken down Holt made a remark to Mr Lakeland, the superintendent of convicts, and was immediately tied back up and given another 50. As soon as the punishment ceased, the men were marched through the streets and loaded on to the *Cyprus*, their backs still bloody, and in this state they were conveyed to Macquarie Harbour.

Some offences caused particular concern and were severely dealt with. Henry Jones Batchelor was transported to Macquarie Harbour for three years after it was discovered that he had altered the convict description register in the police office. The fraud came to light when the chief clerk received a request to check the date when a convict tailor named John Vie would become free. His suspicions were raised when he noticed that the last figure of the year of conviction had been scratched out and re-inked. He went to check the duplicate copy in the colonial secretary's office, but found that that one had also been altered. However, the deed polls that were brought to the colony on board each transport vessel were kept under lock and key. When he consulted these he found that the year Vie had been sentenced to seven years' transportation was in fact 1823, not 1820.

Suspicion fell on Batchelor, an attorney's clerk from Bath, because of the way he formed his 'O's with two distinctive down strokes. His fate was sealed when it was revealed that Vie had made several pairs of trousers for the convict department clerk. As the fraud threatened to undermine the whole stability of the penal colony the case caused some excitement. It raised the possibility that convict clerks might arrange some mass textual escape from penal servitude, rewriting the sentences imposed by the courts in Britain in return for waistcoats, shoes, tobacco and rum. As the editor of the *Hobart Town Gazette* put it 'we feel no small satisfaction at this conviction' despite the fact that the case had been difficult to prove since all the evidence had been 'circumstantial'.

The courts could be particularly severe when it came to sentencing receivers. Margaret Keefe, a servant from County Wexford who had been transported for shoplifting, shared her lodgings in Hobart Town with a man named William Jackman.

At eleven o'clock one night Jackman was apprehended in the act of burgling a storehouse in Argyle Street. He was arrested by the constables as he was trying to make his way out of the building through a gap in the weatherboards. He had in his possession eight incriminating bags of sugar and a further five bags were discovered when he was escorted to his house. Since Margaret Keefe was found 'waiting up', she too was arrested and charged with receiving the goods. Sentenced to be transported for seven years she was one of sixteen female prisoners who served time at Macquarie Harbour penal station.

There were some prisoners who argued the toss in an attempt to wriggle free of the courts. Patrick Kirwin, a sergeant in the Buffs—later to become the overseer of gardeners at Phillip's Island—was put on trial in Launceston charged with having received a gold ring knowing it to have been 'burglariously' stolen. His defence rested on the peculiar argument that, as the thieves had entered the property via an unfastened window, they had not committed an act of burglary, there being no forced entry. In order to effect their exit from the building, however, they had unbolted the back door. The court ruled that there was no difference between a break-in and a break-out, even if one was committed before and the other after the larceny had taken place. Kirwin was sentenced to be transported for fourteen years.

The jury that had pronounced Kirwin guilty was made up of six officers from regiments serving in Australia—civilian juries were not introduced until 1833. In a number of cases these military jurors refused to convict prisoners of stealing goods valued at 40 shillings or more, the threshold at which the death penalty cut in. The same practice was commonplace in Britain. Thus when William Brown, Patrick Lynch and William Young were put on trial, charged with stealing wheat, wheaten flour and canvas bags from a dwelling house, they were found guilty to the value of 39 shillings only. Jurors did not always play the game. When James Higgins was indicted for stealing a watch it was valued at precisely 40 shillings. As a result he was condemned to death, although this was later commuted to fourteen years' transportation.

No matter how they made their way to Macquarie Harbour all prisoners had a tale to tell—and some of those stories were extraordinary. Gottfried Hanskie had been born close to Berlin where he lived, as he put it, 'with my friends' with never a thought of 'becoming a soldier'. That was until the defeat of Prussia in the disastrous 1806 campaign, following which he decided to join the hussars. In April 1809 his commanding officer, Ferdinand von Schill, rose up in rebellion against the French and Hanskie rode out with him. It was a venture that ended in disaster. Those who were not killed in action were either executed by firing squad or sentenced to the galleys. Hanskie was perhaps luckier than most. He was taken in the town of Magdeburg by Dutch troops and thrown into a dungeon. Faced with a set of unpalatable options, he chose to escape life as a galley slave by enlisting in the French army.

His service to the Emperor was short lived. Posted to the town of Flushing, he deserted and made his way to the nearby island of Walcheren. There he enlisted with the 39,000-strong British expeditionary force that lay languishing amidst a mosquito ridden swamp. His new masters posted him to the 2nd Light Battalion of the King's German Legion. Although he was not among the nearly 16,000 British troops who contracted 'Flushing fever'—a mixture of malaria, typhus, typhoid and dysentery—he was sorely tested on the parade ground. Having broken his right collarbone, he found it hard to perform the standard military drill and quickly became the butt of platoon jokes. Ridiculed by his fellow soldiers and repeatedly beaten by his corporal, he resolved to desert once more. Since by now he had been evacuated to the Legion's training depot at Bexhill-on-Sea, he was separated from his home and friends by the English Channel. Undeterred he slipped away one night and with another private seized a fishing lugger.

As a sailor, Hanskie fared even worse than he had on the parade ground. When daylight broke the little boat proved far from inconspicuous. As Charles Landle, the Dover pilot explained, 'she had her mizzen hoisted for a foresail, and the foresail out as a main sail, and one of the men pulling at the sea oar, one of the sails was aback which arose from them not having any knowledge of what they were about'. Recaptured, he was court martialled, sentenced to life and transported on the *Guildford* to New South Wales where he arrived in 1812. Eight years later he was again put on trial for stealing sheep and was sent to the penal station at Newcastle and, when that closed, to Port Macquarie in New South Wales. When he tried to abscond from there he was caught and shipped as punishment to Macquarie Harbour. There he was employed as an armed constable—a position that enabled him to put his experience in three European armies to good effect in the pursuit of runaways.

Other Macquarie Harbour men were 'second transports' who had served a previous sentence in the Australian colonies, returned home, re-offended, and been sentenced once again to be sent to the far side of the world. On their return, they were singled out for special treatment and sent direct to a penal station rather than being deployed as labour elsewhere in the colony.

When the housebreaker Charles Fever was disembarked from the convict transport *Lady East*, it was discovered that he was tattooed on his right arm with a 'mermaid, kangaroo, snake and doves'. It was not the kind of emblem one might expect to find on the skin of a sawyer from Tenterden in Kent, but there again, that was not where Fever had always lived. He had previously been transported to New South Wales on the *Minerva* in 1801 following a conviction for stealing sheep, had served his time, and secured a passage home. When Fever was returned to Australia in 1825 on the *Lady East* he was shipped direct to Macquarie Harbour with orders to remain there until the lieutenant governor should permit his return to the settled districts. When he received his release, however, relief from the torments of a penal station proved only temporary. He was sent back to Macquarie Harbour under a sentence of hard labour for three years—a consequence of being caught 'in a grossly indecent situation' perched on a stool in a cow shed with his trousers around his ankles.

On the *Lady East* alone there were four convicts who had been previously transported. All were transferred to the gaol to await shipment to Macquarie Harbour. They included William Grovenor, who had been sent out on the *Lady Ridley* in 1821, but had escaped from Van Diemen's Land by stowing away on the brig *Deveron*. After he had been discovered he was handed over to a British man o' war in Rio de Janeiro harbour and conveyed to England. From there he was shipped all the way back to Van Diemen's Land. John Williams escaped from assigned service in New South Wales and managed to secure a passage on a colonial vessel bound for Hobart Town. There he signed articles to go on a sub-Antarctic sealing expedition and set sail for Macquarie Island. Armed with his cut from the sealing gang, he shipped first to Batavia in the Dutch East Indies, and then to England on a vessel that was ironically named *Hope*. Apprehended and placed on trial he wisely pleaded guilty and was sentenced to death, although this was subsequently commuted to life transportation 'over the seas and beyond the seas'.

Others were secondarily transported for mutinous conduct. Ten convicts who arrived in Van Diemen's Land on the *Royal George* had participated in a mass riot on board the convict hulk

Coromandel anchored off the coast of Bermuda. The protest had lasted three days and at its height the spirit store had been broken into and a hulk official had been stabbed. In order to make a severe example, two of the ring leaders were executed and the rest were banished to Macquarie Harbour. One of their number, a man named Richard Edwards, had been sent to Bermuda for acting as a clerk to a 'fractious' group of prisoners charged with riotous conduct in the hulks in the Thames. He later changed his name and became a Quaker.

Several others found their way into the settlement as a result of breaches of conduct on board the transport vessels that had conveyed them to Australia. William Thompson, John Morphew and John Becket were sent direct from the *Earl St Vincent* after they had been accused of issuing threats to the ship's surgeon. Four prisoners were sent straight from the *Argyle* suspected of plotting to take the vessel. The trouble had started when William Philips had been caught on deck marking the ship's course on a scrap of paper. It was his former trade that had set alarm bells ringing: he was a seaman from Padstow in Cornwall. Although Philips protested his innocence, several other convicts stepped forward and divulged details of a plot to take the vessel, implicating other members of his mess. In a petition to Governor Arthur, Philips and his friends had strenuously argued that those who proffered evidence against them had done so merely in the hope of gaining some sort of indulgence.

There were others who also found themselves at Macquarie Harbour as a result of testimony provided by men anxious to save their necks. William Jenkins, John McGuire, Jesse Bowhil, Charles Howes and Michael Shaughnessy were all accused of assisting the notorious bushranger and Macquarie Harbour escapee, Matthew Brady. Brady and his supporters had terrorised the settled districts and stretched the military resources of the colony to its limits.

The colonial government was most anxious that all those who had offered succour to this desperate band of bushrangers should be prosecuted to the utmost extent of the law. The problem was that the only evidence against the five men had been provided by George Farquharson who had been sentenced to death for sheep stealing. Farquharson had made his confession shortly before he was marched out onto the scaffold. Having strung up its one and only witness it proved impossible for the Crown to proceed with the case. Undeterred, Lieutenant Governor Arthur sent the five men to Macquarie Harbour anyway.

There were many similar cases. Peter Rainor, a black seaman from Barbados had been placed on trial in the Hobart Town Supreme Court on 14 January 1826 charged with a felony. When the prosecutor failed to show up, however, the judge had no choice but to discharge Rainor by proclamation. Determined that he should not escape justice, Arthur ordered that he should serve the rest of his sentence at Macquarie Harbour. Other cases did not even make it as far as the courtroom. It was suspected that Henry Leonard, Joseph McFarlane, Joseph Bell and William Seymour, all absconders from Maria Island, had committed a felony at Oyster Bay while they had been on the run. As there was insufficient evidence to be sure of securing a conviction they were sent direct to Macquarie Harbour rather than risk the judgement of the court.

Other convicts were spirited to the penal station because they possessed skills that were in demand there—a dubious honour. Seamen were particularly at risk. William Gibbons was working as a sailor and cook on board the government brig *Waterloo* when he was caught swapping a hat with a prisoner for a piece of tobacco. His ad hoc punishment was to be landed at Macquarie Harbour on the next run that the *Waterloo* made to the settlement and to be worked there for six months. Robert

Surrage was confined in gaol in Hobart Town in July 1824 for being drunk. From there he was transferred to the brig *Duke of York* where he was told by the superintendent of the prison barracks that he was to be sent to Macquarie Harbour, but would be delivered back up to Hobart Town in six months time if he behaved himself. Despite an unblemished record at the penal station he remained there for nearly two years, working as a hand in the commandant's boat.

As the cases of many Macquarie Harbour convicts demonstrated, in the penal colony of Van Diemen's Land it was the lieutenant governor who had the last word and not the law of the land. As the colonial government had the authority to select any part of the colony as the place of residence of convicts sentenced to transportation, no court order was required to confine a prisoner in a penal station.

Even when convicts had their day in court, legal niceties were not always followed. William Buelow Gould, who would later paint many detailed watercolours of fish and plants, was sent to Macquarie Harbour for passing a forged note of the Bank of Van Diemen's Land and subsequently destroying the same. The trouble started when he slipped from the Hobart Town Prison Barracks, where he was quartered as a member of the chain gang. Having worked one leg free from his government irons, he attempted to conceal the fact by wrapping the loose chain around the other, and, thus encumbered, he walked into Tapsell's bar. This establishment was also known as the Rock of Gibraltar and once inside he sat down to have a drink with Augustus Traverso, a public work's clerk. Gould ordered a gill of brandy and tendered a one pound note. This was a large sum of money, and since Mrs Tapsell did not have sufficient change, it had to be taken across the street and broken down. Later when doubts were raised about its authenticity, Gould desperately tried to raise the cash to buy the note back. He pawned his box of colours for fourteen shillings and made another three by selling a set of blinds to a barber in Liverpool Street. Together with two shillings that he had in his pocket, and one that he had borrowed from the prison barracks' gatekeeper, he scraped together enough to redeem the offending note. As soon as it was handed back he took it to the prison barracks' cookhouse and threw it in the fire. Despite the fact that no material evidence remained to be produced in court, and no one had been defrauded, Gould was sentenced to a penal station and placed on board the *Cyprus* to be conveyed to Macquarie Harbour for three years.

In official eyes Macquarie Harbour had to remain a site of penultimate punishment. If it was to succeed as a penal station it had to be seen as a place one step short of the hangman's scaffold and the dissecting knife invariably put to work on the mortal remains of those terminated on the gallows. It was important that no prisoner should wheedle their way out of the settlement with lawyer like prose, or should successfully slip beyond its boundaries and walk to the freedom of the settled districts. In a society where prisoners could drink brandy at a bar with one leg in irons and one out, there needed to be somewhere that could be held up as a place of terror—a place where warm draughts of ginger beer could not be quaffed at the end of the working day, or bad notes redeemed with Venetian blinds made for a barber's shop. The very words 'Macquarie Harbour' had to convey to every prisoner a sense of what it would be like to be sentenced to unremitting punishment. Nobody should be left in any doubt that here was a place where day upon grinding day the cold, the wind, the rain, the dull clank of irons and the weight of work would burn callouses into gnarled palms, drive pain into tired joints and fix dread in the firmest of hearts. The point of the place was that convicts should fear being sent there above all else bar a public extirpation via the rough rope of the gallows. If Macquarie Harbour was calculated to strike terror then terror it certainly supplied. The manner in which it did so, however, did not always conform to the carefully scripted plans of colonial administrators and penal station commandants.

Post-execution study of Alexander Pearce the cannibal. This drawing was completed before Henry Crockett set to work on him with the surgeon's scalpel. (Thomas Bock)

4

The law of the sea (as applied on land)

To be condemned twice was no mean thing. It secured the ill repute of those who were sentenced to secondary transportation as securely as the rusting irons that were riveted to their legs for the length of the voyage into penal exile. It mattered little that many of those unlucky enough to find themselves at Macquarie Harbour had been sent there for relatively minor infringements. As far as public opinion was concerned, the place soon developed a reputation for harbouring the most degraded elements of humanity. If further confirmation of this fact was required it was supplied with monotonous regularity by reports from Macquarie Harbour reprinted in the colonial press. The acts of violence committed by those who had been exiled there for the common good of humanity were shocking beyond belief.

Less than a month after Evans had predicted that escape from Macquarie Harbour would be 'next to impossible', two prisoners, John Green and Joseph Saunders, slipped into the scrub. They both disappeared without trace. Six days later another seven convicts absconded. Cuthbertson despatched two soldiers from his small detachment in pursuit together with three convict volunteers, all seamen from the boat crew, equipped with kangaroo dogs. Just as with Green and Saunders, the seven absconders and their five would-be captors were never seen again. The small settlement had now lost ten per cent of its population.

In April a further seven convicts bolted into the bush. This time they returned to Macquarie Harbour to give themselves up rather than starve and were awarded 100 lashes and six months in irons—a punishment that henceforth became the standard meted out to absconders. As the autumn gales set in, the rate of escape attempts dropped until on 20 September 1822 a further eight prisoners spirited themselves away. This time one of their number, a pockpitted labourer from County Monaghan named Alexander Pearce, would make it to Hobart Town, dashing the confident predictions of the deputy-surveyor. When he was eventually picked up, however, no one really wanted to believe the story he told.

Pearce was finally apprehended at Mr Fryett's stock hut in the Western Tiers after an absence of 113 days. He had been in the company of Churton and Davis—two notorious bush-rangers—for a number of weeks, but it was the passage that he had taken from Macquarie Harbour and the fate of his fellow absconders that excited curiosity. Pearce was interviewed at length by the magistrate, the Reverend Robert Knopwood.

Pearce confessed that, although three of the absconders had turned back for Macquarie Harbour after eight days, the remaining five had pushed on until they were out of supplies. On the fifteenth day they came to the banks of a large river and sat down in despair. Here they resolved to cast lots in the tradition of the 'law of the sea' to select one to be sacrificed so that the others might struggle on. Robert Greenhill, a sailor who had been tried at the Old Bailey for having forged one pound banknotes in his possession, volunteered himself as executioner on the grounds that he had once 'been placed by fortune in a similar situation'. In some accounts Greenhill was described as a master mariner—suggesting that he was versed in the nautical tradition that sanctioned the slaying of one in the interests of the saving of others. Thomas Bodenham, a 22-year-old farming lad from Lothian in Scotland with a distinctive blue mark on his upper lip, had the misfortune to draw the short straw. Greenhill killed him with a 'severe blow' from an axe. His former comrades then cut up his body and cooked it on a hastily kindled fire, consuming all but the two missing toes on Bodenham's left foot that had been lost in a previous accident.

As Pearce related, the further on they struggled the more deranged Greenhill became. John Mather, a bread baker from Dumfrieshire, was the next to be slaughtered. He was followed by Mathew Travers, who up to this point had been Greenhill's main partner in crime. The two men had been sent to Macquarie Harbour for the same offence—they had attempted to abscond from the colony in a schooner stolen from the former New South Wales Corps officer, Anthony Fenn Kemp. When Travers was bitten by a 'venomous reptile', however, it made sense to kill him too. Thus, Pearce was spared from Greenhill's axe by the bite of a snake.

The two men pushed on, navigating by the sun and moon and subsisting on 'the flesh of Traviss [*sic*] & what reptiles they could get out of the rotten trees'. At night they eyed each other warily as hunger once more drove them to desperation. Greenhill kept a close guard on the axe, placing it under his head at night while both men tried to stay awake. When Greenhill finally fell asleep Pearce crept through the brush to where he lay and, taking the axe, 'gave him a severe blow on the head which deprived him of his life'. Pearce told Knopwood that, having despatched Greenhill, he left the body and proceeded on his journey, keeping himself alive by living off whatever he could scavenge. After a week he came across a flock of sheep and shortly after that he fell in company with Churton and Davis.

From the start there were concerns that the story was largely fabricated: an attempt to provide cover for his fellow absconders whom it was feared were still at large—harboured, as Pearce had been, in the stock huts of the Western Tiers. Worrying confirmation that the story was essentially true, however, had already been published in the *Hobart Town Gazette*. According to this report two of the absconders who had turned back on the eighth day of the escape had reached the penal station after a further four days in the bush. In a very weakened state they had been taken to the hospital where they related that prior to their leaving the party 'one had been killed to afford sustenance to the rest'.

Pearce could have been tried for murder but this would have been far from a straight-forward matter. Without bodies or witnesses there was no real evidence that could be used against him other than his confession. There was also no supreme court—one was not established in Van Diemen's Land until 1824. As a murder charge could not be heard by a bench of magistrates, Pearce would need to be shipped to Sydney. Instead, he was returned to Macquarie Harbour where he became living proof that it was possible to cut a passage out of the settlement—although this might necessitate going to extraordinary lengths.

As the story of the escape was retold it steadily became embellished. In the account entered into the settlement records by John Douglas, the commandant's clerk, Pearce admitted that Alexander Dalton had also been slain. A former soldier who had been sentenced to fourteen years transportation by a court martial in Gibraltar for deserting from the 64th Regiment, Dalton was one of the three men who Pearce had originally claimed had turned back early in the escape in an attempt to retrace their steps. Faced with the confessions of the two men who had got back to the settlement, however, he decided to change his story. Pearce now revealed that Dalton had in fact been the first victim. Rather than lots being drawn according to the custom of the sea, the former soldier had been set upon—in fact deliberately singled out as he had previously been a flogger. Struck on the head with the axe without warning, his throat had been cut, his insides torn out and his heart and liver broiled on a fire. Pearce still insisted, however, that it was Greenhill who had taken the lead role in the killing.

The murder of Dalton was subsequently retold by a convict who had served time at Macquarie Harbour:

> … a man was then appointed the Wretch that God may forgive him to do the deed taking up the axe he without the slightest notice struck the unfortunate man a blow on the Temple he then took his knife and stuck him in the neck as a Butcher would a sheep and caught his Blood in a tin dish of which he took a hearty drink they then cut some of the Body for their supper the Murderer claiming his Heart which caused a quarrel with another man after a number of blows the other gave in the murderer then cut out the Heart and broiled it on the fire with the greatest Indifference.

It was not, however, the only lurid tale to come out of the settlement.

Somewhere on the banks of Birch's Inlet, William Saul captured a snake. When he refused to share his prize with his fellow convict William Allen, Allen attacked him with a knife, stabbing him first in the face and then the throat and finally the heart. He then set about disembowelling his erstwhile friend, cutting off Saul's penis and decorating a tree with his intestines. When Edward Broughton and Matthew McAlboy absconded from Macquarie Harbour in early September 1830 they survived by killing and eating three of their companions, two of whom were described as old men and the other as a boy of around eighteen years of age. It was an act of such enormity that it was difficult to measure the depths to which the absconders had sunk without resorting to similes.

Bell's *Weekly Dispatch* described them as 'Fifty times worse than the wretched horde of Abyssinians who are reported to cut the flesh as they travel from the backs of living beasts'. It was an account inspired by James Bruce's *Travels to Discover the Source of the Nile*, published in 1790, and was designed to convey an image of McAlboy and Broughton herding their three victims on solely for the purpose of slaughtering them in order to subsist on their butchered remains. The message to the reader was as clear as the cuts made by Broughton's axe. Here were men devoid 'of the least spark of religion' who knew no more of the precepts of Christianity 'than the earth upon which they trod'. In short they were worse, much worse, than the most barbarous heathens.

Some Macquarie Harbour convicts appeared to kill without motive. While walking from the gang boat up the beach to the place where he had been detailed to work, John Mayo unshouldered an axe and drove it into the head of the man in front. Taken completely by surprise, James Bailey Jones was knocked to the ground. While he lay prostrate Mayo got in a second blow to his head before he was secured by the rest of the gang. Although Jones was still alive 'a great portion' of his brain could be seen projecting from both wounds and the man died shortly afterwards. His killer was quite indifferent to his fate and coldly announced that he had no particular quarrel with Jones and would as soon have murdered the next man.

Others were slain for trifling reasons. When John Onely reneged on a deal to supply the slush skimmed from the top of the meat boiler, David McGee attacked him with a crutch. Then while George Driver pinned Onely's hands, Samuel Higgins cut the man's throat. It was not cleanly done. In the ensuing struggle Higgins was covered in blood. One of his mates later testified that he had a nosebleed on the day of the murder and had bled all over Higgins. It was not the best of defences and both Driver and Higgins were executed on the public scaffold in Hobart Town for a killing perpetrated as the result of a quarrel over a few ounces of fat.

Other murders were described as 'cool, deliberate and premeditated'—acts that had been committed 'to the disgrace of humanity'. As the *Hobart Town Courier* said of the killing of the Macquarie Harbour convict Thomas Stopford: 'Never was misery more complete—never was the oat of sin more thickly seared—we cannot describe it.' Despite this declaration the paper proceeded to do precisely that, providing a detailed account of the poor man's last moments. He had been struck while 'fast asleep, and as he lay with his face upwards'. His assailant, a man named Salmon, 'hit him so effectually across the eye and left cheek, that he never spoke. A second blow was with equal force applied to the opposite side, and then a third and finishing stroke was given on the crown of the head, leaving the axe buried in the brain to the depth of four inches'.

John Salmon was said to be 'a stout made, corpulent man' with a short neck and a 'contracted forehead'. The latter was a feature of particular interest to phrenologists—those who believed that a person's character could be determined by their cranial features. As if to emphasise the point, the *Courier* described him as a person 'subject to ungovernable fits of passion'. Originally a ploughman from Havering-atte-Bower, a village near Romford in Essex, Salmon had worked as an assigned servant following his transportation to Van Diemen's Land. It was claimed that he once got so frustrated with a bullock that refused to obey his commands that he beat the dumb animal to death with a plough blade. At another time he was supposed to have stabbed two harmless beasts in the heart with his clasp knife. Yet despite the *Courier*'s attempts to portray Salmon as a demented monster, there is no evidence that he had ever broken the criminal law before he drove the axe into Thomas Stopford's head. He had originally been convicted by a court martial following a botched attempt to desert from the 56th Company of Royal Marines stationed at Chatham. As he had twice tried to run in the previous year and a half, the court sentenced him to be 'Transported as a felon for the term of his natural life' and ordered that he be forcibly tattooed with a 'D' for deserter on his left side just below his armpit. Felon, however, was a strong word for a man whose only act of theft was to attempt to steal himself.

His records show that when he arrived in Van Diemen's Land Salmon was sent to work for the landowner David Gibson where he was charged with 'abusing his master and not taking care of cattle'. For this he was awarded 25 lashes—a routine punishment regularly meted out for minor offences. There is no hint on his conduct record that he ever deliberately mutilated bullocks—let alone that he viciously killed livestock placed in his care. Rather than being charged for a crime of violence, he was sentenced to serve two years at Macquarie Harbour for absconding—an offence that was remarkably similar to the one that had sent him to Australia in the first place. He thus wound up in one of the most notorious sinkholes of the British Empire without having stolen or killed anything, or appearing in any criminal court higher than a magistrates' bench.

Despite being worked in irons, Alexander Pearce absconded from Macquarie Harbour again on either 13 or 16 November 1823 (the records are contradictory). He ran from the gang placed under the charge of overseer Malcolm Logan, but this time only one other prisoner absconded with him. His companion was a man named Thomas Cox, a 24-year-old dealer from Worcestershire who had been sentenced to transportation for life at Salop Assizes. After they had proceeded for a short distance, Cox struck off the irons from around Pearce's legs with an axe. The two men then set out along the north shore of the harbour, avoiding the passage through the interior of the island.

On 22 November the crew of the *Waterloo* schooner en route from the heads to Settlement Island saw the smoke of a fire curling up from the beach. When a boat was despatched to the spot, Pearce was discovered with about half a pound of human flesh in one of his pockets. When questioned, he claimed that Cox had drowned while crossing a river and that he had cut off a piece of his body as proof that he was dead.

The next morning the absconder was conveyed to the mouth of the King River under heavy guard and at bayonet point was asked to point out where the body lay. As Thomas Smith, the commandant's coxswain recalled: 'It was found'. The 'it' was revealing—he did not say Cox's body for it would have been difficult to give the mutilated carcass a name. The head and hands had been severed clean off. The torso had then been suspended from the trunk of a tree and the bowels, liver and heart torn out. Much of the flesh from the buttocks, thighs and calves of the legs was missing. The butchered remains were placed in two rugs and conveyed to the settlement—there was evidence now aplenty, certainly enough to secure a conviction.

As the subsequent trial revealed, the two men had been out of provisions for several days before Cox had been killed. Pearce told John Bisdee, the Hobart Town gaolkeeper, that they had eaten nothing but the tops of trees and shrubs and were starving. They had quarrelled on the banks of the King River when Pearce had discovered that Cox could not swim. The Reverend Conolly, the Catholic priest to whom Pearce gave his final account, related that the two men 'were all the time, from the period they started, without a morsel to eat'. Smith, the coxswain, recalled from the witness box that the only justification that Pearce offered for his crime was that: 'No man can tell what he will do when driven by hunger'.

Yet almost straight away the story became embroidered. According to the report of the trial in the *Gazette*, the eyes of all those in the courtroom 'glanced in fearfulness at the being who stood before a retributive Judge, laden with the weight of human blood'. It was difficult to believe that anyone could 'have banqueted on human flesh!'. It was a revealing choice of words. 'Banqueted' placed a new emphasis on the escape and subsequent killing—it suggested that Pearce had gleefully fallen on the corpse of his unfortunate victim, feasting on it.

There were other tales of cannibalism likely to have been well known in Hobart Town. When the frigate *La Méduse* had been wrecked off West Africa in 1816, 150 survivors were cast adrift at sea on a hopelessly overcrowded raft. The fifteen who lived to tell the tale survived by devouring the bodies of their dead companions. The gruesome event was recounted in a bestselling book published in 1817 that in turn inspired Théodore Géricault's painting, the 'Raft of Medusa'.

The tradition of casting lots at sea to select a man to be consumed can be traced back to at least the mid-seventeenth century, when it was employed by seven seamen adrift in a boat off the Caribbean Island of St Kitts. As the story goes, the lot ironically fell on the man who had first suggested the strategy.

A more recent case was the fate that had befallen the crew of the Nantucket whaler *Essex*. While cruising in the Pacific the *Essex* had been rammed and sunk by a sperm whale. Cast adrift in an open boat the crew cast lots to see who would be sacrificed so that the others might live. In 1821, Owen Chase, one of the eight survivors, published his *Narrative of the Most Extraordinary and Distressing Shipwreck of the Whale-ship Essex, of Nantucket; Which was Attacked and Finally Destroyed by a Large Spermaceti-Whale in the Pacific Ocean*. The account later inspired Herman Melville's masterpiece *Moby Dick*.

What distinguishes the Pearce story from other accounts, however, is the manner in which it was rapidly recast from a survival narrative to an altogether more sinister tale. The surgeon, Henry Crockett, who had treated Pearce in the hospital at Macquarie Harbour, claimed in later years that Pearce had repeatedly persuaded fellow prisoners to abscond 'for the sole purpose of killing them and devouring their flesh'. Another surgeon, John Barnes, told a parliamentary committee in 1837 that Pearce had plenty of pork and bread in his pockets when he gave himself up 'horror-struck at his own inhuman conduct'. In other words it was claimed that he had killed, not out of want or the custom of the sea, but out of choice—preferring human flesh to flour and salt pork. He was even said to have declared that it was 'the most delicious food'. Others claimed that the Pieman River had been named after Pearce—a reference to his former occupation—and that this was the spot that he had been recaptured.

All of these stories are erroneous. The Pieman River account first surfaced in 1854 in an article in the *Hobart Town Courier* that claimed that Pearce had been in the habit of hawking pies about the streets of Hobart Town and had been transported to Macquarie Harbour for 'selling unwholesome meat'. This story clearly owes its inspiration to the 1846 publication of Tom Prest's penny dreadful *Sweeny Todd*—a morbid tale about a Fleet Street barber who slit the throats of his customers dumping their bodies through a trapdoor. From there they were collected by his neighbour, Mrs Lovett, who turned them into pies, which she sold to members of the legal fraternity.

Others sought to inject Pearce's story with even darker tones. As the *Gazette* had put it the whole case had recalled the 'vampire legends of modern Greece'—a subject firmly placed in the popular imagination by the publication of Polidori's *The Vampyre*, which first appeared in Colburn's *New Monthly Magazine* in 1819. Polidori was Lord Byron's personal physician and he had shared the rain-soaked holiday in the Villa Diodati in Switzerland where Byron and the Shelleys had taken it in turns to scare each other witless. It was this bizarre house party that later spawned the Mary Shelley classic *Frankenstein*, but it was Polidori's tale that was the first to make it into print—indeed it was the first vampire story to appear in English. The work, which was initially published under Byron's name, was a runaway success. When it emerged that it was actually authored by Byron's doctor, sales plummeted and Polidori took his own life with a drug overdose. There can be little doubt, however, that it was *The Vampyre* that inspired the *Hobart Town Gazette*'s report of Pearce's trial. It was deep in an entangled forest in Greece that Polidori's demonic Lord Ruthven had engaged in his nocturnal orgy, laughing while he 'opened the vein' of his young victim spilling blood on her 'neck and breast'.

Subsequent writers maintained the connection between the forests and mountains of western Van Diemen's Land and the horrors of Eastern Europe's bloody and supernatural past. David Burn, who described Macquarie Harbour as a place 'unblessed of man, accurst of God', referred to the entire western 'portion of the convict's land' as a vast Transylvania. In this he took his cue from survey maps, which from 1830 used this term to describe the south-west. Transylvania of course had been made famous by the exploits of the fifteenth-century ruler Vlad V of Wallachia, more popularly known as 'Vlad the Impaler'. He was once said to have impaled the inhabitants of a village in Transylvania on stakes while he ate his breakfast surrounded by their bloody corpses.

Nothing did more, however, to revive memories of Pearce's bloody sojourn in the woods than Marcus Clarke's gothic novel *For the Term of his Natural Life*, first published in 1874. Clarke resurrected Pearce in the form of the fictional Gabbett—'a spectacle to shudder at' and a man of whom it could truly be said was consumed by his bestial passions. As Clarke told his readers, he was 'so horribly unhuman'; he looked like an animal 'as he crouched, with one foot curled round the other, and one hairy arm pendant between his knees'. But it was his face that was the most disturbing—'in his slavering mouth, his slowly grinding jaws, his restless fingers, and his bloodshot, wandering eyes there seemed to live a hint of some terror more awful than the terror of starvation—a memory of a tragedy played out in the gloomy depths of that forest which had vomited him forth again'.

In order to give his repellent monster verisimilitude Clarke plundered Pearce's confession and vomited it forth in the pages of his novel. Thus, when the absconders decide first to resort to cannibalism, it is Greenhill who says 'I have seen the same done before, boys, and it tasted like pork' and when just two absconders remain, it is sheer exhaustion which allows Gabbett to approach his sleeping companion 'on clumsy tiptoe' and seize the 'coveted axe'. It was Clarke more than anyone who ensured that forever more Macquarie Harbour penal station would be associated with the horrors of cannibalism.

Yet, as the convict Davis argued in his recollections of life in the penal station, behind the tale of Pearce's macabre forays into the woods lay another story of bloody pursuits of an official nature. The penal station regime was characterised by remorseless legally-sanctioned terror and it was this that drove men such as Pearce to acts of murder and mutilation in their desperation to escape from the place. As he put it, while this 'canot [*sic*] paliate the horrid and dreadful' acts committed by Pearce, the telling of the other side of the story 'will give the reader an idea of the cause'.

James MacKinney

James McKinney, who in July 1823 was bound to the 'fatal wood' while Lieutenant Cuthbertson measured out each cutting blow with the turn of his leather boot. (Thomas Bock)

5

The law of the lash

The most important building at Macquarie Harbour was a small three-roomed weatherboard cottage located behind the stores. It was in this unprepossessing structure that the commandant's clerk, a man named John Douglas, had written down Alexander Pearce's account of his first ghastly, but ultimately successful escape from the penal station. Power at Macquarie Harbour was given immediate effect by the score of the lash. But, other mechanisms were needed to keep power alive—to score it into public memory so that after the scars on the prisoners' backs had healed the marks of their indiscretions could still be read. It was this task that fell to Douglas, a Scot in his mid-thirties who had been tried in the high court in Edinburgh, and sentenced to seven years' transportation for fraud.

Douglas had been schooled in numbers from an early age. His father had worked as the accountant for the Wigton branch of the Bank of Scotland and when he died in 1811, John Douglas succeeded him. It is impossible to know what first tempted him to cook the bank's books, but as the scale of his fraudulent activity grew it became increasingly difficult to conceal. He avoided balancing the books for as long as he could and, when finally ordered to do so, he absconded first to Liverpool and then London. As he was recorded as being a seaman when he was landed in Australia it is likely that he worked for awhile as ship's purser before a guilty conscience got the better of him and he returned to Wigtonshire to face both the wrath of his former employer and the many clients he had defrauded.

Despite his dubious past Douglas possessed the perfect combination of skills for a man tasked with keeping records on a windswept island where everything had to be moved by sea. He recorded the amount of timber sawn, the weight of the supplies off-loaded from brigs and schooners, and the size of the pins required to secure the keel of a vessel. But it is the details of each trial held in the 'small incommodious room' that doubled as his sleeping quarters that proved most consequential for the settlement's convict population. Every quarter, his summary of each trial was forwarded to the superintendent of convicts' office in Hobart Town. There the details of every offence committed within the bounds of the colony of Van Diemen's Land were entered into a central register.

When the lieutenant governor reviewed the cases of men who had been banished to Macquarie Harbour, it was these records that he consulted. They were terse, clipped, scribbled summaries that captured the voice of the commandant, Lieutenant John Cuthbertson, as he pronounced each charge: 'Committing a nuisance—25 lashes'; 'Losing through neglect or disposing of his shirt—50 lashes and 6 months in irons'; 'Destroying through neglect a truss belonging to Govt.—7 days bread and water'; 'Entering the quarters of Lieutenant John Cuthbertson and stealing plums and tea—100 lashes'; 'Absconding into the woods—100 strokes'.

How easily the phrase 'one hundred strokes' slides off the tongue and yet how hard it is to comprehend the savagery of such a punishment. Stripped to the waist, legs splayed and bound and arms secured above the head, the prisoner was fixed like a carcass on a hook—powerless before the flagellator. The lash was 'a formidable instrument'. It was made from nine strands of whipcord each adorned with at least seven overhand knots that had been stiffened with either wax or wire.

At Settlement Island the triangles were anchored on the shingle of the beach just above the high tide mark. They were positioned at right angles to a planked gangway. The surgeon and settlement commandant paced the length of this wooden deck, turning when they had reached its extremity so that throughout the duration of the punishment they could alternately observe the prisoner's back and face. Each stroke was timed to coincide with the turn that brought the gaze of the two gentlemen to bear once more on the bound frame of the convict. One hundred strokes delivered in this manner could take in excess of an hour.

There were times, like the week in July 1823, when the flagellator was excessively busy. Over six days he was called upon to administer 1700 lashes to just fifteen prisoners (a punishment that required him to wield the cat for some seventeen hours). That marathon exercise would have started after each morning's muster and taken place in front of the assembled prisoners. Clad in their different coloured slop clothes stamped with the property marks of government, they would have appeared a motley crew in contrast to the uniformed detachment of the 48th Regiment.

The bare frame of the triangles commanded the attention of both prisoners and soldiers. Also called the halberds, after the axe-like weapons with which sergeants had once been equipped, the triangles were almost certainly fashioned from stout pieces of tea-tree bound at the top and driven deep into the stones of the beach. It was to this 'picture frame for Pluto's land', as one prisoner termed the rough scaffold, that the arms and legs of the fifteen convicts were tied in succession. There they were flogged amidst the most dramatic scenery.

Beyond the outstretched limbs of the prisoner lay the waters of the harbour and the distant peaks, the most prominent of which was Frenchman's Cap. Named because in profile it resembled the Phrygian bonnet that the French revolutionaries had paraded on top of pikes, maypoles and trees as a symbol of freedom, it surmounted the as-yet uncharted forest into which Alexander Pearce had escaped. It was the most ironic of backdrops for a flogging—a symbolism that cannot have been lost on all who surveyed the triangle of cut down boughs upon which the prisoner was strung.

When the punishment was over the cords were cut and the prisoner was carried away, his 'Back like of Bullocks liver and most likely his shoes full of Blood and not permitted to go to the Hospital until the next morning when his Back would be washed by the Doctors mate and a little Hogs lard spread on a bit of Tow'. And often the next man was then strung up in his place.

James McKinney was 23 when his arms were lashed to the tea-tree frame in preparation for his one-hour ordeal. A weaver from County Down in Northern Ireland he had been one of eleven absconders who had been recaptured within four days of each other and had been sentenced to the standard punishment for runaways—100 lashes and six months in irons. This was one of several moments in his life when McKinney was brought centre stage, put on view, written about and described—and because of this it is possible to know something about the man whom the state, over the course of the next 60 minutes, attempted to batter into humiliating submission in view of his fellow convicts.

McKinney's entry in the convict department records can be found in the volume for 'K'—the Gaelic 'Mc' prefix being ignored for purposes of filing. In these leather-bound paper musters the convict population was accounted for in alphabetical ranks listed in the order that they were disembarked. McKinney's police number, 92, marked him out as the 92nd male convict to arrive in Van Diemen's Land with a surname beginning with the letter K. Fate dictated that he would be sandwiched in the record between No. 91 John Kay and No. 93 Timothy Kelly, but beyond this the record was a document of bureaucratic certainty. It was part of an elaborate paperwork penitentiary designed to capture McKinney's life as a prisoner. He was hemmed in, not by gaol walls, but by ink lines ruled on thick rag paper. If the clerk wanted to know what McKinney looked like, he had only to take the register from its shelf, turn to 92K and trace his finger down a line where McKinney's height, age, complexion, hair colour and eye colour were all recorded.

The man whom the superintendent brought down from the gaol and caused to be bound to the triangles on the beach at Macquarie Harbour had brown hair and hazel eyes and stood five feet seven inches tall. At some point in his past, probably in his childhood, he had survived an encounter with smallpox, which had left its tell-tale trace of pockmarks across his face. He could read and write well enough to believe that in 'altering a note of hand of George Owens from one to two shillings' and 'also a note of William Butchers' from two shillings, five pence to ten shillings he would not be detected. For this attempt to defraud eight shillings and five pence he was sentenced by a bench of magistrates in Hobart Town to serve the rest of his sentence at Macquarie Harbour.

The silences in McKinney's record are also revealing. He was originally sentenced to seven years transportation at the Lent Assizes in County Down, but there the record ends. Like hundreds of other prisoners who arrived in Van Diemen's Land, the paperwork which accompanied him to the other side of the world did not include a description of the offence for which he had been transported, despite the fact that it was this that had forever altered the course of his life. There is a simple reason for the omission—once that sentence had been passed it mattered not a jot what it was for. Alongside the other details on his record it would have served no function. The colour of his eyes and hair and the smallpox scars on his face, the place of his birth that fixed his accent, were all important. They could be used to describe him in the pages of the *Gazette*. If he should be wicked enough to attempt to abscond once more, to slip between the trees, his quest for anonymity would be challenged by the power of newsprint. For an hour McKinney would be held a prisoner by the cord that bound his arms and legs. For six months after that he would be held by the irons that shackled his legs. After these were struck off he would still be a prisoner secured by the power of words.

There were other words on McKinney's record that helped to gain a measure of the man. They described him as able bodied and fixed the amount of time to the day that he would have to work for the government. Legally those words wrapped themselves around him as comprehensively as irons and whipcord. They appeared in abbreviated form on the slop clothing that clad him, stamped alongside the B.O. (for the board of ordnance) was the broad arrow, the mark of government property.

When the Crown's clothes were stripped off, a different set of property marks would be stamped directly onto the flesh below.

The lash that was employed at Macquarie Harbour was of a type known as the thief's cat. It was an appropriate weapon with which to mark the body of the absconder who had attempted to steal himself—and mark him it would. Just 50 strokes was enough to cut a man round the throat, under the armpits and across his ribs and belly. A full 100 lashes was designed, not just to turn him into a bloody mass, but to punch the wind out of his lungs and the spirit of resistance out of every inch of his being. As McKinney slumped at the triangles, as his body went limp and as he lost consciousness, he was physically forced to submit to the power of the state. It was a submission which was all the more humiliating for its public enforcement; as first the Crown's clothes were stripped from his back, and then the skin was stripped from his flesh. With that his dignity was stripped away—until that too became owned by the commandant whose calculated pace powered the process of repossession.

In terms of locally useful skill there was not much to be repossessed. Ulster was one of several areas in Ireland and Britain where handloom weaving was a common occupation in the early-nineteenth century. As with many other weaving communities, wages went into decline at the end of the Napoleonic Wars. The wages of Ulster cotton weavers in the period 1813 to 1820 were less than half of what they had been in 1790. As crime and unemployment rates are intricately entwined, the transport ships that departed for the long voyage to Australia contained many who had been brought up in such communities. No wonder that in the years when McKinney was arrested and sentenced to transportation handloom weavers were singing:

> *You say that Bonyparty he's been the spoil of all,*
> *And that we have got reason to pray for his downfall;*

Now Bonyparty's dead and gone, and it is plainly shown
That we have bigger tyrants in Boneys of our own.

It is impossible to know whether McKinney would have agreed with these sentiments at the time of his sentence to transportation. It is nigh on a certainty that he would have done after a year at Macquarie Harbour.

It was the weaver's double misfortune to be landed in a colony that had no textile industry. With no flying shuttles to work or frame looms to rig, transported textile workers were valued for their muscle power alone. They were disproportionately condemned to clear stumps, wield pickaxes and push barrows. Many, like McKinney, found their way into penal stations and other 'places of condemnation' where the coercive instruments of the state were employed to reshape them.

The irons and the lash were weapons of significant proportions. They were designed to carve the will of the state into the frame of the prisoner and yet, somewhere in between the sounds of puncturing flesh and the dull clank of the chain gang, McKinney was taught a new calling at Macquarie Harbour. By 1825 he was working as a sawyer. This is perhaps the most curious aspect of the place. It was a settlement calculated to produce pain, yet it also sought to teach its charges to fell trees, saw in straight lines, steam planks and build launches, whaleboats, brigs and schooners. In the end it was through his new-found skill with a pitsaw, rather than with a dash into the bush, that McKinney escaped the confines of the penal settlement. In April 1825 he was shipped to Hobart Town as one of the crew of a new launch.

This is the story of McKinney as a convict. It is a view of him shaped by the words written by John Douglas and other clerks. These were words which sought to capture the physical likeness of him on the page, that recorded the charges read out in the commandant's office, or were used to measure the amount of timber he cut each week and keep track of every timber dog and compass issued to him. This is not, however, the story of McKinney the man. It is instead the account fashioned of him as a piece of Crown property to be condemned like a cask of rancid salt junk, or whipped like a truculent horse, or entered on a vessel's inventory like any other piece of cargo. The real history of James McKinney lay beneath the skin touched by whipcord and iron. It is an alternative story to that of the hour he spent pinioned to the beach at Macquarie Harbour and it can only be pieced together through his subsequent actions.

Once McKinney had arrived back in the settled districts he was sent to the public works to saw timber for the government. He did not remain there for long. Four months after he had been delivered by colonial vessel from Settlement Island he once more ran into the bush. There he joined a group of bushrangers led by the Macquarie Harbour escapee Matthew Brady. These were men that McKinney knew—he had worked in chains alongside them, shared the same barrack room floor, pulled on the oars of the same whaleboat as they battled the wind and had his legs splayed and arms stretched on the same tea-tree scaffold. Now, despite the fact that he would be freed by servitude in less than a year, he chose to ride alongside them in defiance of all authority. This was an act of rebellion that had almost certainly been wrought on the triangle—proof that the hour that the flagellator had expended upon him had been as wasted as the blood that had seeped into McKinney's shoes.

As bushranging careers go his was long lasting—some seven months. He was captured when rendered lame from the blow to his ankle he received while trying to jump his horse across a stream. Overhauled by a party of convict constables, McKinney was taken, along with two fellow bushrangers who stayed to fight beside their injured companion rather than abandon him to their pursuers. The *Gazette* described the three as 'strong athletic men, with weather beaten countenances, their hair, which they have suffered to grow and project beyond their hats and caps, being bleached by the action of the dew and the night air'. This was the face that the convict artist Thomas Bock sketched as McKinney stood in the dock on trial for his life. Bock, possibly with an eye on future lithograph sales, neglected the disfiguring pockmarks so prominent in the official description filed in the numbered paper pages lodged in the office of the superintendent of convicts. On 5 May 1826 a hood was pulled over that young face and, along with five of his companions, James McKinney was launched into eternity from the public scaffold in Hobart Town.

When McKinney had been strung up to that other scaffold on the beach at Macquarie Harbour a little less than three years earlier, it had been Lieutenant John Cuthbertson of the 48th Regiment who had looked him square in the eye and measured out each cutting blow with the turn of his leather boot. Cuthbertson was a man possessed of extraordinary authority. As the commandant of a penal station he was empowered as both master and magistrate—a circumstance not permitted in the settled districts of the colony. In effect, he owned his charges. He could direct them to work as he thought fit—property rights in their labour having been, for all intents and purposes, transferred to him.

If an illustration of this was required it was supplied by a cutting blow of a different nature. Using some unspecified sharp implement—one must suspect an axe—the convict James Mason chopped off two of his own fingers. Cuthbertson's clinical reaction was to charge Mason with damaging himself 'in order to deprive the government of his labour' and, in an act of official retribution, he sentenced his self-mutilating charge to receive 50 strokes. It was a vengeance of biblical proportions—flesh for flesh. Cuthbertson had been master, judge, jury and, with each turn of his leather-soled boot, had provided the mechanism that wound back the flagellator's arm.

Yet for all of this power, Lieutenant John Cuthbertson remains a surprisingly shadowy figure. Far more is known about each of the convicts who were tied to the triangles during his reign as commandant than is known about the man under whose authority they were held. It is perhaps an unusual circumstance, something that distinguishes early colonial Australia from other places. Since Cuthbertson was not the subject of power, his height, age, eye and hair colour were not recorded. Nor was he, in the world outside of the confines of Macquarie Harbour, a man of particular importance. He did not feature in correspondence between the truly powerful. It is not even certain where he came from, although the evidence suggests that, like McKinney, he too was an Ulsterman—a member of the Cuthbertson family who had first settled in Londonderry in the 1630s before moving to County Tyrone in the 1690s. They were undistinguished small landholders, part of the Protestant ascendency that established themselves in that part of the world in the wars of the seventeenth-century.

The little that is known about his service record provides verification that John Cuthbertson came from a family that was neither wealthy nor influential. When he had been commissioned, aged 21, as an ensign in the recently raised 2nd Battalion of the 48th Regiment on 4 April 1805, he had joined a rapidly expanding army. This was one of 35 new battalions raised in 1803 following the collapse of the Treaty of Amiens. Commissions in the new battalions held less cachet than those in existing line regiments and were thus relatively easy to purchase. As one officer later recalled: 'In those days of raging wars' the officer corps was opened up to all sorts, 'some without education, some without means, some without either, and many of low birth'. Although warfare always provided opportunities for advancement, Cuthbertson's military career was far from meteoric. He received a lieutenant's commission in January 1808, although it is not known whether this was by purchase or promotion, and there his career stalled. Fifteen years later he was still a lieutenant.

Cuthbertson's problem appears not to have been lack of courage. Even his detractors admitted that the one thing he possessed in spades was bravery. His service record was distinguished—he had participated in '12 general engagements' which included many of the most horrific encounters of the Peninsula War. As a poetic epitaph written in his honour put it:

> *Undaunted spirit! oft has thou been seen*
> *Foremost and bravest in the battle scene!*
> *Where at thy word fast binding man to man*
> *Thro' ev'ry rank electric vigour rang.*

Warfare, however, is not poetic. Cuthbertson had survived the slaughter at Albuera when the 2nd Battalion of the 48th Regiment had been cut down after it had been caught in the open by French cavalry. He had been slightly wounded at Talavera and more seriously at the Battle of the Pyrenees. He had been in the British assault party that had stormed the breach at Badajoz—an experience which it would have been impossible to forget. The hole punched in the fortress wall by British artillery fire had been as dark as the 'infernal regions' until illuminated by the light of exploding grenades and barrels of powder. Witnesses recalled that burning bodies had been tossed into the air before falling back into the water that had inundated the bottom of the breach. During the night, the 4th Division, of which the 48th was part, attempted 40 times to assault the breach in the walls. By dawn they had taken 2000 casualties. When he saw the carnage, Wellington, the Iron Duke, was reduced to tears.

If Cuthbertson was no green novice to war, neither was he a harassed man of mediocre talents who 'in the Army's view, deserved no better reward' than a posting to this ultima Thule. It is true that he had been passed over for promotion; but in the Georgian army this was no sure sign of a lack of talent, but rather a lack of sufficient financial resources to secure a captain's commission. At 1821 prices this would have set him back £1100, even after accounting for the sum of money he would have received for selling his existing lieutenant's commission. A popular toast in the army was 'to a bloody war and a sickly season', since high death rates lowered the price of commissions and created more opportunities for promotion through merit alone.

After the ending of the Napoleonic Wars such opportunities were severely diminished. When a vacancy became available the offer of purchase was first made to the most senior eligible officer. Such men had, if you like, first right of refusal. Once a position had been filled each lieutenant shuffled up the line. Cuthbertson was given command of the cutting-out party charged with establishing the penal station at Macquarie Harbour because he was the most senior lieutenant in the battalion, not as some de facto punishment designed to sideline a man of little ability.

The command at Macquarie Harbour represented an opportunity for Cuthbertson. Success, combined with long service and a distinguished record in the Peninsula, might well earn him promotion. As he was aged 39 it was possibly his last chance to gain a captain's commission. All that stood in his way were the wild winds that stripped off the Southern Ocean, the scurvy which loosened the teeth of his charges, the dysentery that loosened their bowels, and the obstinacy of men like McKinney who absconded no matter the odds. All these things had to be kept in their place. That was what was meant by command. Words that would fast bind each 'man to man', words that would erect windbreaks, pile up soil, construct quarters, cut timber, man boats, build vessels, fasten leg irons, fix bayonets, unload brigs and flog absconders, until 'thro' ev'ry rank electric vigour rang'.

A military court martial was empowered to hand down punishments of literally hundreds of lashes and soldiers were flogged for offences as trivial as being drunk or making away with their kit. But without recourse to a court, a regimental commanding officer could not legally order a flogging. As a result they were relatively rare, although other summary punishments, including forcing a man to drink salt water or to trot in circles, were more regularly doled out. It is the monotonous regularity with which Cuthbertson resorted to the lash that secured his reputation among his charges as: 'the most inhuman Tyrant the world ever produced since the Reign of Nero'. As one put it: 'Oppression and tyrany [sic] was his Motto he had neither justice nor Compassion for the naked starved and wretched'. It was a reputation reinforced by his 'custom' of taking a constitutional walk while a prisoner was flogged.

A style of walking can be as forceful as a tone of voice. It can denote class and power, dictate rhythm and command notice. Cuthbertson was both trained and equipped to do all these things. Officers wore boots that drew attention to their choreographed steps. They wore tailored coatees with high decorated collars and epaulettes that accentuated their ramrod backs. On the top of their heads they wore shakos replete with the crowned plates of government and plumes that exaggerated their height. Their arms sported gilt buttoned cuffs faced with their regimental colours. All of these things magnified the power that emanated from their uniformed movements. But Cuthbertson took this one stage further.

By constructing a walkway to measure his military gait he controlled the surface on which he walked. In so doing he ensured that the sound of boot on wood would punctuate the silences between the swing of the flagellator's arm. He also ensured that his pace, the turn of his head, the fix of his stare on McKinney's back and face would time the whole bloody performance. Walking placed him back in command as surely as the convict runaway was now bound and could not move, and the rank and file of the 48th stood to attention with their muskets loaded and bayonets fixed, and the mustered convicts were held in serried ranks to watch this exercise of power in which only power moved.

After a few strokes McKinney's back would have been red with blood. As a spectacle it competed for attention with Cuthbertson's coatee. Ever since Cromwell had selected the colour, the British army had been clothed with cloth dyed with cochineal fixed with tin to produce a bright red. Unlike Cuthbertson's jacket, however, the red on McKinney's back was not fixed—it ran down his legs into his shoes. There must have also been a considerable spray propelled by the force of whipcord across the ground at right angles to the triangle. In this context, another motive for walking emerges—one that had a more practical purpose. In order to view McKinney's back and face it seems likely that the triangles would have been placed midway along the walkway, with the flagellator on the far side. Thus, every blow would have sent blood in the direction of the strolling commandant. If the command to strike, however, was signalled by Cuthbertson's turning boot, walking ensured that the splatter never landed on black military leather. Between strokes it was Cuthbertson who ground the blood of the absconder beneath his feet before walking took him clear in preparation for another strike.

It is ironic that Cuthbertson should die before McKinney met his own untimely death on the public scaffold in Hobart Town. On 22 December 1823 the *Governor Sorell*, a new schooner of 35 tons, broke its moorings in a storm and threatened to drift onto the rocks at Rum Point. Growing increasingly impatient at the failure of his convict charges to retrieve the situation, Cuthbertson set off by boat to supervise the operation personally. In the event the schooner was driven through heavy surf onto the relative safety of a sandy beach and, seeing there was nothing more that could be done, Cuthbertson signalled a return to the shelter of Settlement Island. The journey back would require the boat crews to pull against a rising gale and the voyage quickly turned into a tussle—a battle between land and sea, power and knowledge, free and unfree. There were two whaleboats, one tried and tested and the other newly constructed. The new vessel, named the *Bucephalus* after the famous horse that Alexander the Great is said to have tamed as a boy, was straight off the slips and until that day had never been in the water. Cuthbertson desired it to be put through its paces and against the advice of his two convict coxswains, Revell and Anderson, he commanded the crews to race each other.

In vain, James Revell begged the commandant to travel with him in the older vessel. It was advice Cuthbertson should have heeded. Revell was the settlement shipwright. Cuthbertson may have commanded the *Bucephalus* to be built, he may have named her, and seen her as an extension of his will, but Revell knew her frame by frame, plank by plank, nail by nail. The commandant replied that he 'would go home with Anderson', that the *Bucephalus* 'had brought them safe out and he could not see that there was any danger as she would have to meet the sea in place of going before it', and with that they set off into the surf.

There was no doubting Anderson's seamanship. A sailor in his mid-thirties he was 'a perfect master of his Business' having previously served as a mate on a whaler and as 'Master of a Slaver and a west Indeaman [*sic*]'. Despite having Anderson on board, the *Bucephalus* was out-pulled half a mile in every four by the older boat. Seeing the race lost, and that the gale was increasing in intensity, Cuthbertson ordered Anderson to turn the *Bucephalus* about, although the coxswain pointed out that to do so in such a heavy sea was to court disaster.

Cuthbertson, a soldier who knew little about the ways of the ocean, was convinced that they would be swamped if they maintained their course, so he commanded Anderson to obey. As they turned the waves met them side on, first swamping, and then capsizing the boat and tipping commandant, coxswain and crew into the sea. Anderson had had enough—he unshipped the stern oar 'and placed it under his breast and whent [*sic*] before the wind and sea' to safety. Cuthbertson, 'Determined to have his own way' in this as in everything else, ordered the remaining crew to stay with the upturned boat. All who followed his orders drowned with him.

Cuthbertson could order timber to be cut, vessels to be constructed, boats to be manned, high seas to be crossed and winds to be tamed by the erection of fences, but none of this could actually be achieved without the co-operation of his unfree charges. Herein lay his problem. The small detachment of soldiers at his command was incapable of preventing the prisoners from breaking ranks and running. Instead, he relied on geography and the elements to ring the settlement with water, steep gullies, horizontal scrub and thick mud. It was landscape that channelled absconders like McKinney north via the mass of sand dunes piled up on the fringe of the beach. Yet even armed with this knowledge, Cuthbertson still relied on one group of prisoners to catch another.

It was convict oarsmen who pulled the whaleboat from the pilot's station north and who made it possible to convey a military detachment ahead of a party of absconders and round them up as they tried to cross the river mouths.

So it was in a myriad of other things. The commandant required the skill of prisoners to handle boats, to fell tall trees, and make charcoal from unfamiliar timbers so that convict blacksmiths could use the heat of a forge to drive carbon into iron. There would have been no windbreaks, jetties, boats, water casks—no means of reliable transport—without the co-operation of the men whom he had been ordered to punish to the point where they would never forget the experience of penal labour. Cuthbertson may have aspired to command the elements and he was certainly empowered to beat a man until all will to resist was flogged out of his head—but this did not make, nor would it make, his command any more secure. The exercise of power, the choreographed turn of a boot, an order shouted into a gale, could not on their own deliver success. Without the knowledge to turn trees into windbreaks or to ride out a gale by holding a boat into the weather with a steerage oar, his little settlement would meet the same fate as the ill-starred *Bucephalus*—it would be blown flat and swamped by the elements. Without the co-operation of those whom it was also his duty to punish, without listening to their advice, he, like every commandant at Macquarie Harbour, was bound to fail. Yet, as Cuthbertson discovered, the moment he turned his red coatee those same convicts absconded into the bush or broke into his quarters and consumed his plums and tea.

The harbour was slow to give up its prize. Nine weeks passed before Cuthbertson's decomposing body was located and forwarded to Hobart Town. The month following its arrival, and nearly twelve years after he had charged into the bloodied breach at Badajoz, his promotion to captain was finally gazetted.

Walkers, it is said, 'are known by the company they keep'. As Cuthbertson paced out McKinney's punishment it was Henry Crockett who kept time with his uniformed stride. Crockett was the settlement surgeon and he had to be present to ensure the punishment was legal. If Cuthbertson's turning boot was the signal for the flagellator's arm to begin its forward swing, then it was the assistant colonial surgeon (to give the man his proper title) who could have issued the order to stop the whole bloody proceedings. Crockett did not stop the count. On this occasion, as on all bar one of the times that he kept pace with Cuthbertson's measured stride, he let the punishment run its course. In fact the surgeons at Macquarie Harbour rarely used their powers of intervention to cut across the commandant's will. Out of a total of 1268 floggings administered over the life of the settlement punishment was curtailed on just ten occasions because the surgeon was of the opinion that the prisoner 'would not bear the remainder'.

The only time that Crockett intervened was on 14 November 1823, when a prisoner named John Taylor was sentenced to receive 50 lashes and work three months in irons for cutting up his shirt. After exactly half the punishment had been administered Crockett put a stop to Cuthbertson's turning boot 'being of the opinion' that Taylor could bear no more. His decision may have been influenced by Taylor's deformity. The man's left hand and wrist were crippled and it is likely that he could only have been bound to the triangles with some difficulty. That Crockett kept pace with Cuthbertson's epaulette sealed his reputation among the settlement's convict population. It is not immediately clear, however, that Crockett had anything in common with the older man with whom it was his duty to walk.

A graduate of the Royal College of Surgeons in London, Crockett had arrived in Van Diemen's Land as a paying passenger on board the convict transport *Prince of Orange*, equipped with a letter of recommendation from the Earl of Bathurst. Jobs for young medical graduates were scarce in London. The city was served by some 4000 surgeons, physicians, druggists and apothecaries. Per capita this was twice the number who competed for a living in Paris. To make matters worse, many hospital appointments were honorary positions or, as at Guy's Hospital, paid their physician surgeons miserly stipends of the order of £40 a year. Competition for jobs in the London hospitals was nevertheless fierce as additional income could be gained from lecturing fees and a hospital post presented opportunities to establish a lucrative private practice. There were other opportunities to be had abroad. The East India Company, for example, employed several hundred surgeons. Death rates in the tropics ensured a continuous supply of vacancies for those who were willing to chance their health on the subcontinent.

Employment in the Australian penal colonies held other opportunities. Ever since Linnaeus had devised his famous system of botanical classification based on the form and function of the reproductive parts of plants, dissecting the natural world had become a medical preoccupation. The colonisation of far-flung places increased the fascination. Merchant captains suddenly found a profitable sideline in retailing specimens collected in exotic climes and sailors increased their wages by 'hawking stuffed animals, shells or foreign artefacts'. Travel to distant parts of the empire held attractions for young surgeons wishing to make a name as men of science. Australia, with its bipedal mammals that reared their young in pouches, and trees that shed their bark and not their leaves presented opportunities to the would-be collector. A further fascination was the ready supply of corpses for dissection. Cadavers were hard to come by in Britain. The only ones that could legally be used were those of executed criminals who had been condemned to be hanged and then anatomised.

In Hogarth's famous series of prints, The Four Stages of Cruelty, dissection was the subject of the fourth stage. Entitled, the 'Reward of Cruelty', Hogarth depicted the body of the executed criminal in the process of being hung, drawn and quartered at the hands of the demonstrating surgeon and his assistants. The practice was also unpopular with the lower orders; they rioted against the power of the surgeons to slice the criminal's body into unrecognisable parts in the belief that thus dismembered there would be nothing left to resurrect on the day of judgement.

The supply of legitimate corpses fell far short of those required for anatomical demonstration in the expanding surgical colleges. In Thomas Hood's satirical verse, 'Mary's Ghost, a Pathetic Ballard', the ghost of a young woman appears before her fiancé after her grave has been desecrated by 'resurrectionists' in order to supply Sir Astley Cooper, the pre-eminent London surgeon, with material for the dissecting table.

> *The cock it crows, I must be gone,*
> *My William we must part:*
> *And I'll be yours in death although*
> *Sir Astley has my heart.*

Fewer questions were asked about the bodies of the dead in New South Wales and Van Diemen's Land.

When he arrived in Hobart Town Crockett presented himself at the office of the colonial surgeon, James Scott. His patronage was essential for those who aspired to a position within the colony's medical establishment. Having seen Crockett's diploma, and having read 'various other testimonials of Medical education', and having otherwise 'subjected' him to his examination, Scott wrote to Lieutenant Governor Sorell to recommend him as a 'proper and desirable Gentlemen for the appointment'. His first posting was to Macquarie Harbour. The salary of £136.17.6 compared favourably with that provided by Guy's Hospital, especially considering that quarters and rations were thrown in.

The remote west coast of the colony also provided the opportunity for the scientifically minded to exercise their passions. One of Crockett's successors at Macquarie Harbour, Dr William de Little, employed the convict artist William Buelow Gould to make a series of detailed watercolours of the various fish and plants to be found in the vicinity of the penal station. In each of the plant drawings the reproductive organs are clearly visible or have been slit open with a surgeon's scalpel to provide a detailed view of their contents. It is a remarkable record of a desire to understand the environment by capturing it and ordering it on paper. Others kept records of the rainfall and tidal movements or raised echidnas as pets, feeding them with ants. Crockett's collecting passions lay in other directions. He had a particular fascination with phrenology, the study of the connection between head shape and character.

Viewers of violent acts can disengage themselves by turning the subject of violence into a mere thing. It is possible that Crockett inured himself to the physical pain inflicted by a flogging by concentrating on the nature of the process itself. A flogging was after all little more than a bloody form of vivisection. It was popular to see the body as a machine—a set of muscles and bones and sinews that operated in harmony. Just as the surgeon's knife laid bare the spatial arrangement of those various anatomical structures, the lash exposed their dancing movements—or at least it did until the body of the flogged man slipped into a state of unconsciousness. Anatomical knowledge provided a method of capturing the subject, of knowing it as a set of related systems, and simultaneously not recognising it as a writhing human mess.

Alongside other men of science of his time, Crockett shared a fascination with the heads of runaways. The colonial surgeon, James Scott, commissioned the convict artist Thomas Bock to make a series of post-mortem drawings of executed bushrangers laid out on the dissecting room slab. Drawings survive of two Macquarie Harbour convicts—the bushranger James McCabe and the infamous cannibal Alexander Pearce—who, post-death, were cut open by Scott.

These dissections were conducted in a room on the top floor of the Hobart Town Hospital. His probationary stint at Macquarie Harbour completed, Crockett was back in Hobart Town when Pearce's corpse was carried into the dissecting room in July 1824. Scott zealously guarded his monopoly of the corpses supplied to him in his capacity as colonial surgeon. Indeed, he later fought a protracted battle with Dr William Crowther, a surgeon in private practice who had been trained by Astley Cooper, the subject of Thomas Hood's satirical verse. Crowther wished to gain access to corpses for the edification of his own medical students. As assistant colonial surgeon, Crockett was one of the privileged few invited to witness the dissection of Pearce's cadaver. He would have played an important part in Scott's demonstration. Crockett had known Pearce in life—he had even treated him in the hospital at Macquarie Harbour.

And so it was that the surgeon completed the work that the judicial arm of the state had started. It may have been the hangman's noose that snapped the life out of Pearce, but it was the surgeon's scalpel that removed his identity cut by cut until he was no more than butchered meat on a slab. Scott allowed Crockett to keep a souvenir of the bloody work. After the flesh had been cut from the cannibal (and surely there was an irony here), Crockett was presented with Pearce's skull. Anatomists had long been collectors of human body parts. The Austrian Franz Joseph Gall, who had popularised phrenology in the early-nineteenth century, had a vast collection of skulls and plaster casts. The skulls of individuals who suffered from particular pathologies, or who had exhibited abnormal behaviour in life, were especially sought after. The skull of a convict cannibal was indeed a prized specimen.

It is difficult to determine whether McKinney met a like fate. Was his lifeless corpse taken down from the scaffold after his body had been left to dangle for an hour? Was he delivered to the upstairs room in the hospital where the layers of his skin were peeled back and his ribs cracked open and his organs exposed? Since McKinney was not found guilty of murder, under the terms of the Dissection Act his body should not have been delivered into the hands of James Scott. As in Britain, however, it is apparent that the terms of the Act were often ignored. Bodies that were not claimed immediately after death frequently found their way into the dissecting room. If McKinney was dissected, however, we can say with some certainty that Henry Crockett was not present.

His tour of duty on the western shores of Van Diemen's Land completed, Crockett purchased a substantial house in Hobart Town, 'Woodlands' on the corner of Campbell and Bathurst streets. From here he ran his own private practice, securing a second income to augment his government salary paid to him for his work as assistant colonial surgeon at the town hospital. He started to move in polite circles. He was first introduced to the Reverend Knopwood in October 1824 when he pulled a tooth that had been troubling the clergyman. Thereafter Crockett attended Knopwood on several occasions, sometimes in the small hours of the morning. He bled his clerical patient and administered laudanum to him and made a point of calling the next day to inquire after his health. Between November 1824 and August 1825 the two men dined together on no less than sixteen occasions. Often they shared the company of other men of society, of the likes of Major Morley of the 3rd Regiment; the surveyor general, G. W. Evans; the former provost-marshall, John Beaumont; the Reverend Bedford, and Josiah Spode, grandson of the founder of the famous Staffordshire pottery works which bore the family name.

Knopwood and Crockett took the air together—they rode to the suburb of New Town where they dined on strawberries. Perched high above the street where the lower orders walked, this was company that Crockett would have been happy to be associated with. On these occasions the two gentlemen no doubt talked about phrenology and other matters which stemmed from Crockett's experience at Macquarie Harbour. It was an association, however, that terminated abruptly.

Knopwood payed his last social call to 'Woodlands' on 2 September 1825. Thereafter Crockett rates only two further mentions in his diary. The terse entry for Friday 30 September reads: 'At court all the day. Dr Crockett's ill conduct'; and the entry for the following Saturday: 'Dr. Westbrooke and Mr Ross called on me about Dr Crockett but refused to see him.' James Ross was a particularly powerful friend. He was editor of the *Gazette*, the paper that had earlier published the description of

McKinney the runaway, and it may have been this friendship that kept the scandal out of the press. It is clear, however, that Crockett had been brought before Knopwood in his capacity as magistrate and that he was accused of committing an act that was not merely illegal, but one which was the cause of considerable embarrassment.

The bench book for 1825 has not survived, so in the absence of newspaper reports it is difficult to be precise about the nature of what Crockett referred to as his 'imputed crime'. The broad outline, however, is clear enough. Five days after his appearance before his erstwhile riding companion, the Reverend Knopwood—an occasion which must have been intensely embarrassing for both men—Crockett made an application to marry Emily Ann Vardon without publication of banns. As his wife-to-be was under the age of 21, her legal guardians had to vouch for her. Miss Vardon's mother had remarried and her new husband was a man possessed of a name with Dickensian overtones, Joshua Eynon Drabble.

Mr Drabble was superintendent of the female factory, a position for which he received the measly salary of £50 a year. Crockett and Drabble moved in different circles. The superintendent belonged to the class who walked out of necessity rather than for effect. He would not have owned a horse, nor did he rate a mention in Knopwood's diary, and he was certainly never invited to share the reverend's dinner table. Instead, Drabble was forced to write petitions to the lieutenant governor seeking some improvement in the quarters that he and his family shared with the nearly 'one hundred turbulent, depraved and diseased characters' who inhabited the factory.

The young Emily Vardon had grown up, as Drabble had put it, exposed to the 'disgusting, yet dangerous because daily, spectacle of vice, deaf to admonition, destitute of fear, and insensible to shame, setting at naught every institution both human and divine'. As well as the moral dangers that might ensue from constant contact with the worst aspects of lower order morality, there were the physical dangers of 'contagion and disease'. While the circumstances of her upbringing may have titillated the society doctor, as a marriage partner Ms Vardon had nothing to recommend to a man with social pretensions.

Married they were, however, on the very day after the application had been signed suggesting that there was some urgency about the whole affair. The union solemnised in St David's did not extricate the young surgeon from his predicament. The bench appearance assured that all in Hobart Town who mattered knew that the young society doctor had sexually interfered with Mr Drabble's daughter. After the wedding, Crockett wrote to James Scott, to tender his resignation. 'I feel it due to myself' he explained, 'to assure you in the most solemn manner on the word of a man and the Honor of a Gentleman, that I am the victim of a deep laid and most infamous Plot; of which fact I can now from the mouth of Mrs Crockett most fully convince you'.

As the marriage register reveals, however, Mrs Crockett was still very much a child. She was aged just fourteen and even by early-nineteenth century standards this was young. That it transpired that she was not in fact pregnant counted for little in the scheme of things. 'I cannot report that I have fallen a victim to conspiracy', Crockett wrote to Arthur in a futile attempt to rescue the situation, 'without wounding the character of her whom I have vowed to cherish, support and maintain'. In so doing, of course, he further sullied the reputation of the girl who had presumably been one of his patients. By failing to resist the 'impulses of his nature' Crockett had displayed his lack of gentlemanly qualifications.

Crockett wrote twice to Arthur requesting a grant of land, so that he could escape into the interior and assume a life of solitude as a settler cut off from the polite society that had turned its back on him. It would have been an act of escape not so different from that attempted by McKinney; but in the event Crockett found his path into the woods blocked by officialdom. Arthur scrawled a note on the second application: 'At the time I refrained from making a minute inquiry into his case, inform him that if I was to accede to his request I would have to do so now.' Crockett refrained from writing again. The following year, however, the colonial secretary did receive a letter from the young Emily Ann Crockett. She too requested a grant of land and listed the rental value of 'Woodlands' as proof of income. Since married women did not have access to their own property, let alone their husband's, until after the passage of the Married Women's Property Act later in the century, it seems certain that Henry Crockett had by then left the colony. Whether he took his young bride's heart with him we will never know.

He did, however, have an insurance policy of a different kind tucked into his luggage. When he absconded from his marriage he took with him Pearce's skull—a souvenir that he subsequently hawked like a common sailor to William Cobb Hurry, a Calcutta-based agent who collected crania for the Philadelphia phrenologist, Dr Samuel George Morton. Pearce's skull is now in the collection of the Pennsylvania Museum of Archaeology and Anthropology. The catalogue entry ends with the words, 'Mr Crockett, from whom I had this account, and who gave me the skull, is the Colonial Surgeon, and attended Peirce [sic] in the Hospital both before and subsequently to his crimes'. The version of the story peddled by Crockett was particularly lurid. He claimed that Pearce had lived on the edge of the settlement, but had periodically slipped in only to try and persuade another deluded convict to abscond with him in order to provide a fresh victim to feed his craving for human flesh. Thus it was that the former colonial assistant surgeon sensationalised the story of one absconder in order to help fund his own escape from the social wreckage he had left behind in the penal colony of Van Diemen's Land.

And what of the man who performed the punishment, who slammed the knotted cord into James McKinney's back? It is often assumed that the flagellators of convicts were soldiers, men from the garrison who pounded out each stroke to the beat of a regimental drum. In fact they were always fellow convicts, although the popular account is not entirely without foundation. As was the case elsewhere in the colony, the flagellators at Macquarie Harbour had all served under the King's colours or before the masthead prior to being lagged 'across the herring pond' to the far side of the world.

Despite what Pearce had said about Alexander Dalton—the first man that Greenhill had butchered—convicts did not volunteer to work behind the triangles, but were selected for the job on the basis of their prior military experience. The man who wielded the cat on that day in April 1823 was an agricultural labourer from Cork named John Flynn. Flynn had been court martialled at the Royal Marine Barracks in Plymouth in March 1820. In his case, as in so many other things, the power of the state to know its subject proved less than perfect.

For all his apparent service credentials, Flynn having signed up with the Marines on no less than three occasions, his actual military experience amounted to no more than a handful of hours. He had first attempted to enlist at Salisbury under the name of John Foror, but on arrival at Portsmouth he was rejected after the division surgeon had discovered that he was suffering from a rupture that had occurred sometime after his initial examination in the country. Undeterred, Flynn, if that was his real name, walked to Bath where he signed on with the Marines once more under the name of George Keefe, collecting the bounty of ten shillings plus a day's pay.

Placed under the charge of Corporal William Price he was marched out on the road to Plymouth. On route he 'hitched' his leg behind Price and gave the corporal such 'a hard blow with his closed right hand' that he threw him backwards onto a heap of stones. Not only was the rupture apparently a thing of the past, but Flynn demonstrated an uncanny level of dexterity. As Price cartwheeled through the air, the Irishman grabbed his pay book from the breast pocket of his jacket and absconded with the substantial sum of five pounds, ten shillings and sixpence in government recruiting expenses. It was a thing neatly done, as Corporal Price attested, but Flynn was not yet finished with the Royal Marines.

Having defrauded the Plymouth division he returned to Salisbury to try his luck once more with its Portsmouth-based counterpart. This time he signed on 10 February and deserted the next day. When he was finally apprehended and put on trial before a court martial he offered nothing in his defence and threw himself on the mercy of the court. He was sentenced to be transported as a felon for fourteen years.

Was Flynn pressed into service as Macquarie Harbour's flagellator? Could he have declined to perform the bloody duty with which he had been tasked? The evidence would suggest that he could indeed have exercised some degree of choice. There were plenty of other sailors, marines and soldiers at Macquarie Harbour—men who had far more experience of the trials and tribulations of armed service. He could, presumably, have pointed this out. He could have protested that he was as ill-qualified for the position as any other of the thousands of southern Irish labourers who crossed into south-west England every year in search of harvest work. Instead he chose to keep his mouth shut and thus it was that the right arm that had knocked down Corporal William Price by the Old Down Inn on the road from Bath to Plymouth, was turned to the service of the state on a remote small island in the middle of a wild harbour.

The rewards that befell the collaborator were not inconsiderable. He escaped the sodden grind of ganged labour and swapped the cramped confines of the penitentiary for a more comfortable billet. In the four years and two months that he worked as flagellator, Flynn was called upon to administer an average of 2.7 floggings a week, a task which would have called him to wind back his arm 123 times and would have taken him about one and a half hours to complete. There were of course low points, like the week in which McKinney was punished when he had to inflict a total of 1700 strokes. But even though he was also expected to work at night as a watchman, his duties were far less physically demanding than those performed by the mass of prisoners.

Flynn's conduct did not always meet with the approval of his superiors. He was once described as 'A great liar & not to be depended upon'. Nevertheless, he was released from Macquarie Harbour seven years before his sentence to a penal station was due to expire. This indulgence, the then commandant explained to the colonial secretary, was no more than Flynn merited for the 'good character' he had exhibited in his role as station flagellator. Others would disagree. Shortly after his return to Hobart Town, Flynn was assaulted in the prison barracks by a convict named William Hopper. Hopper lunged at Flynn, 'upbraiding' him in this most public of convict spaces for 'cutting the men's flesh at Macquarie Harbour'. It has not been possible to determine whether Hopper's calls for the other prisoners in the barracks 'to ill use him' were heeded, or indeed, how many other taunts, jibes, boots and fists Flynn had to endure in private retribution for his service aft of the triangles. If the words of the convict ballad 'Jim Jones at Botany Bay' are anything to go by, the opprobrium of his fellow prisoners may have been something he commonly encountered:

> *But it's bye and bye I'll slip me chains and to the bush I'll go*
> *And I'll join the brave bush rangers there, Jack Donahue and Co.*
> *And some dark night when all is quiet I'll slip into the town,*
> *I'll shoot those tyrants one and all, I'll gun the floggers down.*

Flynn was literally the arm of the state, but he was also an agent in his own right who had to negotiate the space between official duty and below decks opinion. He himself was bound to the triangles at Macquarie Harbour on no less than six occasions receiving a total of 130 lashes. It is the second of these punishments that is the most revealing.

On 5 November 1822, Flynn was charged with 'Raising false reports by saying that a person named Alexander McCurdy that was punished yesterday for losing or making away with his shirt was punished innocently'. McCurdy, a former private in the 11th Light Dragoons who had been transported for looting while serving in France with the post-Napoleonic War army of occupation, had indeed received a 50-stroke punishment for losing his shirt on the previous day. Yet if Flynn felt the same sympathy for his fellow countryman, James McKinney, as he had for McCurdy the previous year, then this time he kept his thoughts to himself and ground out the punishment blow-by-blow as McKinney slumped down on the triangles.

By 1827, Flynn was back in the Hobart Town Prison Barracks where he was charged with a string of minor offences, including gambling in the mess room and neglect of duty in not attending a flogging. In March 1829 he was sentenced to a further seven years' transportation for stealing a coat and was shipped once more to Macquarie Harbour. After his release he worked as flagellator in the Bothwell district before finally serving out his sentence. He was granted his free certificate on 24 March 1836. Thus it was that Flynn the collaborator who had performed his duty at the triangles negotiated a circuitous route to freedom. He appears to have died of tuberculosis in Sandy Bay, Hobart Town, on 22 September 1863. This was a decade after the last convict transport had pulled into Hobart Town.

By then, McKinney, the man whose back he had ripped ragged on a beach at Macquarie Harbour 40 years earlier, had long since turned to dust. Cuthbertson, the commandant who had timed each stroke with the turn of his leather boot, had also been buried in his lead and cedar coffin in the ground for four decades. Crockett the surgeon who could have stopped the punishment as he kept pace with Cuthbertson's cochineal-dyed jacket had died a social death that had just as effectively removed him from colonial memory. Macquarie Harbour, 'that place of tyranny', where tyranny it had been Flynn's lot to uphold, had been abandoned once more to the wind and the tea-tree. Even Van Diemen's Land, the name of the colony to which he had been transported, was a thing of the past.

Each of the 1273 floggings that were ordered at Macquarie Harbour was a staged event. They were designed as theatre to be watched by an audience that was literally captive. Floggings, however, were not isolated moments—up to an hour of time that could be measured by the drip of blood into a man's shoes and then set to one side. They were events that tied the participants to one another—that created bonds of subservience and revenge, order and disorder as strong as the cord that held each flogged prisoner to the triangle's wooden frame. It is impossible to understand a penal station by simply reading the correspondence enclosed in official despatches sent to Whitehall or the instructions supplied by colonial governors to successive commandants. The plans of colonial officials were never perfectly translated at ground level because, as powerful as writing was, it could not shape the everyday in the way that something like the lash could. In order to understand penal station society it is necessary to construct it from the ground up—from the rock cut by picks, the fences erected by blocks and tackles and the muster yards reclaimed from the sea with hard-fired brick and rubble.

A 'walled castle': north-east of Settlement Island showing the fences erected to break the passage of the wind. (Artist unknown)

6

Fifteen acres

Not every prisoner rejoiced when Cuthbertson drowned, despite the blood that had been spilled during his rule. This was because the commandant was said to have promised that when his period of office was over he would take up to Hobart Town with him 'as many as the schooner would carry and burn the Black Book as he said that it would be no more than fair that his successor should have a little trouble in finding out the characters of the men and that he said would give the boys an opportunity of brightening the nails in their shoes'. Not only were these good intentions frustrated by the commandant's untimely death, but his replacement, Lieutenant Wright, proved in the words of one prisoner to be possessed of all of Cuthbertson's faults but was devoid of his only virtue, bravery.

This was a point that Wright would have hotly contested. The new commandant, like Cuthbertson, had fought his way through the Peninsula War and had been wounded at Albuera and Bayonne. Yet there can be little dispute over the frequency with which he resorted to the lash. Throughout Wright's term as commandant, the office would continue to be a place where men were regularly condemned to be tied to the triangles.

Having endured 'the extreme inclemency of the weather' and the 'hardships and privations' of Macquarie Harbour for two years, the superintendent, Richard Ray and John Douglas, the commandant's clerk, were rewarded with tickets-of-leave and returned to Hobart Town. Douglas was replaced by a man who confusingly bore the same surname. The new clerk, Neil Douglas, had much in common with his predecessor. He too was a prisoner and also hailed from Scotland, having been born in Dundee. By contrast Ray's replacement, Thomas Warton, was a freeman. The son of a clergyman from Winchester, Warton had served as an officer in Cuthbertson's regiment, the 48th, before being convicted and transported. Pardoned by Macquarie, he was selected for the position of superintendent at Macquarie Harbour because, in addition to being 'extremely well educated', he had the military credentials to suggest that he could command a body of secondarily convicted men.

The appointment was a disaster. Now that Warton had served his time he wished to forget that he had ever been a convict. He styled himself 'a free man and a free gentleman'. He set out to use his posting to elevate himself to something approaching his former position in society. He was thus horrified to find that he had to share his small three-roomed cottage with Neil Douglas, who was not only a time-serving convict, but whom under any circumstances he would have regarded as his social inferior. As he put it in a letter to Wright: 'the relative distances between your Clerk and myself are as great as the distance between Your Worship as Magistrate and Commandant and myself as Superintendent'.

Technically Warton had a point. Even under the best of circumstances clerks occupied a lowly position within the British social order. They were neither working class, nor possessed of the wherewithal to pass that crucial test of middle class membership—the means to hire a servant. But the truth was that the superintendent was trapped between several states of being, as surely as his six foot two inch frame was wedged into his small 'incommodious' quarters. He was neither officer nor civilian, convict nor free, lower order nor, despite his protestations to the contrary, a gentleman.

In a colony where reputation was everything it should have counted that, like Cuthbertson and Wright, he too had fought and been wounded in the Peninsular War; but all that now counted for naught. Ever since he had been sentenced to seven years transportation at the Somerset Quarter Sessions for misappropriating regimental funds, Warton had become little more than an embarrassment to his family, his regiment and his social class. It no longer mattered that he had been gazetted for the part he had played at the Battle of Salamanca, an action which ironically gave its name to a section of the Hobart Town waterfront. His subsequent career had rendered this of so little consequence that the page of the *Gazette* that bore his name may just as well have been tossed before the winds.

At a loss to know what to do with him, Governor Macquarie had set Warton free after he had been in Sydney for little more than a year. For a while he had occupied the position of teacher at the public school at Richmond until he was dismissed for retailing spirits without a licence. When he failed to pay the fine, he had been imprisoned for a while before he took ship to Van Diemen's Land, possibly in the hope that there he might escape his past. He fashioned a living in Hobart Town as a memorialist, writing petitions and letters for those who lacked his literary flourish. Separated from his family by both physical distance and the depths of the social abyss into which he had so comprehensively sunk, he grasped at religion as a means of breaking his fall. As he told the supreme court in Hobart Town when he was subpoenaed to give evidence as a witness: 'I was once a gentleman, I am now a Christian'. The position of superintendent at Macquarie Harbour provided him with the opportunity to be a gentleman once more and he set about this task with the same zeal with which he proclaimed his new-found faith in God.

Shortly after he had disembarked from the brig at Settlement Island, Warton met the man with whom he was to share his quarters. Neil Miller Douglas had been sentenced to seven years transportation at the Old Bailey for fraudulently eliciting money from an unemployed clerk on the promise of securing him a job at the East India Office. Before his appearance in the dock, Douglas had worked in the King's Printing Office where he had operated a letterpress, and like Warton he was highly literate. It was unclear how he had found his way to Macquarie Harbour, but it appears likely that it was resulting from some further misdemeanour. According to his conduct record he was charged on 30 October 1823 while working as a clerk in the commissariat office with 'neglect of duty'.

Although the apartments of the two men abutted each other, Warton refused to socialise with Douglas. Instead he laboured at night on letters and poems with which he hoped to ingratiate himself with his social superiors. Thus, having heard that the newly arrived lieutenant governor, Colonel George Arthur, had lost a small child at sea on the voyage to Van Diemen's Land, he penned the following lines:

All flesh is as grass!—***Psalms***
Epitaph on Master Arthur
Had ruthless time; whose harvest is each hour!
Made, but 'one pause' to view this lovely flower,
In pity t'would have turned his scythe away,
And left him blooming till another day;
But restless he moved on! And it alas!
Too soon fell withering, with the common grass.

His nocturnal scribblings were interrupted by the sounds of Neil Douglas's 'midnight revelries' that penetrated the thin partition of wood that separated the two men's quarters.

It is clear from Douglas's Old Bailey trial that the young Scottish clerk was fond of a drink or two—the offence that had sent him to Van Diemen's Land had been plotted in a string of London taverns. Seized by religious zeal and the desire to distance himself from those he regarded as his social and moral inferiors, Warton railed against the hard drinking and foul language that he encountered daily at Macquarie Harbour. Douglas, for his part, was convinced that the weather and the pressures of the job had 'disordered' the superintendent's brain.

The superintendent's duties were onerous. He had to supervise the day-to-day running of the fifteen-acre settlement in all its minute detail. There were many things little and great that needed attending to; for a man new to the job, who was barely on speaking terms with the settlement record keeper, the task was daunting. To make matters worse, although Warton outwardly exuded self-assurance in his own moral superiority, he was inwardly wracked by guilt. Every Sunday he read and reread the last letter that he had received from his mother and wondered how he could possibly respond to the family he had so severely disappointed.

On 30 July 1824 he at long last put pen to paper and told his mother and sisters that he had passed the last five years 'in regret, in penitence; and in tears of remorse'. His experiences, he assured them, had shown him exactly what were the 'fruits of passions detested reign and sensual appetites indulged'. He wrote also to his daughter, Eliza, whom he would 'never behold more' and asked his mother and sisters to give her a lock of his dark hair which he enclosed in the folds of the letter; although one wonders whether this was an act motivated by the desire to be remembered or more by the fear of being forgotten.

Rather than sending the letter direct to his family, he enclosed it in another addressed to the lieutenant governor. 'I am induced', he wrote, 'to beg one favour of you' and with that he requested that Arthur wrap the missive to his parents in a copy of the *Hobart Town Gazette* that bore the news of his appointment as superintendent and forward it on. Perhaps not surprisingly, the lieutenant governor refused to be used as a mere postal clerk and the letter, separated from its discarded lock of hair, was neatly pressed into volume 271 of the colonial secretary's correspondence files where it remained forgotten.

It was part of Warton's duties to lock the prisoners into the rooms in the main penitentiary at eight each evening. Most of the settlement buildings had been erected in the lee of the slopes and were further protected from the elements by tall fences. There were exceptions, however—buildings that were deliberately constructed to catch the full force of the wind. Their existence confirms that the early settlement surgeons were anti-contagionists who were dismissive of the idea that infection was spread by personal contact. Whereas the causes of deficiency diseases like scurvy were well understood by the 1820s, knowledge of water-borne infection was still rudimentary. Many, including leading public health reformers, thought that sickness was spread by 'pestiferous "miasmas"'. In other words, that bad air was a dangerous enemy. Polluted water, sewage and industrial waste were all thought to be unhealthy because they emitted rank odours—in short, if it smelt bad it was bad, because it was the contaminated atmosphere that was the transmitting agent.

It was because of miasma theory that the first site chosen for the hospital was Small Island. Continually flushed by fresh draughts of air the island had the added advantage that its relative isolation allowed Cuthbertson to separate the female convicts who were employed as hospital orderlies from their male counterparts in the penitentiary on Settlement Island. Due to poor access and general discomfort the hospital was soon removed. Its new location, however, was still governed by the dictates of anti-contagionism. It was located on the exposed western side of the island where the wind could continue to sweep the structure clear of pestilent miasmas. The only other building located on this exposed shoreline was the penitentiary, another place where foulness could be dealt with by the cleansing properties of the wind.

While the single-storeyed brick and weatherboard penitentiary was more spacious than its counterpart on Small Island, it was still hopelessly cramped. Later, a new two-storey stone penitentiary was constructed at the back of the old building. Although this was a more substantial structure calculated to provide a greater degree of comfort, it was still draughty. While each of its three rooms was furnished with a large fireplace, narrow slits had been left for windows on the sides of the building that faced the weather. They were designed to ensure that the structure was continually flushed by circulating currents of air. It was described by the settlement commissariat officer as 'strong, capacious and airy'—as though airy was definitely a good thing.

When the bell rang for morning muster, the convicts in the penitentiary had to turn out from wherever they had been sleeping and assemble for work. The fence that was joined to the back of the building was designed not just to catch the wind, but to funnel the prisoners down to the wharf where they were ranked up in front of Warton to be counted. Not all of the convicts on Settlement Island were housed in the cramped confines of the penitentiary—some were permitted to reside in detached huts. The servants who attended to the needs of the various settlement officers slept in the kitchens at the back of each house. The gardener was quartered in a hut of his own where he could keep a close watch on the potato fields to check that they were not robbed in the dead of night. The boat crews slept in three conjoined rooms located to the front of the nail makers' forge. From there they could be roused at any time their services should be needed. Other prisoners who were employed as artisans were also permitted to share huts as were the clerks. Warton's semi-detached cottage was thus hardly a special privilege.

After muster, it was Warton's task to despatch the various work parties to their daily tasks. Lieutenant Governor Arthur had insisted that the convicts at Macquarie Harbour should be strictly classified. The prisoners of the very worst description should be given the hardest tasks; those who were deserving of reward, the lightest. Wright had replied explaining that it was difficult to achieve a precise alignment between severity of work undertaken and the various grades of conduct into which the ranks of the prison population might be separated. It would be unwise, for example, to employ the chain gang on the mainland hauling and rafting logs, as even though they were encumbered by irons there was every chance that they would abscond as Alexander Pearce had done when he ran for the second time. The prisoners classified as the worst therefore escaped the heaviest species of labour—although the disadvantages of being accommodated on Small Island went some way towards redressing the imbalance.

Instead of working on the mainland, the chain gang was employed in the considerable task of transforming the shape of Settlement Island itself. They quarried stone from the cliff face, shaping it into ashlars, or carved blocks, with which to build some of the more substantial buildings. They constructed caissons of timber from logs considered too poor to cut into planks or fashion into the ribs of a ship. Notched so that they could be slotted together 'pig's stye style' and fixed with large wooden pegs called treenails, these were filled with stones and used to extend the sheltered side of the island out into the shallow waters of the harbour. The reclaimed land was used to enlarge the lumber and shipyards.

The chain gang was also employed improving the thin sterile soils of the island which were often no more than '4 to 6 inches in depth with a sand or gravel bottom'. Timber was burnt in huge quantities and the wood ash mixed with earth and thousands of pounds of lime, all of which was painstakingly brought over from the mainland by boat. In addition to potatoes, it proved possible to grow a number of other fruits and vegetables in the more sheltered parts of the gardens for the consumption of the settlement officers. The north face of the island was transformed too. A roadway was cut into the solid rock of the cliff so that the chain gang could carry timber from the stockpile to the lumberyard without having to negotiate the uneven ground of the beach—a task which caused them to move, irons clanking, along the line of the paling fence that marked the edge of the neat gardens belonging to the commandant and surgeon.

The lumberyard was a place that caused the superintendent no end of trouble. While it was ringed by stockading, the sheer volume of prisoners that collected there and the number of tools and materials in circulation made it difficult to adequately police. It was Warton's task to guard 'against the constant plots and experienced villainy of the prisoners' who laboured there. Part of the problem was that the various buildings were so 'jumbled together as to afford no adequate security'. Although it was part of the superintendent's duties to view the place 'frequently in the course of the day' it was amazing what found its way out of the yard. As a place where the chain gang came into contact with the convict mechanics, it was not surprising that the yard was a site of exchange. It was impossible to stop the two classes of prisoner mixing, as all heavy objects, like large pieces of compass timber from which the knees of ships were fashioned, had to be carried in on the shoulders of those undergoing punishment. Within its confines those who were most likely to contrive to escape came into contact with men who had the tools and skills to fashion articles that would facilitate any such attempt.

Although the entrance to the place was protected by both a gatekeeper and a sentry, they were not always accorded the greatest respect. Prisoners simply refused to be searched and told the sentry that they did not 'give a damn for him or anyone'. Those employed to secure the place could not always be trusted. Thomas Morrison had to be dismissed as lumberyard watchman when he was caught passing out a flint and steel to a ganged convict.

At times the prisoners acted in concert to thwart the will of the superintendent. William Hawkins was sentenced to receive eighteen lashes when he was detected giving notice to some prisoners of the superintendent's approach. On another occasion Benjamin Horton was punished for providing a similar warning to a prisoner who was caught working in the nailors' shop on a piece of iron which had been cast into the shape of the storekeeper's hall door key with the aid of 'an impression made in soap'.

The stores were another place that needed to be vigilantly guarded. The commissariat was under the charge of a man named Parsons who had a veritable army of underlings to assist him, including two store-porters, an issuer and assistant issuer of provisions and a store clerk. It was their responsibility to keep all the settlement provisions safe and secure. This did not stop things going missing. On one occasion Parsons discovered footprints on some flour bags. Someone had stepped in a pool of brine that had seeped from a beef cask and left an incriminating trail of prints. The storekeeper climbed up on the stack of wheat flour sacks to reach the loft. There he discovered that the boards that partitioned the store from the adjacent sifting house were loose. Sergeant Reid was placed on guard and it was he who challenged William Argent when he caught him lowering himself down from the loft. Argent, who had been working in the sifting house, had climbed up with the aid of some barrels and wriggled his way through the gap in the boards. When he drew a ten-inch store knife Reid shot him, killing him outright. The body was carried to the mortuary where it was stripped by the dispenser of medicines who found a container manufactured from the bladder of some large animal and an eel skin bag concealed in one of his pockets. When filled they could hold some eight pints of spirits. In the subsequent audit it was discovered that, after accounting for leakages and evaporation (popularly referred to as 'the angels' share') some eleven gallons of spirits were missing.

The engineering store was directly under Warton's charge. It contained tools, equipment and other supplies essential for the completion of any number of tasks. Warton had to ensure that a list was kept of everything received into the store and all that was issued out of it. It was essential to know who had been given what and supervising the process occupied a great deal of his day. The list that was kept recorded the workings of the settlement in exacting detail. On 5 June, for example, he issued 250 clout and 400 clasp nails to Maynard, the carpenter who continued to work on the leaking quarters Warton shared with Douglas. A further 400 clasp and 300 shingle nails were supplied to Griffiths, who was conducting repairs on the commandant's house. A new spade was doled out to a man charged with turning the soil over in Wright's garden. Keefe, the shoemaker, was given enough leather and hemp to make five pairs of shoes and 150 hobnails with which to decorate their soles. Reeves and Smith, the boat builders, had nearly finished a new lighter for the pilot. They requested eight pounds of red lead, half a pint of linseed oil and some rosin (a translucent resin extracted from pine) to help finish her off. They were also issued with twelve oars made from celery top pine. Fisk was repairing the boat crew hut and was issued with a quantity of spike nails and 200 pounds of iron to complete the job.

Dr Garrett and Reeves each requested a sheet of tin—possibly for use as chimney vanes to help reduce the wood smoke in their quarters. The sawyers Knight and Yates asked for two new axes and three files. Osborne, the house painter, was issued with six panes of glass to fix some unnamed official's broken window. Later in the day he returned to collect some black paint to work on the pilot's boat. By then Reeves had turned his hand to the repair of the water boat and returned to the store to collect 200 timber nails. Fitzgerald, a former theatrical performer from Dublin, was issued with a quarter of a pound of twine and three old shirts in order to patch some of the men's clothing and four new piggins (wooden ladles) were supplied to the cookhouse for distributing skilly to the various messes. At the very end of the day a prisoner named Clayton, who had been employed driving piles, was issued with a new maul (a large two handled mallet), presumably because the one he had been working with was no longer fit for the task. All these things had to be accounted for in minute detail.

On Saturdays at one in the afternoon the prisoners were exempt from labour; but, although he was free, Warton was kept hard at work. He had to issue shoes and clothes from the store to all those who required them, reporting any who attempted to pass in articles that had been 'wilfully damaged'. At three o'clock he had to visit the penitentiary and muster all of the bedding, inspecting each article. In fact Warton's day was longer than that worked by the convicts. He had to supervise the ringing of the bell before dawn and the muster of the prisoners in the penitentiary every night at eight. It was his job to check that at least one constable had been left in each room, that the doors were securely locked, and that the watchman had been placed on duty. Only then could he turn in for the night—in the knowledge that he would be interrupted every twenty minutes by the watchman's call of 'all's well' and the sentry's answering cry from the wharf. The only day he was not busy was the Sabbath, but this was almost certainly little comfort to him. Despite the superintendent's religious fervour, it was Dr Garrett who was selected by Commandant Wright to read out the church service to the assembled prisoners.

As if Warton did not have enough to contend with, he also had to battle the elements. The hours of labour kept at Macquarie Harbour varied. In summer they were between six in the morning and six in the evening and, in winter, from seven until five. An hour was set aside in the 'forenoon' from nine until ten and another in the afternoon from one until two for 'breakfast and dinner'. The weather could play havoc with these times. In the darkest months of the year, from 25 May to 25 July, the evening bell was rung at half past four to take account of the dwindling light. At other times the wind and rain made it difficult to conduct any kind of work.

Even when the elements were kind, it was difficult to run the settlement according to the prescribed timetable. The men from Small Island often arrived late to muster owing to the difficulties of getting them off their isolated rock, and the detached gangs at work on the mainland hardly ever returned on time. Sometimes they were early and had to be supervised to prevent them from lolling around the wharf and, on others times, particularly when the weather was 'boisterous', they arrived late, wet and very much done in. It was the superintendent's duty to orchestrate all of these things. He had to battle the weather with the settlement bell in an attempt to impose industrial time on the vagaries of the elements and season.

The weather in July 1824 was particularly severe. A series of heavy gales from the north and the north-west made working conditions miserable. Wright was particularly anxious about the state of the prisoners' clothing. Many of them were labouring 'at this inclement season rolling logs in the swamp without shoes and almost without trousers'. It was perhaps not surprising that no prisoners had attempted to abscond in such conditions. Bad weather meant that on some days it was impossible to dispatch the gangs to the mainland. Indeed on some days it was difficult to organise any sort of outdoor labour. A priority on such occasions was to make sure that the chain gang at least were kept at hard labour. It was the superintendent's duty to get the key of the sifting house from Parsons, the storekeeper, and place the prisoners in irons inside and have a constable watch them grind flour for the settlement. Thus the timber walls of the sifting house ensured that those in the punishment gang did not 'escape with impunity' from hard labour on the frequent occasions that the weather was too wild to send a gang out to battle against the force of the wind.

Sorell's instructions to Wright, which were subsequently repeated by Arthur, were that the commandant was to maintain a rigid system of work discipline, even if this consisted of little more than 'opening cavities and filling them up again'. While the work undertaken by the ganged convicts was certainly severe it seems to have been driven more by pragmatic needs than purely the desire to punish no matter what. When prisoners were forced to work up to their waists in water, or arrived home late at night and soaked to the skin, for example, Wright insisted that they were provided with a measure of rum for nothing encouraged the prisoners to exert themselves more 'than the prospect of getting a little spirits'. As a result he used to issue cheques for the stuff 'at all hours of the day and night'. It was a system that Warton found difficult to adjust to. He railed against what he saw as flagrant breaches of Arthur's instructions—the lieutenant governor had been adamant that prisoners in a penal station were to be deprived of all spirits, tobacco and other comforts. As a result of Warton's complaints, Wright was forced to abandon the practice. It was a turn of events that ensured that the superintendent was detested by everyone with the possible exception of John Harris, his servant.

A whitesmith by trade, Harris was transported to Macquarie Harbour after he absconded from George Town in northern Van Diemen's Land and was found at large in the bush armed with a pistol, a canister of gunpowder, a quantity of lead and five large knives. Skilled he may have been in dressing tin and mending kettles, but there is little to suggest that he knew how to dress a man who had formerly belonged to the officer class. It was not skill, however, that drew Harris to Warton's attention but the way that he spoke—both men had been born in Dorset. It is a striking coincidence as less than half a per cent of all convicts transported to Van Diemen's Land were convicted in this small west country county. Within the confines of Macquarie Harbour their representation was even less. Harris was the only prisoner retransported to the station to claim Dorset as his place of birth. Perhaps it was because his accent reminded Warton of happier days before 'passions detested reign', as he put it, had induced him to plunder the regimental funds, that the superintendent requested that the man be brought over from Small Island to act as his servant. Perhaps the decision to ameliorate the lot of a man who spoke in ways familiar allowed Warton to indulge in the illusion that, loyal retainer at his side, he was on his way to regaining his former rank and position.

During the day, while Warton attended to his many duties, Harris would collect firewood and water from the boats that had been sent to gather these items from the mainland. He would clean Warton's quarters, make up his cot and cook his evening meal, and at dusk he would light the whale oil lamps. Like the commandant and the assistant colonial surgeon, who were also furnished with servants at government expense, Harris' presence ensured that Warton did not have to sully his hands with duties that were beneath a man of status. If access to a servant had been restricted to the higher officials in the settlement, then Warton could have contented himself with the knowledge that he was once more counted among those of some rank.

Such, however, was not the case. Lucas the pilot, who had been born illegitimate and had served at sea as a warrant officer, had a servant. Indeed, he had been assigned a female convict for the purpose with whom he cohabited and had several children. Not only was Parsons the storekeeper provided with a servant, but so was his clerk. Even Neil Douglas had been provided with his own man, effectively ensuring that, though a convict, he acquired a form of status beyond the reach of the vast majority of free men of his station. This must have seemed like the ultimate insult to Warton. Indeed the only official indicator of the division in status between the two men was the difference in their weekly ration scales. It was, when all was said and done, a few pounds of salt junk, some sugar, a little tea and about two pints of spirits that served to officially separate the two men—and as Warton had sworn off the grog following his disastrous appointment as a schoolmaster in New South Wales, his spirit ration did not count for much at all.

The winter gales of 1824 played havoc with more than labour schedules. The schooner *Waterloo* had finished loading timber for the return run to Hobart Town on 7 July but had been kept inside the heads for a further 22 days by the rough weather. The rain fell in torrents, washing the exposed soil off the vegetable plots. Cooped up in their cramped quarters under a leaking roof, the relationship between Warton and Douglas festered until things finally came to a head.

On 29 July the pilot tried to guide the *Waterloo* through the heads, but in the heavy swell she struck the bar and her rudder irons were carried clean away. Hearing the news, Commandant Wright dispatched a long boat to pull her back into the harbour so that the damage could be properly assessed. When she was finally refitted and ready to sail on 3 August he sent Douglas down to the heads in a boat with some correspondence to be placed on board. The clerk did not return until eight o'clock at night—he was soaked through, his shoes were torn and he was very tired. The boat crew pulled into the commandant's jetty so that he could give Wright the news that at last the *Waterloo* had cleared the bar.

This duty performed, Douglas called in next door to see Dr Garrett with whom he supped. Since he was drenched through, Garrett offered him a few glasses of punch. The colonial assistant surgeon was fond of a drop or two. Reading between the lines, Garrett and the convict clerk settled in for the evening drinking and—in the parlance of the time—it appears that they 'fathomed the bowl'.

The next morning after muster a befuddled Douglas tried to get new boots fitted. No sooner had the shoemaker started the task than John Harris came into his quarters to call the man away to attend to the superintendent's needs. Later when Douglas was trying to give instructions to the sawyers, Warton interrupted shouting at him from over the lumberyard fence to stop interfering and 'ordered' him to 'go about his business'. This public put-down incensed Douglas. He stormed up the path to see the commandant but en route thought better of matters and popped in to the quarters of his friend, Dr Garrett. When he emerged he found that Warton had gazumped him and brought his own charge to the commandant. Thus it was that Douglas was placed before Commandant Wright and charged with being insolent while under the influence of strong liquor.

Wright dismissed the case out of hand. Warton was furious. He wrote a letter of complaint to the commandant, which he ordered his servant to deliver by hand. To do so, Harris had to walk past the bakehouse, the tannery and gaol and through the turnstile in the gap in the fence below the military parade ground. There he would have had to inform the sentry of his errand and receive permission to pass.

On the other side of the parade ground was another fence that marked the boundary of Civil Row where the commandant and doctor resided. Some 'taste' had been exercised in the construction of the range of buildings which accommodated the settlement officers. The terrace included seven apartments, the final three of which were reserved for the commandant. His drawing room, which was the last in the range, was possessed of a rather 'handsome' circular front which, looking out towards Frenchman's Cap, commanded a view over 'a landscape of rich and varied magnificence'. It was a room that in shape and aspect mirrored the great cabin of a man-of-war.

When Warton had tried to argue that the social distance between himself and the convict clerk was as great as that which existed between the rank of superintendent and that of commandant, it was the spatial geography of the settlement with its intricate network of fences that exposed the absurdity of his argument. The point could be reinforced by reference to smell. There was one building in the settlement that most definitely stank. In order to prepare hides for tanning they had to be soaked in a solution of fermented faecal matter. The excremental odours that emanated from tanneries were notoriously stomach churning for all who were not seasoned to the stink. The commandant and surgeon resided upwind from such unpleasantries. Even the common soldiers in the barracks were protected by the prevailing breeze. Warton, however, was accommodated downwind from the stench.

Yet the superintendent's behaviour only served to accentuate his physical isolation from Civil Row. Over the coming days he put every little grievance in writing, sending a sequence of little folded missives by way of John Harris. It seemed an absurd thing to do—to converse in writing with someone who resided less than a hundred yards away. It was a huge mistake—it was to communicate as the commandant would, by written order and not face to face with cap in hand. As Wright said, the written counter charges were 'an insult to him as a magistrate'.

Warton and Wright inhabited a world where polite talk was an important social art. This would have been true whether they had met over a card table, in a coffee house or regimental mess.

It was especially true of Macquarie Harbour where there were so few people who had been brought up versed in the art of conversation. As Joseph Addison, the editor of the *Spectator* wrote, conversation was 'nothing else but an intimation and mimicry of good-nature, or in other terms, affability, complaisance and easiness of temper reduced into an art'. Every letter Warton sent was a substitute for a conversation that never happened, a sign of the extent to which he had cut himself off from the daily talk of the weather, the finer points of the vessel under construction and the peculiarities of the fauna and flora of the harbour. It was a miscalculation that condemned him to the continuing squalor of his incommodious quarters and the stink of the tannery. By contrast, Douglas was very much part of settlement society. He took constitutional walks in the gardens behind the comman-dant's house, played cards with Mr Parsons, the storekeeper, and conversed with the surgeon over a glass of punch.

Although in matters of religion Lieutenant Governor Arthur was an Anglican, albeit one with an evangelical bent, he did not think that clergymen from his own denomination necessarily made good missionaries. He had toyed with this idea during an earlier posting to Honduras. While he thought Anglicans were men of superior education and were generally more affable, and the kind of people one might choose to mingle with in society, when it came to proselytising to slaves and common criminals he was in no doubt that Moravians and Wesleyans were better equipped. He thought that as men of 'low estate' and humble disposition, they might succeed in effecting lasting change in the attitudes of ignorant and disorderly peoples while those who adopted a more condescending attitude were bound to fail. It was a view Warton's haughty and ill-conceived communications may well have reinforced.

The lieutenant governor now sent instructions to Wright to construct a house for a Wesleyan missionary. Despite being the son of a well-connected clergyman who had received a superior education Warton was now forced to watch as the settlement carpenters busied themselves preparing the frame for the new chaplain's house. While it was a structure destined to be occupied by a man of simple education and possessed of few social graces, it was nevertheless one that was to be erected within the confines of the paling fence that ringed the commandant and surgeon's quarters, up-wind of the tannery.

Fences were important at Macquarie Harbour. They defined the routes that linked the various areas of the settlement like the hatches and the companionways of a ship or the doors of a house. Perhaps it was not surprising, therefore, that Warton now applied for permission for a fence to be constructed to separate the yard at the back of the building, half of which he shared with Douglas, so that he should not be forced to come into contact with the time-serving felon. Indeed he went as far as to refer to the commandant's clerk as 'a convict dog'. Wright's patience was now sorely tested and he resented the manner in which his petulant superintendent constantly challenged the daily running of the settlement. He refused to sanction Warton's garden fence and so the two men occupied a space that remained undelineated by anything other than mutual loathing. Socially isolated but otherwise trapped in a space lacking in privacy, Warton was now convinced that there was a conspiracy to unseat him. He accused Douglas of having announced to 'Mr Parsons' table' that the superintendent was a 'sodomite' and that he engaged in 'unnatural practices' with John Harris, the sounds of which could be heard through the patently inadequate partition that separated their quarters. Wounded by the 'dagger of slander', Warton once more wrote to Wright requesting that Douglas be put on trial.

As Parsons denied that any such thing had been said at his table, Wright could not see much point in pursuing the case. To Wright's complete annoyance, Warton refused to drop the matter. It was clear that he would have to go.

When he had first arrived at Macquarie Harbour Warton had been shown a number of boxes at the back of the engineering store which he had been told belonged to absconders. He now had them pulled out and broken open as he was assured had been the custom in the past. He gave the contents of one box to the settlement flagellator, John Flynn. It turned out, however, to contain the property of a convict constable named James Wilkinson. It had long been the tradition at sea that when a sailor died that his box would be opened at the masthead and its contents auctioned. Often the dead man's shipmates would pay over the odds for the scattering of possessions in order that a bereaved family ashore would receive some small compensatory payment. In the penal station this ritual was turned on its head. When a prisoner absconded their box was taken out of the store and broken open and the contents distributed among the constables and watchman—in this Warton was only following tradition. It was a powerful dishonouring act that pronounced the absconder dead and simultaneously repossessed him by taking his private things and distributing them as rewards among those responsible for securing the settlement.

To treat a constable like an absconder—to pronounce him dead and distribute his clothes—was an act which Wright could not tolerate. The man had no respect for the delicate protocols of the settlement and in this regard, he did not act like a gentleman. Wright dismissed Warton on the spot and ordered him to collect his things and remove himself to the brig to await his passage to Hobart Town. On 13 August the superintendent sailed away from the station convinced that Macquarie Harbour was a place full of 'such damned scoundrels' that for '½ a pint of rum they would swear a man's life away'.

Warton never appears to have recovered his former position in society. In 1828 he was penniless and living in Launceston when he wrote the last of a long series of letters to Arthur soliciting money or a grant of land. By then he had received news, first of the death of his father and then of his wife and two of his children. His ultimate fate remains unclear. Neil Douglas died in Hobart Town on 21 November 1845 aged 49 years. The death was reported by a friend named Thomas Maxwell, resident in Bathurst Street, who—when asked for the occupation of the deceased—replied, 'gentleman'.

It is not exactly clear when the long-awaited clergyman arrived at the settlement, but when he did get there he lasted even less time than the ill-fated superintendent. The appointee returned to Hobart Town in shock to report that Lieutenant Wright was openly cavorting with the wife of one of the soldiers. Others repeated the story although, as they told it, Wright had a rival for the woman's affection in George Way Eldridge, the doctor's mate and a man with whom Neil Douglas was in the habit of walking in the government gardens. Eldridge was employed as dispenser of medicines at Macquarie Harbour, in which capacity he assisted Dr Garrett in the hospital.

It was a settlement rule that prisoners were strictly prohibited from entering the barracks—a place where the soldiers' wives and children were housed as well as the military detachment. Early one morning Wright spied Eldridge making his way into the building. As the story went, the commandant ran after him only to meet a sailor from the schooner *Waterloo* who was on his way out. It appears that Wright had rivals aplenty and that the barracks, upon which the security of his command rested, had been turned into a common brothel. Having detained the seaman, Wright instituted a search of the building but no trace of Eldridge could at first be found. Eventually he was unearthed by the commandant concealed 'in a large chest in the lady's bedroom'. George Way Eldridge was only charged with one offence in the time he was at Macquarie Harbour. On April Fool's Day 1824 he was placed in solitary confinement on a diet of bread and water for seven days for 'absenting himself from quarters after hours & being found concealed in a box in one of the soldier's huts'. The story would thus appear to be substantially correct.

For years the house constructed for the missionary remained empty and prayers were said by the settlement surgeon on a Sunday to the prisoners assembled around the sawpits. As one prisoner recalled, religion continued to be 'an affair that was not thought about at that place', and since the weekly service lasted such short a time 'the men did not trouble about it'. Arthur, by contrast, thought about Macquarie Harbour a great deal.

If the lieutenant governor had shown little interest in the place, Warton would have been left to rot in his cramped quarters while the roof leaked, and Douglas and the rest of Mr Parsons' table drank themselves unconscious. Far from it, however, Arthur pored over every scrap of correspondence that came out of Macquarie Harbour. Although he never visited the fifteen acres of Settlement Island he knew its confines intimately through writing. The stench that oozed through Garrett's floor as a result of a blocked drain in Wright's backyard, the details of an eel-skin bag found tucked inside William Argent's waistcoat and the contents of Constable Wilkinson's box were all unlikely details to which the lieutenant governor was privy. As he wrote to the under secretary of the Colonial Office, he spent much of the first two years as lieutenant governor trying to put the penal stations under his control on a 'better footing'. He 'freely confessed' that although it was a task that had absorbed his 'unremitting' labour 'there has not been any corresponding appearance of improvement'. In the end he approved the dismissal of Warton, despite the fact that the man had done little more than try and impose the lieutenant governor's orders. He did so because a penal station was too important a place to be left to go to rack and ruin, destroyed by petty squabbles and rumours about sexual peccadilloes.

Convicts at work in the sawpits, with the commandant's quarters with its 'handsome' circular front in the background. (Thomas Lempriere)

7

The mills of empire

It had been eighteen months since Neil Douglas had arrived at the settlement. Despite the relative comfort of his billet he was beginning to feel the effects of scurvy, having subsisted, as he put it, 'on a salt diet, whilst almost nothing in the shape of an antiscorbutic can be procured'. When Commandant Wright had left Macquarie Harbour in April 1825 he had promised his clerk that he would present his case to the lieutenant governor. It was now June and there was still no news.

Wright's replacement, James Butler, was a newly promoted captain in the 40th Regiment. Like his predecessors, Butler had fought his way through the Peninsula War. He had been promoted to the rank of lieutenant in 1809, the year of the battle of Talavera, but had to wait until his posting to Macquarie Harbour to receive his captaincy. The delay might be explained by factors other than poverty. Butler, who hailed from Dublin, was a Catholic. Under the terms of the penal laws, Catholics were not permitted to serve as officers in the British Army. This prohibition was watered down in 1793 by the provisions of the Catholic Relief Act, which allowed them to hold commissions within Ireland, but not outside. In reality the Act had been a farce from the outset. Butler was far from the only Catholic officer serving in the British Army. When the Duke of York refused to approve a commission on the grounds that the young man was a Catholic he admitted that there were many of a similar religious persuasion who were officers in the militia and even the regular army. Even Butler's commanding officer in the Peninsula turned a blind eye to the situation, despite the fact that the Duke of Wellington was a noted opponent of Catholic emancipation.

Butler's religion created other problems. Under measures passed in 1673 every public office holder had to take a sacramental test—a measure designed to debar Catholics and dissenters from positions of authority. The provision was not repealed until 1829. The test involved a repudiation of the doctrine of transubstantiation, the term used by the Catholic Church to describe the conversion of bread and wine into the body of Christ during the Eucharist. Without taking the test Butler could not technically be sworn in as a magistrate and until this occurred he was not empowered to punish any civilian, whether they be free or convict. Distance, however, provided a solution and in the end he was appointed a magistrate in a letter sent from Hobart Town, thereby avoiding a swearing-in ceremony.

The delay in the receipt of the appointment forced him to act outside of the law. One of the first prisoners that he detained illegally was Neil Douglas. Despite explicit instructions to the contrary, the commandant's clerk had broadcast the names of the prisoners Lieutenant Wright had recommended for release. Butler was furious but there was little he could do other than cause

Douglas to be locked up for a day. Butler kept Douglas in the dark in other ways too. It was vital that word about the commandant's lack of magisterial status did not leak out to the convict population as had the names on Wright's confidential list.

Douglas must have wondered why it was that he had not been formally charged. Over the next month he found himself distinctly under-employed. Week after week went by without a case being tried. May was nearly over before he was called upon to write anything into the settlement 'black books', although several prisoners had been shut up for short periods without being put on trial. By then it must have been obvious to everyone that something was up. On 27 May a gang of twenty men put the issue to the test. They downed tools and refused to work. Butler spoke to them in person, admonishing them for insubordination and threatening to punish the next man who stepped out of line. Scarcely had he turned his back when William Pierce, a 22-year-old former sweep from Maldon in Essex, 'urged the others not to labour any more' announcing to all and sundry that 'the Commandant could not flog but merely confine them'. Tellingly he added that while 'they could well bear' confinement, 'they could not stand flogging'. They were words that would ring in Butler's ears in the years to come. When the constable in charge of the gang attempted to shut him up, Pierce called him a damn villain. This was tantamount to mutiny and the commandant now had little choice but to act. He hauled the man into the office and ordered him to be awarded 25 lashes. To cover for his lack of legally constituted authority, however, the commandant did not institute formal court proceedings and made sure that he swore no-one in to give evidence.

The whole experience put Butler off the idea of confinement and henceforth he pretty much abandoned the expedient in favour of flogging. When John Popjoy, a member of the pilot's boat crew, refused to obey James Lucas's orders Butler sentenced him to 25 lashes. On the same day he sentenced Robert Badkins to 50 lashes for being insolent. Before the punishments could be inflicted, however, he remitted both sentences.

Despite the fact that winter was well and truly upon the settlement and the rivers were in full spate, making any attempt to run difficult, six prisoners absconded. When they were brought back Butler sentenced them to labour in irons for six months. He deprived other offenders of their rations, ordering them to be placed on bread and water. Finally he resorted to sentencing prisoners to work with the chain gang, grinding wheat in the sifting house. Even after his position as magistrate was confirmed he rarely resorted to solitary confinement. Over the next three years, he caused prisoners to be locked up as punishment on just eight occasions. Over the same period he ordered those placed on trial before him to be tied to the triangles and flogged on 612 separate occasions, sentencing them to receive a total of 23,696 lashes at an average of a little under 39 strokes per man.

In relying so heavily on the lash, Butler departed from the current penal ideology, which increasingly advocated the use of confinement over physical punishment. His habit of sentencing convicts to work at the hand mills, however, was more in line with the thinking of prison reformers. Treadmills were all the rage in the early nineteenth century, especially following the installation of William Cubitt's improved device in the Suffolk county gaol in 1819. This engineering masterpiece consisted of two treadwheels, each five feet in diameter and twenty feet long, set back to back. The apparatus was designed to be operated by 56 prisoners (28 working on each side) and the power that they generated was sold off to a local miller at six pence per bushel ground. By 1842 over half the 200 gaols and houses of correction in operation in England, Wales and Scotland had treadmills in place. Initially they were used to grind grain, crush beans, cut cork, beat hemp, power looms, break rocks and pump water.

Quickly, however, the treadmill became a machine designed to regulate toil, rather than to put the labour of prisoners to productive use. Many were disconnected from the millstones or other mechanisms to which they had once been attached and the hand cranks placed in cells were used to turn little more than sand. Prisoners were charged with making a certain number of revolutions each day, but the effort they expended was otherwise wasted. They were machines, as the philosopher Jeremy Bentham argued, 'for grinding rogues honest'. Like the penitentiaries in which they were installed, their principle aim was to regulate the prisoner by inculcating the habits of industry; but beyond this they had no utility.

Although there were plans to install a proper treadmill at Macquarie Harbour these came to naught. Handmills were far more practical as they did not need to be housed in a purpose-built structure. The punishment, in this respect, was designed to fit into the existing routine of the settlement and not the other way round. Rather than small rotary querns—the type of handmill that was still in use in western Ireland and the Hebrides—the mills at Macquarie Harbour were probably turned by capstans. In September 1829 a convict in the chain gang was sentenced to receive 25 lashes for 'impeding the work of one of the mills by mis-screwing part of the machinery', a wording that suggests a more complex device than a rotary quern. On another occasion three prisoners were awarded 50 lashes for 'scorching wheat whilst employed in the mill', presumably as a result of generating too much heat by grinding too hard. The charge implied that all three operated the same piece of equipment—capstan mills were powered by wooden bars that had to be pushed around in a circle by a team of prisoners. Mills of this type were certainly in use elsewhere in colonial Australia—one designed to be manned by Aboriginal convicts, for example, was constructed on Rottnest Island.

Rather than being condemned to meaningless labour in the confines of a penitentiary cell, the prisoners in the sifting house worked under the same roof where they sweated and grunted while the air filled with dust. If they were to be ground honest it was to be at the expense of the calluses on their hands, the threat of the lash upon their backs and the shout of the colour sergeant as the capstan bars were propelled round and round. There was no room here for quiet contemplation and the public good produced by their exertion was measured in sacks of flour.

A similar observation could be made of the whole system of punishment in the Australian penal colonies. As its critics pointed out, it was the labour of prisoners that turned the economy—they ploughed the fields, split the timber, built the roads, minded the flocks and packed the wool that was spun into cloth in the textile mills of northern Britain. This was to extract punishment not according to the principles of justice, but the dictates of the market.

When the First Fleet set sail in 1787 there appears to have been no firm concept of how convict labour was to be used. Many among the prisoners thought that transportation was punishment enough, and although they had been banished for a term set by a court in the British Isles, they were free to do as they liked while in exile. It was not an idea without precedent. An earlier scheme to transport convicts to the island of Lemane, many miles up the Gambia River in West Africa, proposed that they should be left there to organise a society of their own. Although there was to be a superintending officer, he was to reside on a hulk in the river and his main duties were to act as a mediator between the colony and neighbouring peoples. The convict colony was to be placed under the rule of a chief elected from their ranks by the prisoners themselves.

When the flotilla under Captain Arthur Phillip's command sailed into Cape Town en route to Australia they encountered a society that presented other options for organising labour on a more coercive level. From the earliest days, slaves were imported from the Dutch East India Company possessions in the Indian Ocean. Many Cape slaves worked alongside indentured Khoi, the indigenous people who, as pastoralists, were useful to the expanding settlement. By the late-eighteenth century the Khoi had lost their independence, having been subsumed by the advancing frontier and reduced to virtual slaves. Among the last of those to resist were a handful who were shipped to Australia as convicts. Convicts were also imported into the Cape. They came from places as diverse as Mocha in Yemen and Tidore in the Moluccas, many having been transported for political offences—for fermenting unrest in the Company's far-flung possessions.

The British in Botany Bay had fewer choices when it came to labour. Although they quickly came into contact with Aboriginal peoples these proved to be very different from the Khoi. They were not pastoralists, despite the Australian Agricultural Company's best attempts to turn them into minders of sheep, and they showed remarkably little interest in the European concept of labour. There were also no slaves, nor any possibility of importing them. At the time the First Fleet set sail, British slaving interests were engaged in a rearguard action against the powerful abolitionist lobby. Indeed Phillip, who had been given command of the expedition, was careful to insist that the new colony would be run according to the laws of England and not some slave code. From the start therefore the convicts formed the only practical supply of labour and Phillip assumed that property rights in their labour were assigned to him as governor.

He referred to them as 'servants of the Crown' and treated them as though they were indentured labourers bound to serve for a period of time fixed by the courts in Britain.

The arrangement mirrored the seventeenth- and eighteenth-century practice of selling transported felons as indentured servants in the Caribbean and the American colonies. The language that developed in New South Wales to describe the civil status of convicts betrayed the connection with the Atlantic experience of transportation. Convicts still under sentence were described as in 'servitude' and those that were free as 'emancipated'—terms that explicitly aligned convicts with other categories of unfree labour.

There were other similarities between New South Wales and seventeenth- and eighteenth-century America. It was generally the practice to give indentured labourers a payment on emancipation in order to provide them with some means to establish an independent future. In some places this took the form of a block of land. It was hoped that this would help populate Britain's overseas possessions with what was sometimes referred to as a 'stout yeomanry'. Such men and women might best be described as the kind of independent small scale farming class that could answer the call to arms should the occasion arise. There were additional advantages, landed people have for long been considered safe. A block of land gave a person a stake in the future, whereas a landless labourer was seen as a potential source of discontent. It was better to anchor former servants in the soil, so the argument went, than leave them to drift from place to place.

While such payments were rarely made to emancipated convicts after the mid-eighteenth century—they were abolished in Virginia in 1753 for example—Phillip resurrected them. Upon their emancipation, he supplied former convicts with small blocks of crown land of between 20 and 80 acres. The practice was important in that it provided transported men and women with the prospect of future independence.

The policy was nurtured in other ways too. The largest purchaser of goods in early New South Wales was the commissariat store. It was responsible for supplying rations to prisoners, soldiers and others who were listed in the muster returns as 'on the stores'. Wheat and meat were purchased from local settlers on a quota system that guaranteed a share of the market for all those who tendered produce. By this means the government provided a source of income to smallholders, protecting them from direct competition with larger, more efficient landholders.

There were other ways in which early colonial Australia was surprisingly free. Colonial custom quickly placed limits on the rights that the Crown had in convict labour. After government hours the prisoners' time was restored to them and they were free to work for wages until the official start of the next day. Weekends became times of particular industry as government time ended at midday on Saturday and did not commence again until sunrise on the Monday morning. It was a bizarre arrangement but one that was necessitated by the lack of government infrastructure. Before the completion of Hyde Park Barracks in Sydney in 1819 there was little government accommodation for prisoners and as a result there was no real option but to let prisoners participate in the economy in order to provide them with the necessary means to pay rent.

As Phillip understood that property rights in convict labour had been assigned to him, he assumed that he had the authority to both pardon prisoners and to transfer those property rights to others. Accordingly, he provided some of the colony's early farmers with convict labour hoping that this would make them more productive. In an economy where free labour was notoriously expensive, attempts by the government to establish a monopoly over the services of prisoners were always likely to be challenged. In the three years between Phillip's departure and the arrival of his successor, New South Wales was run by the senior military officers. The latter promptly expanded the practice that Phillip had established, effectively privatising a proportion of the available convict labour. The early governors had all been naval men. They looked out to sea—trying their best to limit the growth of the tiny settlement under their control. Their remit was to maintain Port Jackson as a small outpost where ships could be overhauled and refitted on the model of the Dutch East India Company station at Cape Town.

The New South Wales Corps officers in particular had other ideas. Australia was far more than just a posting for them—the place represented their future. They saw themselves as the elite of a new colony and actively attempted to foster its growth. In contrast to their naval masters, they looked to the interior, attracted by the prospects of large acreages and the potential riches of a new continent. They also allocated sizeable tracts of crown land to themselves. They were careful to provide grants to others, too, calculating that this would make any attempt to reverse their actions both administratively and politically difficult.

As the practice of assigning convict labour expanded, many convicts were distributed to colonial farms and, as in urban areas, they tended to blend in with the colonial lower orders. On small farms run by emancipists, it was notoriously difficult to tell the difference between convicts and their masters. They worked alongside each other, ate at the same table and dressed in the universal garb of the colonial lower orders—the kangaroo skin jacket. They were also often paid. In an economy where there was an acute shortage of cash, such payments were usually made in kind. It was thus common for shepherds to be paid a third of the increase in the flock, and thus acquire the means to support themselves. In this society it was not uncommon for convicts still under sentence to own property and even run businesses. Some became wealthy long before they were emancipated—the entrepreneurial Jewish brothers, Joseph and Judah Solomon who opened their first store while still under sentence being a case in point.

All of this started to change in the aftermath of Wellington's victory at Waterloo. When the Napoleonic Wars came to a close the army and the navy were dramatically reduced. The scale of the demobilisation was such that it sent shock waves through the British economy. As competition increased for jobs, many were thrown out of work and crime rates rose. During the war the number of convicts transported to Australia had been reduced to a mere trickle. The large post-war increase had worrying financial implications and the British government despatched a commissioner of enquiry to investigate ways of ensuring that Britain's far-flung penal colonies remained viable. Transportation needed to be both feared by the British working class and cheap enough to keep the taxpayer happy. The alternative was the construction of a string of penitentiaries on the lines of those advocated by the English philosopher, Jeremy Bentham. This would certainly be costly, but it was argued by its proponents that it would provide a more effective remedy to rising crime rates in that penitentiaries were better calculated to curb recidivism. The man selected for the job was John Thomas Bigge, a former chief justice from the British slave colony of Trinidad, and the report that he wrote had a profound influence on the future development of New South Wales and Van Diemen's Land.

Bigge thoroughly disapproved of the policy of granting small blocks of land to time-expired convicts. He looked askance at their farms, which he regarded as slovenly ramshackle affairs. Rather than encouraging the habits of industry, he thought the provision of land to emancipists merely permitted the maintenance of indolence. Others concurred, describing small properties in Van Diemen's Land as littered with wool, bones, sheepskins and wasted manure. They were gathering points for 'a numerous tribe of dogs and idlers; the former barking, the latter lounging about'. It would all have seemed very odd compared to what Bigge had seen in Trinidad. In the years he had been posted to that colony, plantation sugar production had greatly expanded. In 1813 there were 25,000 slaves on the island, most of whom had been engaged in intensive monoculture production for export markets. Food crops were important too; indeed agricultural land was valued as much as that under cane since the maintenance of the slave population depended upon the cheap local production of victuals. What Bigge found in Van Diemen's Land and New South Wales must have seemed the very antithesis of the productive order he had observed in the Caribbean.

He recommended that, in future, crown land should be granted only to respectable migrants—those who could demonstrate that they had at least £500 capital. Rather than being split up into small blocks, land should be alienated in large tracts. He had been particularly impressed by the estates of the Macarthur family in New South Wales, which he thought provided a model for the future direction of the colony. If the Macarthur experience could be replicated across the Australian colonies the place could become a production house for fine merino wool, lessening the dangerous dependency of the British textile industry on imports from the European continent. Rather than being a drain on the treasury, Australia could be turned into a sheep walk.

The policy was attractive since the necessary incentives to make it happen were readily at hand. The colonial government could control the allocation of land and provide the additional carrot of cheap labour. A settler was entitled to request the services of one convict for every hundred acres of land received. The post-Napoleonic War influx of convicts could thus be turned to advantage. Rather than swelling the ranks of the government gangs in Sydney and Hobart Town where they were a direct drain on the treasury's coffers, they could be distributed to migrants with capital who would clothe, house and feed them instead. Bigge calculated that the saving to government would be considerable—£24.10 a year for every convict placed in private service.

He also disapproved of the way in which the commissariat store operated, noting that it amounted to little more than a government-subsidised scheme for keeping small-scale farmers on the land. His recommendation that the quota purchasing system be abolished altogether was adopted in January 1822 and henceforth the store operated on a competitive basis, refusing to accept tenders below 100 bushels of wheat and 2000 pounds of meat. This effectively put it beyond the reach of the vast majority of small farmers.

The policy shift had the dual advantage of saving the government money and assisting in the social transformation of land holding patterns. As the new settlers would be drawn from the respectable classes, Bigge was confident that they could be depended upon to inculcate their convicts with the values of the large estate. In future, prisoners would be taught to tug their forelocks and curtsey to their betters. To refuse to do so would be to run the risk of being dragged before the bench. An additional advantage was that the bulk of the convict population would be scattered across the countryside where they would be locked within a deferential landscape away from the urban temptations proffered by the taproom, gambling house and brothel. The whole scheme was calculated to turn idle prisoners into a compliant and obedient working class.

In fact even before Bigge tabled his three reports before the British Parliament, the Australian colonies had started to change. The publication of a series of emigrants' guides, several of which were advertised for sale in *The Times*, encouraged free migration. From November 1818 onwards the same paper carried regular advertisements for passages to Van Diemen's Land.

The arrival of increasing numbers of migrants with capital spelled an end to the untidy flocks of Persian fat-tailed sheep that had been run by emancipist farmers. They were replaced by improved breeds noted more for their wool than their eating. By the mid-1820s cloth manufactured from wool exported from Van Diemen's Land had already achieved a high reputation. The land was now taken up by pastoralists at a far greater pace than before. Settlement in New South Wales broke out of the Cumberland Plain, crossing the Blue Mountains, while in Van Diemen's Land all of the good land between Hobart Town and Launceston was made over to settlers in a little more than a decade. The markers of property appeared on the landscape. Fences were important in protecting improved stock from unimproved and by the late 1820s the first of a string of fine stone-built houses had been erected with ornamental gardens and carriageways at the front and service quarters, farm buildings and male convict barracks around the back.

There were, as one might expect, voices of dissent. As a 'freedman' put it: 'If no immigrant had come out here, to claim not only the exclusive possession of the soil, but also of all the powers, emoluments, and honors [*sic*] of the state, would not the original regulations have still been adhered to, of giving small land grants to free men?' Under these circumstances, he asked, would not the colony now be 'more populous, more rich, more cultivated, more advanced in every thing but aristocratic feeling'?

The reality was, however, that Commissioner Bigge's report cut off the convict's route to independence. It ensured that henceforth the end of one sentence would merely mark the start of a second as the convict passed into the ranks of the colonially waged. The 'assignment era', as the post-Bigge order was described, was geared not just to extract labour from prisoners while they were still under sentence, but also to train them to be a dutiful worker for life. The reformed convict, in this sense, was a man who kept a 'still tongue in his head' and did what he was told. The only reward for years of service as a prisoner would be the ability to earn a wage and freedom from the coercive control of the Convict Department under whose rules he could be flogged for the smallest disagreement with his master.

Indeed the 1824 Transportation Act attempted to cement private property rights in convict labour, providing masters with the legal right to hire out the labour of prisoners that had been assigned to them or even to sell them on to third parties for profit. It was as though masters had title in their assigned servants in the same way as they held title over the land that had been granted to them. Certainly, a strict interpretation of the Act was that it cut across the governor's right to recall assigned servants, or pardon them before the termination of their sentence without compensation. It is perhaps not surprising that it was never fully enforced in the colonies where the Act became a matter of political and legal controversy. Nevertheless, the legislation provided a vivid demonstration of the extent to which the British government thought that security in property rights in convict labour formed a crucial underpinning to colonial economic success. Events elsewhere provided ample evidence that this might indeed be the case.

In 1820 an attempt was made to settle the Eastern Cape in South Africa using nothing but free migrants. The problem was that in a place where cheap land was abundant few people were prepared to work for wages unless these were equivalent to that which could be made from working the land as a small holder or by running livestock. The scheme came to naught when the would-be labour force decamped to the frontier in search of land of their own. Some form of bonded labour was crucial if the park-like lands of Britain's antipodean colonies were to be brought to productive use.

The message was reinforced by warnings provided by several prospective colonial gentry who migrated to Van Diemen's Land. As one put it, if the emigrant intended to bring servants with them 'these should be bound in England under an indenture to serve for a given time, and under penalty if they should quit their master in this country before the period agreed expires'. In the colonies every migrant wanted to be his own master and regardless of his class, those who arrived free adopted a 'certain nonchalance' that appeared 'to acknowledge no superior'.

The convict, anchored in place by the threat of the lash, provided the necessary cheap labour to ensure that capital invested in New South Wales and Van Diemen's Land was likely to yield returns. It was thus no accident that convict legal freedoms declined steadily in the 1820s and 1830s at a time when their labour was seen as crucial for transforming the colonial economy. Their rights and freedoms were curtailed in other ways too. Increasingly the hours that they worked were regulated and opportunities to earn money limited. Following the completion of Hyde Park Barracks in 1819 it became the norm for public works prisoners to be housed behind government walls at night. The system of passes was tightened up, regulating travel from one place to another, and the colonies were divided into police districts, each complete with its own magistrates' bench. The latter were empowered to punish prisoners for infraction of the rules and regulations governing convict labour. Indeed, Chief Justice Forbes in New South Wales thought that for all intents and purposes assigned convicts were slaves. Others agreed—Arthur said as much to every prisoner who arrived in Van Diemen's Land.

Part of the ritual of the colony was that after convicts had been disembarked they were addressed by the lieutenant governor in the yard of the prison barracks in Hobart Town. The whole shipload was told that they would now find themselves in a degraded state, one that, as they would discover, could be compared to slavery. Arthur later repeated the claim before a British parliamentary committee. When asked to describe how the convict's condition related to that of the slave, he replied that it differed in no respect 'except that the master cannot apply corporeal punishment' (this could only be inflicted following a magistrates' bench) and had 'property in him for a limited period'. It was an assessment that Arthur was well placed to make. He had formerly been superintendent of British Honduras, a place where slave labour was used to procure mahogany for the manufacture of fine furniture.

As with slavery, the chains that held the convict in place were ideological as well as physical. The very fact that all prisoners had been convicted of breaking either the criminal law or the Articles of War was used to justify the levels of exploitation to which they were subjected. Any attempt by the prisoner to challenge their condition merely confirmed that they were at best ungrateful, and at worst wicked and depraved. It was a point underscored by the damning lines that could be entered against their name in the register of offences kept in the superintendent of convicts' office.

The 'black books' were the centrepiece of the post-Bigge convict system. They had initially been created in Sorell's time

(1817–24) but Arthur employed Edward Cook, a transported law stationer, to reorganise the volumes. It took him a year to write out a summary of the offences for which 12,305 convicts had been charged before the various benches of the colony. At times he worked for fourteen or fifteen hours a day, his pen illuminated by spermaceti oil burnt in lamps. It was a huge task, and one that as he later confessed greatly injured his health.

The purpose of the registers was to chart the course of each and every prisoner so that when they applied for permission to marry, or to be removed from a place of suffering like Macquarie Harbour, their record could be quickly retrieved. Each case could then be dealt with on its merits. The official would know with certainty how many times a prisoner had appeared before a magistrate and the outcome of each hearing. The black books were an essential tool of convict management, one that could be used to separate the sheep from the goats and the deserving from the undeserving.

Yet if Edward Cook's eyes had been sacrificed for a slightly different purpose, an alternative view of convict Van Diemen's Land would have emerged from a perusal of his labours. If the offences for which convicts were charged were reassembled according to the skills they brought to Australia it would have been possible to discern that a clerk like Neil Douglas was three times less likely to be flogged than a tailor. Over the course of his sentence, a carpenter received on average nineteen strokes of the lash, whereas weavers and cotton spinners got nearly 60. The difference in the degree of judicial punishment they received reflected the fact that carpenters and clerks were much in demand. Indeed, fewer men with these skills were transported than there were colonial positions for them to fill. As a result they were on the whole well treated. This was particularly true for those who were assigned. Advice commonly given to settlers thinking of migrating to the distant penal colony was that it was far better to reward assigned servants for good behaviour than it was to punish them for bad. This was particularly the case for those with useful skills. A trip to the magistrates' bench could result in a valued convict being sent to a road party or, worse still, a penal station, and there was no guarantee that the replacement would be a man who was half as useful.

By contrast, far more tailors were transported than there were jobs available. As a result they were given tasks such as clearing stones off fields or grubbing out the stumps of trees. This was work that required little beyond raw muscle power. If a poorly skilled prisoner's services were lost to the chain gang then little damage was done—an application could simply be made for a replacement. This is why agricultural labourers received on average 28 strokes of the lash per man over the course of their sentence while common labourers, with little or no experience of shearing or handling draught animals, were awarded 45.

The rate at which convicts were charged also varied according to the seasons of the year. Assigned servants were one and a half times more likely to be brought before a magistrates' bench during the two harvest seasons than they were in August, the least busy month in the agricultural cycle. Some masters undoubtedly used the bench to encourage increased participation in an attempt to squeeze more labour out of their assigned servants. Convicts may also have played up at harvest in the knowledge that, as their services were in particular demand, the master had less room to manoeuvre and was more likely to cave in to their demands. It is likely that in other cases tempers simply snapped, and that during a time when the demands of farm labour put a stress on one and all, routine disputes were more likely to end up being settled in court. Whatever the explanation, however, the entries entered into the black books are revealing. They demonstrate that the charges brought against convicts were shaped by the realities of the colonial labour market. Thus the lines of 'indiscretions' that Edward Cook copied out late into the night were as much a product of economic circumstance as they were the moral failings of the individual.

That prisoners were aware of this is borne out by the language they employed to describe their situation. They referred to themselves as bond men and women or crown servants, prisoner servants or indeed slaves. These were all expressions that emphasised the extent to which they were forced to work against their will. The term 'slave', of course, was particularly emotive, suggesting a gross level of exploitation. Its use had the effect of turning the spotlight away from the prisoner and focussing it instead on those who profited from the exploitation of transported labour. The term 'convict' by contrast had degrading overtones of moral failure. It was an explicit reference to the conviction passed on every man and woman who had been lagged to Australia.

Just as in the plantation world, ideology played an important role in the labour extraction process. The very fact that every prisoner had been found guilty was important in justifying the levels of exploitation to which they were exposed. Thus, those who laboured in positions of trust were permitted to do so as they were said to be deserving of reward, while others were forced to crush aggregate or drag logs through the dense scrub in order to atone for their insolence, idleness or other misdemeanours.

The penal landscape that emerged in the wake of the Bigge report was structured like some earthly representation of Dante's vision of hell. Each convict was allocated to one of six types of labour. The uppermost level, reserved in theory for the best behaved, contained those who had been awarded a ticket-of-leave. This piece of paper allowed convicts to earn their own wage. Indeed, they needed to do so or they'd starve since ticket holders were no longer entitled to a government ration. To feed, clothe and house themselves they had to search for work. It was a kind of probation designed to prepare the convict for waged labour proper. The second level contained the vast majority of prisoners—those who were either in assigned service or employed by the government as masons, clerks, butchers, seamen or any of the numerous roles required to maintain the various departments of government.

A further level below were the road gangs where prisoners were worked in long lines under the constant supervision of an overseer. It was the overseer's job to make sure that there was no let-up in the rate of production; he did this by singling men out for punishment. His presence ensured that those sentenced to the roads were far more likely to collect further damning entries in the black books. For those that re-offended the iron parties formed the next stop on the downward slope. Here prisoners were encumbered with three pounds of wrought metal riveted to their legs, which could not be removed unless struck off by a blacksmith. Many of those sentenced to work in irons were absconders and the chains that rubbed the skin off their ankles anchored them to their daily labour, considerably reducing the possibility of future escape. Finally, there were the penal stations. First Maria Island, reserved for the prisoners whose misdeeds were considered to be not of the very worst description, and for the others—the outcasts of the penal colony—the gates of hell beckoned.

When Arthur was first informed of the kind of labour undertaken at Macquarie Harbour it must have conjured up memories of his time in Honduras. In that colony, parties of slaves were sent up-river in August every year to cut timber. Suitable trees were scouted out by a 'huntsman' and then felled by axemen standing on platforms. The bulk of the work was undertaken by gangs who cleared roadways through the forest, cutting the underwood with cutlasses and removing stumps and rocks with hoes and pickaxes. Once the logs had been cross cut and squared they were dragged to the water's edge by ox teams before being floated downstream.

The variety of different tasks undertaken at Macquarie Harbour ensured that the penal station provided opportunities to retrain convicts whose skills were not useful in the colonies. As Butler wrote to Arthur, there were many who laboured at Macquarie Harbour 'such as weavers, tailors, cotton spinners and other sedentary trades, who are unfit for and disinclined to outdoor labour; and I should conceive a very troublesome and useless set for settlers'. This was indeed the case—convicts with skills in the textile industry were over-represented among the ranks of prisoners at Macquarie Harbour. Indeed twice as many were sent there as one might expect given their general distribution in the convict population as a whole. Once these prisoners had been disciplined however—fashioned by the rhythm of work into what might be called docile bodies—they could be re-skilled. Taught to handle an axe or put to work in the sawpits or perhaps even the lumberyard where they could learn to shape the frames of a brig with an adze, they became useful to the colonies at large.

Butler spelled out the advantages that might flow from this. Once released, former penal station convicts would work hard and without complaint, for the consequences of insubordinate behaviour had been impressed upon them by the horrors of working in a timber rolling gang. At the very least they would be better suited to manual labour, to clearing and breaking land. Many, however, would be returned to the settled districts with superior skills 'which independent of the reformation effected in their habits' could not be 'otherwise than beneficial to a community where such high wages are demanded by mechanics'. The price of skilled free labour was a constant complaint among settlers in Van Diemen's Land. This was particularly true of workers in wood who were in much demand. One of the many remits of Macquarie Harbour was to help address the situation. It was not just a machine for grinding rogues honest, although that was one of the things that it set out to do, but part of a wider mechanism designed to drive down labour costs.

One of the results of this was that the punishments experienced by prisoners at Macquarie Harbour were not borne equally. Those who were sent to the penal station for absconding, for example, received on average 60 strokes of the lash per man and spent 45 days in irons over the course of their sentence to secondary transportation. This was a fearful rate of punishment significantly greater than that meted out to other categories of offender. Convicted burglars, for example, received 42 strokes of the lash per man and spent an average of just fifteen days in irons. Men who had been retransported for crimes of violence, cattle and sheep duffers, receivers of stolen property and common thieves were all significantly better treated than those who had been banished to the confines of Macquarie Harbour for attempting to run. What is peculiar about this is that absconding was not a criminal offence and as such could not be tried by a superior court. Thus one of the many ironies of the penal station was that the bulk of the punishment meted out fell on those who had been sent there on the orders of a magistrates' bench. By contrast, convicts who had received sentences of secondary transportation in the supreme court, even those who had been reprieved from the gallows, were punished far less frequently.

It was an anomaly created by the economics of transportation. The vast bulk of absconders ran from road and iron parties. They took to the bush in order to escape the fly-blown rations, constant work and general misery associated with punishment labour. The decision to run condemned them to the greater horrors of penal station life, yet it was lack of bargaining power that had caused many to be cast into road gangs in the first place. As the Quaker missionaries Backhouse and Walker observed, it was in the master's interests to charge their less skilled assigned servants since this was a convenient means of turning over their labour force. For every convict lost to a road party the master received a replacement from the government and there was every likelihood that the new man would be either more skilled, or more compliant, or perhaps both. Those possessed of little in the way of colonially useful skills fared no better in a penal station. Carpenters, blacksmiths and other mechanics were far better treated than those who had little to offer other than muscle power. Mechanics spent on average eighteen days in irons and received 37 lashes per man compared to 32 days and 49 strokes for convicts with less useful skills.

The point was underscored by the fate of agricultural labourers. As skilled farm workers were valued as assigned servants, comparatively few found their way to Macquarie Harbour. Although convicts with agricultural skills accounted for one in four of all male prisoners landed in Van Diemen's Land between 1817 and 1839, they accounted for less than one in seven of the convicts at Macquarie Harbour. Although proportionally few in number there was little for them to do once inside the confines of the penal station. There were no teams of oxen and the agricultural land at Macquarie Harbour, such as it was, was tilled by hand hoes rather than ploughs. The inclement weather and acidic soils that ensured that crops either rotted in the ground or were blown flat condemned secondarily transported farm hands to the drudgery of ganged labour. As a result they received nearly half as many lashes again per man as mechanics and spent twice as long working in irons. This was precisely the kind of arbitrary system of justice calculated to attract the ire of penal reformers and it was no accident that Macquarie Harbour featured prominently in subsequent enquiries into the efficacy of transportation. In other respects, however, it was a process that worked in that it ground out goods in the form of ships, pine furniture or sawyers crafted from the bodies of textile workers.

Arthur placed a great deal of faith in Butler as the man responsible for keeping the mills in the sifting house at Macquarie Harbour turning. He lamented his loss when the 40th Regiment was ordered to depart for India in 1829, ironically the same year that saw the repeal of the law prohibiting Catholics from holding office. The lieutenant governor described him as cool, determined and sensible and generally approved of his methods, even if these paid little attention to the precepts of penal reformers—and well he might. The penal station was always far more than a place for disciplining recidivists. As the offences for which prisoners were sent to the settlement illustrated, it mattered little whose bodies were actually used to sate its appetite. The role of the place was to power the economy by fear—a fear calculated to increase the rate at which labour could be extracted from all convicts, no matter where they were stationed. While it functioned under the cover of judicial retribution, the true purpose of the station was revealed in the uneven marks that it scored on the backs of its charges.

A mountain trout, the native fish that could be caught using small hooks and lines made of bark or twine. (William Buelow Gould)

8

Mr Douglas's list

Neil Douglas's teeth continued to rattle in his jaw, despite the issue of potatoes three times a week from the supply cultivated at the heads by the boat crew. As long as the plans to grow vegetables at Farm Cove were reduced to naught by the thin soils and the vagaries of the weather, it was the small amount of vitamin C in the skins of the potatoes supplied by the pilot that kept the worst effects of scurvy at bay. On 18 June 1825 the Duke of York finally brought relief in the shape of a passenger who knew the settlement well. John Douglas, now holding a ticket-of-leave earned as a reward for his previous services as commandant's clerk, had arrived under instructions—as he put it—to relieve his namesake who was now free to return to Hobart Town to nurse his scurvy-loosened teeth.

To Butler's irritation, however, no letter of appointment had arrived with the brig to confirm the new arrival's story.

Worse still, those at the settlement who knew John Douglas gave varying accounts of his former conduct. As he had been in regular correspondence with Neil Douglas, he knew about the comings and goings of the settlement, of Warton's ill-temper, of past acquaintances who had been punished, and of others who had received new billets. If the two clerks greeted each other like long lost friends, however, others were less welcoming. James Lucas complained that when John Douglas had last left Macquarie Harbour he had swindled him out of £28.10. Butler was less than impressed. As he wrote to the colonial secretary, this did not strike him as an appropriate qualification for a confidential clerk.

In his defence, Douglas claimed that the money had merely been borrowed. He had always intended to repay the debt as soon as he was furnished with his ticket-of-leave. As he wrote to the colonial secretary, 'no event of my life has given me so much uneasiness as this business of Mr Lucas'. This was a lie. When the audit of the Wigton branch of the Bank of Scotland had been completed in 1817 it was discovered that Douglas had made off with £1384, a veritable fortune by the standards of the day. Explaining his way out of that little mess had caused him a great deal more trouble than the affair with Lucas. Indeed he owed his neck to Mr Hamilton, his defence counsel, who made much at the subsequent high court trial of the long and faithful service that Douglas's father had given to the bank.

Although the sum that he had defrauded from Lucas was far less, he had found it difficult to earn sufficient money to reimburse the pilot. Work in Hobart Town proved hard to come by as Lucas caused it to be known that the clerk was a cheat who could not be trusted. When Douglas attempted to go up country in the hope that there his reputation had not preceded him, he was thrown from a horse. He injured his left shoulder so badly that he was unable to move around for several weeks. In the end he had no choice but to request that he be posted back to Macquarie Harbour to take up his old position once more, although this time his salary would be paid to Lucas until the debt was settled.

Record keeping was important in a place where so many things went missing. One of John Douglas's tasks was to account for every prisoner at the settlement in black and white. Each quarter he made out a detailed list of each man and woman upon the station, noting the day they had arrived and the length of time they had been ordered to serve. He compiled lists of absconders, recording those who got clean away from the settlement and those who returned half starved to death or had been brought back under the charge of the military.

The record he kept made grim reading. According to this official history, 93 per cent of all escapes ended in the death of the convict. Some were thought to have been murdered by their comrades, others to have drowned, or been speared by the Mimegin, Peternidic, or one of the other bands of Aboriginal peoples who moved up and down the coast. A few were shot by soldiers sent in pursuit, but mostly they were presumed to have starved to death in the bush. Despite this the convicts at Macquarie Harbour continued to seek to defy the confident pronouncements that declared escape from the place to be nigh on impossible. At times so many absconded that they pushed the capacity of the military to its limits and kept Douglas's quill busy, scrawling reports of each escape and recapture.

The large number of prisoners who had been sent to the settlement for running compounded the issue. Macquarie Harbour was seen as the place of choice to send those who had attempted to bust out of other penal settlements. Over the course of the 1820s, at least 114 runaways from other penal stations in New

South Wales and Van Diemen's Land were despatched there as this was a place from which escape was 'never accomplished without loss of life, either by perishing in the woods, or by some other miserable end'. This was of course an allusion to the grisly fate that had befallen those who had attempted to escape with Alexander Pearce. It was, as the *Hobart Town Gazette* put it, a fitting place to banish 'notorious and abandoned characters'.

It was a view that was shared by many others in colonial Australia. It was considered that the 'rugged, closely wooded, and altogether impracticable country' would ensure that prisoners exiled there would be kept to hard labour for the term of their sentence. Even British parliamentarians knew that to attempt to escape from Macquarie Harbour was folly in the extreme.

When John Barnes had served as colonial assistant surgeon at Macquarie Harbour he had acquired a copy of the list of absconders kept by Douglas. Later when the surgeon had returned to London, he was called as a witness before the Molesworth Committee, charged with investigating the continued efficacy of transporting convicts to Australia. Barnes furnished the committee with the piece of paper drawn up by Douglas and the return was duly printed in the papers and proceedings of the British Parliament. The committee closely questioned the former assistant colonial surgeon. Why was it, they wanted to know, that prisoners continued to attempt to run from the settlement when the fate of those who had tried to effect their escape was so well established? Barnes explained that 'there were constantly rumours coming by fresh batches of convicts, that such and such a party of men who had left the settlement at such a time, had made their escape from Launceston or Hobart Town, or some place that the ships visit'. Indeed, he confessed that the 'impression which convicts at Macquarie Harbour had was, that the greater part of those who had absconded and were not heard of, had made their way to some settled part of the country'.

There is a certainty in written lists: once cast on to paper a thing takes on the illusion of fact. The fact was, however, that the administration had no idea what had happened to the runaways who had slipped into the blank sections of the map and had never been apprehended. The aim of the list was to pronounce the absconder as dead and the escape as failed. It was literally a paperwork exercise that sought to traffic in the bodies of escaped prisoners—moving them from a figurative column labelled 'success' to an inked column labelled 'dead'. It was a literary trick that may have worked with commandants, surgeons, lieutenant governors and parliamentarians, but it had little effect on the rank and file condemned to life in a penal station. As Commandant Butler confirmed, the prisoners believed every little rumour that filtered back to circulate among their ranks. It turned out, however, that it was not just the map that had blank sections on it. There were prisoners marked as perished on Douglas's list who survived their sojourn in the bush to turn up alive and kicking elsewhere.

When it came to breaking out of the place, those who had been sent to the settlement for absconding played a prominent role. They accounted for half of the participants in all Macquarie Harbour escape attempts although they represented less than a third of the convict population. Many were seasoned campaigners who had previously spent many months in the bush. Among those who had been sent to the settlement for absconding from Port Macquarie in New South Wales were men who had walked over 100 miles 'subsisting on such garbage as they could pick up'. By the time they were apprehended some were 'covered in scabs from top to toe, having endured extreme hardships'. Such men did not need Mr Douglas's list to inform them of the odds stacked against the runaway. When it came to weighing their chances in the bush, they did not employ the logic of an accountant. However remote the probability of shaking off the shackles of convict life, the belief that this might be possible outweighed all that might otherwise be said against the venture. 'It was', as one said, 'impossible to give an idea of the hardships and misery' which were suffered at a place like Macquarie Harbour and many, rather than endure it, would go to extreme lengths. As he continued, he felt himself 'as it were shut out forever from society, and utterly wretched' and it was in this miserable state that 'he determined to brave everything in order to put an end' to his present suffering. He was filled, as he put it with an 'uncontrollable desire' to run.

John Davis had been transported for life for cutting the gold seal from the watch ribbon of a man in the pit of the Royalty Theatre. A Jewish shopman from Woolwich, he was transported to New South Wales but was again convicted in the criminal court in Sydney and banished to Port Macquarie. From there he escaped, was apprehended and shipped to Macquarie Harbour. He arrived at the settlement on 7 January 1823 but absconded just fourteen days later in company with six other prisoners. According to Douglas, all were 'supposed to have perished in the woods'. Yet, like Lazarus, Davis resurfaced. He was convicted at the Campbelltown Quarter Sessions in New South Wales on 18 January 1840 for 'being at large with fire arms' and was sentenced to transportation for life for the third time. Despatched to Norfolk Island, he occupied his time in the writing of a history of Macquarie Harbour, that dreadful place of condemnation from which he had escaped all those years previously.

Davis's case was certainly not unique. William Vincent was said to be 'a man of forbidding countenance with unusually dark, projecting eyebrows'. A former soldier who had served in the

Royal Horse Artillery, Vincent was sentenced to seven years' transportation by a court in Monmouth and conveyed to Hobart Town. From there he was sent to Macquarie Harbour for a year after a bench of magistrates had found him guilty of insolence and disobedience of his master's orders. Shortly after arriving he absconded into the bush and was recorded on Douglas's list as having perished in the woods.

According to a report submitted by the Quakers Backhouse and Walker, however, Vincent not only managed to escape to the settled districts, but succeeded in effecting a passage all the way back to Britain. There he joined his wife, but was taken again for a different offence and sentenced once more to transportation. Having arrived in Van Diemen's Land for a second time, he again escaped. Once more he secured a passage home, but by now his wife had taken up with another man. Apparently this rendered him 'still more reckless' and he was soon apprehended again. Sentenced to transportation for a third time, he was landed in Hobart Town where he was ordered to be sent direct to Macquarie Harbour. Before he could be despatched, however, he absconded once more—this time he appears not to have been apprehended. His conduct record has scrawled across it 'supposed to have died on board the ship *Norfolk* in 1833 at sea'.

In December 1824, Edward Evans attempted to run from Macquarie Harbour with two other convicts. A shoemaker from Wexford who had been sentenced to life transportation for stealing a handkerchief, Evans had previously lived in a stock hut at the Black Brush near New Norfolk. Described by the *Hobart Town Gazette* as a man possessed of 'considerable intellect', he had some knowledge of the high country beyond Hamilton and Bothwell and that was where the three escapees headed. They pushed on to the north of Frenchman's Cap, and had even caught a glimpse of the western lakes, before they were enveloped by 'extremely wet and foggy weather' which drove them off the high ground and into the scrub and deep gullies.

Rather than press on they went back to the settlement and gave themselves up. When Evans absconded again on 10 January 1826 he was favoured with much better weather. In April 1827, Butler wrote that word was circulating around the settlement that Evans had sent a message back to his friends instructing them to avoid the scrub and the valleys in which Pearce's party had become so hopelessly ensnared by following a chain of mountain ridges.

The route over the central plateau was not the easiest way of getting out of Macquarie Harbour, but it certainly was possible to walk out that way. In March 1828 James Goodwin and Thomas Connelly escaped from a timber cutting detail stationed some distance up the Gordon River. The attempt was well planned. The river was low in March, the autumn rains having yet to set in, so they paddled upstream in a canoe that they had fashioned from a log of Huon pine, reasoning that the further up the Gordon system they went, the closer it would take them to the settled districts. When James Goodwin was apprehended in a hut on Macquarie Plains on 9 May 1828 he claimed that he had made the journey from Macquarie Harbour in just seven days, although it seems more likely that it took him three weeks. When news of the achievement became known, others tried to emulate the feat. In general, however, the coast was much easier to negotiate than the direct route taken by Pearce and Goodwin. It may have taken longer to reach the settled districts travelling north via the beach, but the going was much easier.

Thomas Kent proved as much less than a year after the settlement had been formed. He had been sent to Macquarie Harbour for entering the dwelling house of John Biffen at Launceston and taking a quantity of potatoes. Described by the court as an 'incorrigible villain', he arrived at Macquarie Harbour in March 1822. This was before the limekiln had been established on the banks of the Gordon River and Kent was sent to the heads to burn shells plundered from Aboriginal middens. He recalled that on 22 December at about twelve at night a runaway named Edward O'Hara crept into his hut. O'Hara was a determined absconder. Originally convicted in Armagh, he had been transported for life and sent to Hobart Town. In January 1821 he had been tried for bushranging and sentenced to be transported once more. He was sent first to the penal station at Newcastle where he was awarded 100 lashes for 'mutinous conduct, refusing to work and exclaiming for liberty'. Transferred to Port Macquarie, he absconded from there, was recaptured, and then sent to Macquarie Harbour as punishment.

There was quite a store of provisions in the hut, including 21 pounds of flour, seven of salt meat and a quantity of ale, but the runaway was after more than rations. Kent later swore that O'Hara forced him to join the escape for fear that he would alert the pilot; but since he knew something of the geography of northern Van Diemen's Land he was useful to O'Hara in other ways. The two men set off northwards keeping to the paths made by natives. When their supplies ran out they survived on provisions plundered from Aborigines or the carcasses of snakes and other scavenged bits. At Robinson's Passage on the north-west coast of Van Diemen's Land they were picked up by a sealer's boat. They were first conveyed to King Island and then Albatross Island and finally Hunters Island, before travelling back to George Town. En route O'Hara got onshore and made his escape, leaving Kent to face the music.

There was some uncertainty about what to do with him, especially as his sentence to transportation had nearly expired. In the end it was Kent who forced the issue. He slipped from his captors but was apprehended breaking into a house and stealing sugar, tobacco and cloth. On 1 June 1824 he was sentenced in the supreme court in Hobart Town to a further term of transportation for seven years at Macquarie Harbour. His arrival there would have provided yet further confirmation, if confirmation were needed, that escape from the place was distinctly possible.

On 26 October 1824 he absconded for a second time. This time he ran with Robert Cowbarn, a cotton spinner from a village near Preston who was tattooed on his left arm with a sailor and a crucifix. It was perhaps a lucky sign—for once more salvation appeared by sea. On 29 November the two men were picked up in 'the most exhausted state' by the schooner *Australian*—they had been reduced to crawling 'along the shore in search of cockles'. They were taken to Hobart Town and from there returned to Macquarie Harbour, arriving on 14 February 1825.

Kent now had a second piece of useful information to impart. While the route north along the beach presented opportunities for absconders, the way south was blocked by Port Davey, a significant, perhaps insurmountable, barrier. By now the prisoners at Macquarie Harbour were privy to more information than surgeon Barnes was to provide to the British Parliament. Kent's name was a notable omission from the list that he handed over to the Molesworth Committee.

Having escaped into the blank bits of the map and emerged on the other side, Thomas Kent was a man with a story to tell. At least three absconders from Macquarie Harbour were interrogated by their captors and all recounted much about the nature of the country through which they had passed. In part they responded to prompting and fielded questions aimed at them by magistrates. Notably these magistrates were also settlers and pastoralists and, as such, were eager for news of exploitable tracts of land. Now they had been apprehended, the absconders had an opportunity to turn in the country through which they had passed.

All obliged, coughing up details likely to aid the process of recording and extending property rights over land that had previously been uncharted. Both Pearce and Goodwin talked of finding beautiful plains that they had mistaken for stock runs. The country was so good that they could not believe that it had not already been colonised. It was Kent, however, who made the most of the opportunity. Interviewed by the magistrate and mineralogist A. W. Humphrey, he recalled seeing great drifts of Huon pine stranded on bars at the mouths of the rivers. In places, he had passed 'very fine grass'. At one point he had 'got upon a hill and the clear land seemed to extend as far as I could see from the coast'. At other times he observed rich black soil.

It was as much garbage as the pieces of found trash that the two absconders had lived off, but he was careful to weave in known details to give the story verisimilitude. He recounted, for example, how they had come across the remains of a vessel they assumed was the *Phatisalam*, wrecked the previous year with much loss of life. As a stratagem it was a grand success.

Kent and Pearce escaped punishment altogether and Goodwin was employed in a survey team sent to map the good land over which he claimed to have traversed. They were rewarded in other ways too. Goodwin's name was inscribed on the map—Convict Peak and Goodwin's Creek were both named after him. The large river that Kent had found, the second to be encountered walking north from the heads, quickly became known as the Pieman. It was a reference to Kent's trade—indeed no-one outside the convict department referred to the diminutive baker from Southampton by anything other than 'the Pieman'.

While a handful of escapes were written up in detail, the movement of absconders mostly went unrecorded. When they ran into the uncharted area of the map they also engineered an escape from the archive, a point underscored by the last word entered on their colonial record: 'run'. From henceforth they too became uncharted, slipping between the lines of ink that had kept them prisoner. Even when absconders were subsequently picked up, it was unusual to record details of the route they had taken, or the means that they had employed to navigate, cross rivers and live off the country.

After Thomas Kent had shown that escape to the north was possible it became the route of choice for Macquarie Harbour absconders. The first time Gough had tried to abscond from the settlement he had been apprehended on the northern beaches. A black sailor from the Isle of Wight, Gough caused havoc at Macquarie Harbour. While there, he received 625 strokes of the lash, spent nineteen days in solitary and was sentenced to serve two and a half years in chains. He broke out of his irons, cut up his blanket, broke into the stores and pulled down the fences that had been erected to break the passage of the wind. He also threatened all who stood in his way. In company with six other prisoners he ambushed a detachment of the 48th Regiment, seizing their flintlocks. The absconders were apprehended at the Pieman Heads after a stiff firefight. It was not the only armed struggle to take place on this isolated stretch of beach. In September 1831 Private John Corrigan of the 63rd Regiment was shot through his left shoulder in a 'conflict' with seven prisoners, some of whom had managed to secure muskets from those sent in pursuit of them.

One of the assailants was a man named Robert Hansler who had absconded from the settlement twice before. He had even succeeded in getting as far as Circular Head. There he tried to pass himself off as a freeman by the name of Robert Johnston, but was taken into custody and was forwarded by Edward Curr, the superintendent of the Van Diemen's Land Company, first to Launceston and then overland to Hobart Town. He made the trip south in a cart, heavily ironed and under an escort of soldiers and constables. He was eventually sent back to Macquarie Harbour with orders to serve a further three years there. He immediately furnished information about the route that he had taken to other runaways enabling them, too, to reach the Hampshire Hills where they survived by robbing huts belonging to the Van Diemen's Land Company. Edward Curr wrote a letter of complaint to the colonial secretary. By that stage, company employees had already apprehended twelve absconders from Macquarie Harbour. They had better things to do than round up the convict department's lost property and Curr requested that a military detachment be posted in the district.

Arthur received another letter from the commandant at Maquarie Harbour begging leave to submit 'the impropriety of sending back prisoners who have made their escape from the settlement, as their knowledge of the country may be the means of inducing others to abscond'. There was no easy solution to the problem. Macquarie Harbour was the worst place of punishment in Van Diemen's Land; not to return an absconder was, in effect, to reward a man for escaping.

The problem did not just extend to runaways. Butler desisted from using all but the most trusted convicts to apprehend absconders. He even found that the boat crew could not be relied upon. When they were employed to catch prisoners he reported that they 'never fail to talk of what they saw and thus enable future absconders to be more cautious'. By the time he wrote the warning, however, the secret of the route north was well and truly out.

Kent reckoned that he and O'Hara had covered 25 miles in one day travelling along the beach. The rivers, however, presented serious obstacles. As the two absconders had found, they could only be safely crossed at the mouths. Whenever runaways gained the northern shore of the harbour, and especially when they were known to have passed the King River, the pilot was despatched with a party of soldiers with instructions to make for the Pieman. There they would wait until the prisoners attempted to cross. If the absconders had seen the whaleboat on its passage north, they would sometimes play a waiting game, hiding in the dunes until the party of soldiers gave up because their rations had run out and trudged back down the beach or sailed back in the whaleboat.

Equipment was essential for survival in the bush. The military parties that went in pursuit of absconders carried lengths of cord. The strongest swimmer would carry these across the rivers in his teeth or tied to his arm and they were then used to haul over a raft upon which the arms and other provisions were stored. Rope was prized by absconders for similar reasons. When Edward O'Hara escaped he took with him a canvas bag, an axe, a tinderbox and a three-gallon kettle. The canvas bag proved particularly useful as it could be cut into strips and used to lash up a raft. Tinder boxes and steels were important items. Without them, runaways were forced to eat food raw, or attack Aboriginal encampments in the hope of seizing firesticks. Some absconders took other comforts with them. A party of soldiers walking through the scrub at dusk were alerted to the presence of two runaways when one tried to light his pipe by snapping a musket to ignite the powder in the pan. They had taken the firearm from three soldiers whom they had overpowered. When they were apprehended at the Pieman Heads they were found to have sixteen rounds of ball cartridge and Private Edward Wilmer's boots in their possession.

Many escapes were well planned. Most absconders avoided the winter months, not so much because of the cold, but as this was the period in which the rivers were in full spate and at their most difficult to cross. The most popular months to abscond were December through to April. Some escapees proved particularly adroit at raft construction. In June 1825, a vessel was recovered from the bush near the mouth of the Gordon. The contraption had been built by one of the convicts employed in the lumberyard, who had absconded on it with the settlement baker the previous year. They had taken with them a goodly amount of flour and a kangaroo dog belonging to Mr Parsons' clerk. They were never apprehended. Shortly after the discovery of this vessel, a similar craft was discovered concealed in the bottom of a sawpit under a covering of grass and sawdust. Constructed from boards that had been caulked with pitch and grease, the ingenious device was thirteen feet, seven inches long and two feet broad.

There was not much in the bush that could be readily eaten. The Quaker James Backhouse reported that the hills around Macquarie Harbour were covered with a lichen that resembled reindeer-moss. It was incredibly prolific, growing to the size of a cauliflower. Its taste, however, was insipid. Alexander Pearce related that on his first attempt to escape, Mather had boiled some fern roots, but when he consumed them he became violently ill. Over time, however, prisoners worked out what could be safely consumed. Goodwin and Connolly subsisted off mushrooms, grass roots and the berries of the native olive. They also caught small 'mountain trout' that thrived in many highland and coastal streams. Absconders frequently took fish hooks with them and lines fashioned from either twine or strips of bark. When George Clay drowned attempting to escape from Small Island, his body was found upon the beach 'perfectly rotted, with some fish hooks tied around his neck'. Many of the creeks and streams of the west coast were also home to the giant freshwater crayfish—considered to be excellent eating. It is possible that other absconders learned how to catch crows and gulls from observing Aboriginal peoples. The trick was to hide under a mound of kelp and use a piece of offal as bait to attract unsuspecting winged scavengers.

For practical reasons, runaways from Macquarie Harbour were drawn to country frequented by Aboriginal peoples. These were invariably the places where the pickings were most abundant—where mussels and ear fish, as abalone were universally called, could be prised from the rocks. Besides, hunting grounds were open tracts of country that could be easily crossed and in other coastal areas there were native paths along which both migrating Aboriginal peoples and absconders travelled. As a result they frequently met with one another.

Thomas Kent reported seeing hundreds of natives as he made his way north to the large river that would soon be named after him. Further north still he encountered a large number gathering shellfish. He recalled that their 'fires spread along the sea coast for about a mile'. Many absconders recounted how they had charged Aboriginal people while they sat round their fires, attempting to drive them off so they could eat whatever they were roasting. Goodwin and Connelly armed themselves with sticks for this purpose, which they pointed as though they were guns, and Greenhill and Pearce charged a group armed with an axe and a wooden club.

In June 1825, a party of absconders were taken at the Pieman Heads after they had rushed a soldiers' fire they had mistaken for a native encampment. Although the risks were significant, such tactics could yield rich pickings. When Kent and O'Hara managed to surprise an Aboriginal man and woman, the woman dropped two baskets before running off. To their joy the absconders discovered that these contained a large number of cray and ear fish.

It is perhaps not surprising that hostilities ensued. By early 1827 Butler reported that the Mimegin, who frequented the coast to the south of the heads, routinely speared absconders who were 'an easy conquest' owing to 'their debilitated and emaciated state'. The skeletons of many runaways were said to have been found along the coast, although it was impossible to determine whether they had died from starvation or Aboriginal attack. When Joseph Geary absconded in January 1825 he was speared to death the same day. The Mimegin even harassed detachments of the military who patrolled the beach and were 'extremely hostile' to the pilot and anybody else who strayed from the settlement at the heads.

By the early 1830s there was conflict up and down the coast. Some Aboriginal women told George Augustus Robinson that they had maimed two white men, probably absconders, whom they had found on the beach near Macquarie Harbour. Penderoin, a man from Robbins Island off the north-east tip of the colony, told him that he had seen three convicts killed with waddies. Another convict was speared to death near Mount Cameron and one of his companions was struck twice with spears in his left shoulder and once in his right side. When the man retreated into the bush he was assaulted with volleys of sticks and stones. This attack had the hallmarks of a ritual spearing—retaliation perhaps for an assault the absconders had launched a few days earlier on an Aboriginal encampment.

The conflict was certainly fuelled by the garrison. On at least one occasion the 63rd Regiment were reported to have fired on a party of Aborigines while out hunting and it was 'said that the Buffs ill-treated the natives very much'. It is simply pernicious nonsense to argue that in the early 1830s, the west coast of Van Diemen's Land remained a 'pristine region, untouched by the colonial presence'. Conflict had its consequences. When Robinson placed a party of the Peternidic people in the lower floor of the penitentiary on Settlement Island they reported that the prisoners 'did all they could to annoy them'. They poured water down through the boards, hammered on the floor and pissed through the cracks. It was an atrocious thing to do, but it was an act played out against a history of attacks with axes, muskets, sticks, spears, waddies and stones.

If Aboriginal attack and the rugged nature of the country failed to deter absconders so too did the instruments of law. William Allen was a 23-year-old card brusher from Manchester who had been transported for life. He had been sent to Port Macquarie from Sydney after he had fallen in company with a seaman named William Poole, who had convinced him that he would be able 'to conduct them through the interior of the country to Timor'. In preparation for their long trek the men had committed a series of burglaries and it was for this that they were put on trial and sentenced to death, although they were subsequently pardoned on condition of transportation to a penal station for life. From there the two men absconded and after many trials and tribulations they were recaptured and put on trial once more and condemned to hang for having broken the conditions under which they had previously been reprieved. The *Hobart Town Gazette* expressed its astonishment at Poole's naivety. As the paper put it: 'regardless of the extent of mercy so graciously bestowed, he voluntarily rushed into the arms of death!' The point, however, was that to be condemned to cut cedar in a remote penal station for year upon grinding year was not mercy 'graciously bestowed'.

Allen escaped the gallows but was sent as punishment to Macquarie Harbour. On 25 August 1824 he absconded from the rolling gang at Kelly's Basin with a prisoner named Saul. He returned alone to the settlement on 8 September with a tale of misery. He said that they had crossed the Gordon and proceeded in the direction of Port Davey. When they approached the coast they had been attacked by the Mimegin and were both wounded with spears. Saul had died on the return journey to the settlement. Yet, as Allen lay in the hospital awaiting his 100 lash punishment 'he declared his conscience would not allow a moments rest' till he confessed to having murdered Saul by 'striking him on the head with a knife, cutting his throat and otherwise mutilating the body'. The confession ensured that Allen would escape corporal punishment and affect a permanent escape from Macquarie Harbour by other means. He was sent to Hobart Town, put on trial for murder and sentenced to death.

In order to ram home the futility of attempting to escape, he was sent back to Macquarie Harbour with two other capitally convicted convicts to be executed there. Instead of playing the penitent, Allen mounted the scaffold in a state of jubilation, kicking his boots into the crowd and to the cheers of the assembled prisoners he 'rushed into the arms of death'.

Others chose to starve in the bush rather than risk returning to the settlement to be flogged. As a result, the standard punishment of 100 lashes and six months in irons for recaptured runaways was reduced to 50 lashes and three months in irons for those who gave themselves up. There can be little doubt but that the rate of punishment inflicted on the backs of prisoners encouraged many to abscond. Some harboured dreams of exacting their own revenge. In June 1824 fourteen prisoners seized a boat from Kelly's Basin and having first tied up the overseer, constables and all those who were not 'in the conspiracy', hid in the bush where they lay in wait for Commandant Wright. The latter had spent the morning fishing with the surgeon, Dr Garrett, before instructing his boat crew to pull for Kelly's Basin so that he could inspect the gangs at work. The two men landed and had walked a short distance through the swamps when Wright became suspicious, not being able to hear the sound of axes. He ordered a retreat to the beach and upon seeing this the prisoners broke cover and attempted to rush the party. The commandant only just managed to make it to the safety of his boat. Garrett was not so fortunate—he was captured by the absconders. The prisoners' immediate focus, however, was Wright and they launched the gang boat in a desperate attempt to cut off his retreat to Settlement Island. The man who took the steer oar, however, was unfamiliar with the waters of the basin and ran the craft onto a mud bank. By the time they had got her off, Wright had too much of a head start to be overhauled and they gave up the chase.

Although Garrett may have expected the worst, he was treated with civility. James McCabe, a waterman who had been transported from Dublin for stealing a tablecloth, addressed him in the name of all the prisoners. He thanked Garrett for attempting to soften the severe treatment that Wright had ordered to be inflicted on the backs of so many of the men. He told him that if they had captured the commandant they would have ordered him to receive 200 lashes with a couple of cats that they had fashioned from the three and a half inch-thick rope that was used to lash the rafts of pine together. Indeed, he went as far as to venture that if the doctor had been of the opinion that the commandant could take more, they would have increased the punishment—as the cats that they had made were 'of a moderate size and not like those murdering things on the settlement'.

Wright assumed the absconders would try and make for the ocean beaches to the west and then work their way along the coast to the north of the colony. Indeed before they had left Garrett, the escapees had implied that it was their intention to walk to the settled districts. The commandant duly despatched a party of soldiers to the Pieman Heads with the intention of intercepting them. The absconders had other plans, however. They ambushed the gang boat in Farm Cove on the morning of 9 June and forced those on board to carry her over the isthmus dividing the cove from the rest of the harbour. There were at this point only thirteen of them, one of their number having lost his way in the bush overnight. As the launch that they seized was a fourteen-oared boat they asked for a volunteer and were joined by James Tierney, a 24-year-old stable boy who had been born in Barbados. Of those on board at least five were experienced seamen who knew how to handle a vessel in open water. They were well prepared in other ways too, having secreted under their clothes the canvas from their bed ticks, which they now fashioned into two lugsails and a jib.

They made for the heads as fast as they could. News of the seizure was slow to reach Settlement Island. When it did there was a further delay as word was sent for Wright who was out shooting with his dog Pluto, named in honour of the god of the underworld. By the time a vessel was sent to the pilot station, the absconders had slipped out into the vastness of the ocean. They reached the River Derwent ten days later and immediately set about plundering properties in order to gather supplies.

It was the most famous convict rebellion that Van Diemen's Land ever faced and certainly the most dangerous. At its height there were real concerns that it would develop into a general insurrection. As the attorney general put it, they 'spread terror thro' the colony'. Matthew Brady, who assumed command of the absconders, was particularly audacious and the war that he now waged on colonial society was shot through with symbolic gestures. William Faber, an emancipist herdsman, reported that when Dry's house at Quamby's Brook was attacked, the bushrangers seized Dry's nephew. In a complete reversal of the normal relations of the country estate they enquired of the assembled assigned servants as to their captive's character. Thus, for a brief moment, the unfortunate nephew's fate hung in the hands of the estate's unfree workforce. The latter pronounced him a 'good man' and he was released, the convicts having exercised a paternalist prerogative usually the preserve of the magistrates' bench. It was a tactic that had also been employed by pirates in the Atlantic in the early eighteenth century and was designed to destroy the master's hold over his charges by placing him forever in their debt.

When they attacked a property at the Lake River in February 1826, Robert William Lawrence reported that he 'heard two shots fired while I was in the Kitchen, they told me that Bramsgrove [the overseer] had been wounded by Brady—but that if that did not kill him he should not live six months, as his Character was so bad all over the Country for ill-treating the Men'. There were good grounds for the bushrangers' charge. Thomas Bramsgrove, who survived the attack, had already been cautioned for a 'violent assault' on an assigned servant and was later dismissed from Lawrence's service for a similar offence. Before departing, the bushrangers exacted a heavy toll on Lawrence, setting fire to and completely destroying his wheat fields, house and outbuildings.

It was suspected, however, that the bushrangers' real target was Macquarie Harbour—that place of tyranny where so many of them had suffered. They had said as much to Robert Peate, an assigned servant to the surveyor John Helder Wedge. They told him that they intended to go there in order to liberate ten of their former colleagues. Butler was most alarmed when he was informed of these plans. He petitioned the colonial secretary, requesting an additional ten privates and two corporals to augment his small garrison. He warned that if Brady and McCabe should make an appearance, his situation would be truly desperate. He would have no easy means of stopping the anticipated flood of absconders from joining their ranks, as any detachment that he sent in pursuit ran the serious risk of being isolated and overpowered by the bushrangers. He speculated that their first target would be the pilot station, and that once they had command of the heads they would 'render themselves formidable' descending on Settlement Island by boat. As the prisoners would 'be tainted with the spreading infection' of rebellion, he would be left powerless and his little wooden-walled citadel would inevitably fall. Although Arthur promised to send a strong party after the bushrangers if they should make such an attempt, he had his hands full attempting to contain their attacks in the settled districts. The convict Davis estimated that the whole affair cost the colonial government £33,000 plus an immense 'sacrifice of private property and many lives lost in the warfare'.

Further insurrection was to follow. On 5 August 1829, the brig *Cyprus* set sail from Hobart Town bound for Macquarie Harbour. The weather was terrible. This was her second attempt to make the passage—on the first she had been forced back after losing her anchors and cables on a shoal and damaging her windlass. The experience had been punishing for all on board, but especially the prisoners locked down in the hold. When the *Cyprus* set out again some were let out on deck and had their irons struck off in order to help sail the vessel. After battling high winds off Bruny Island, the ship's master decided to run for Recherche Bay where he intended to ride out the storm.

It was here that the vessel was seized. The prisoners picked their moment. Lieutenant Carew, the ship's doctor and the mate were away fishing and Harrison, the master, was down in his cabin when the sentries were knocked unconscious with belaying pins. Harrison heard the scuffle and came on deck, but was struck flat on his back with a blow from a scrubbing brush. By this time all the prisoners were on deck piling anything they could find on the hatch to the soldiers' quarters to jam it shut. As they did so they shouted 'keep the buggers down, keep them down'.

Although the detachment fired several shots up the hatchway in order to try and clear it, the mutineers retaliated by pouring boiling water on them. They then threatened to 'throw down a kettle of lighted pitch to smoke the ship, and smother them all'. This had the desired effect and the detachment passed their arms up through the hatchway. When Lieutenant Carew returned with the fishing party, Matthew Pennell levelled a musket at him. He pulled the trigger, but the weapon merely flashed in the pan. Carew called on the prisoners, impressing upon them the dangers of continuing in their bold enterprise, but they replied 'we have our liberty, and we shall die to a man before we give her up'. Then for a second time Pennell, the man who had so helpfully bent the spring on the alarm bell on the back of the treasury door, levelled a musket at Carew and snapped it in his face. No further violence, however, was offered and the soldiers, crew, passengers and those among the convicts who did not wish to join the enterprise were put on shore. Then Fergusson, a servant from Colerain in Ireland, put on Carew's regimental uniform and sword and strutted on the deck while the convicts shouted 'the ship's our own'. At half-past five on Saturday morning, 'they gave three cheers, and sailed with a fair wind'. The event was later celebrated in song:

Play on your golden trumpets boys
And sound your cheerful notes
The Cyprus Brig's on the ocean boys
By justice does she float.

Among the stores with which the mutineers sailed off were; six razors, 72 hair combs, 200 ship's blankets, 632 fathoms of rope, 27 ship's blocks and enough flour, oatmeal, peas, salt junk, tea, sugar and spirits to feed an entire penal station for weeks. There was also a large quantity of paint, and the mutineers lost no time covering up the tell-tale yellow streak on each side of the captured brig. They also cut off the figurehead and changed the name painted on the stern of the ship's boat to the *Edward*. The absconders made first for New Zealand and then the Chatham Islands, before sailing on to Japan via Savage Island. They finally scuttled the vessel at Whampoa on the Pearl River. Most were eventually apprehended but, like the bushranging rebellion that Brady had led, the exercise cost the British government a great deal in time and expense.

In his official reports Butler was rather dismissive of prisoners' attempts to escape. Some ran, he claimed, almost as soon as they arrived—before they had any chance to gain an intimate knowledge of the surrounding topography. He reported the attempted escape of William Dorrell with near disbelief. Not only had the man just arrived, but one of his arms had been amputated as a result of a previous accident. It was perhaps not surprising that he was never heard of again. At times, however, Butler's command was stretched to the limit. Unseasonably good weather could trigger a whole raft of attempted escapes requiring parties of soldiers to be dispatched in several directions at once. August and September 1825 proved particularly difficult months.

On Friday 2 September, the gang boat arrived at its usual station at the mouth of the Gordon River. The gang had no sooner disembarked than the vessel was seized by four runaway convicts who had been hiding in the scrub. The four men 'compelled' six of the gang, including the coxswain, to row them across the Gordon. On reaching the southern bank the absconders abandoned the boat and disappeared once more into the scrub. As a parting gesture they partially disrobed the coxswain, an American sailor named William Simpson Lindon. Being a skilled prisoner, Lindon wore his own clothes, rather than ill-fitting government slops. The four absconders relieved him of his jacket and his comforter—a type of woollen hat. It was an act that would have unexpected consequences.

The runaways were all young men. John Ward, a 24-year-old shoemaker's apprentice who was also known as 'Flash Jack', had been transported to Macquarie Harbour for absconding from the public works and remaining absent for six months. If his previous experiences gave him some confidence in his ability to survive in the bush, the short length of time that he had left to serve might have caused him to exercise a greater degree of caution. He had less than half a year remaining of his seven years sentence of transportation passed on him in the Old Bailey for stealing four shifts, two gowns and a shawl from a drying ground in Chelsea. Not Commandant Butler, nor Lieutenant Governor George Arthur, nor any other official in the British Empire for that matter, had the power to keep him at Macquarie Harbour beyond this date unless he was sentenced by a court for a new offence.

Samuel Bews was 22, although he had been sentenced to seven years' transportation at the tender age of sixteen for stealing a coat by using a hook to filch it from a basement railing. He too had been sent to Macquarie Harbour for absconding and, like Ward, had less than a year of his sentence left to serve. Daniel McClean was a weaver in his mid-twenties whom Butler regarded as 'a principal promoter of insubordination'. A native of Carlisle, he had been transported to Van Diemen's Land for seven years for 'stealing a watch from the person'. Assigned to Major de Gillern, he had found his way to Macquarie Harbour after his master had charged him with neglect of duty and absenting himself without leave. He had a little more than two years of his sentence to serve.

Compared to his fellow absconders, James Buckley had much less to lose. A 25-year-old labourer from Cork, he was described by Butler as 'a good workman but much dreaded as a violent character'. He had been sent to Macquarie Harbour for the term of his natural life for killing an assigned convict named Solomon Booth in a drunken fight.

Having crossed the Gordon, the four absconders skirted Birch's Inlet and headed towards Port Davey. While attempting to swim a river the two younger men, Ward and Bews, got separated from their companions and decided to turn back. They stumbled into an outpost of the settlement on 15 September after thirteen days in the bush. Buckley and McClean pushed on. McClean eventually surrendered himself at the pilot station four days later and Buckley on the next day. He was scarcely able to walk and in a much worse condition than any returned absconders that Butler had yet seen.

The commandant had to wait three weeks before the settlement surgeon thought Buckley fit enough to bear his punishment of 100 strokes. For the other three men, who had absconded so close to the expiration of their sentence, Butler had other plans. He was determined to make an example of them so severe that it would act as a deterrent to other would-be absconders—a punishment calculated to make others think twice before running into the woods.

At the same time as Buckley, Bews, McClean and Ward were trying to cut their way through the bush to the south of the harbour, there were another five groups at large. Butler was, he confessed, put to much 'trouble and anxiety in intercepting them'. He attempted to keep them on the move in the knowledge that the constant searches of the beaches would deprive them of easy ground to move along, driving them into the scrub where their clothes and shoes would be destroyed and they would be forced to expend so much energy that they would eventually have to give themselves up, exhausted. As he put it, 'for once a man gets reduced in the bush he has no means whatever of recruiting his strength'.

Nevertheless, the commandant was worried that when the warm weather arrived the prisoners would be off in droves. The gangs were in such a feverish state, he reported to Arthur, that he dared not send men up the Gordon River to burn lime. Even William Jarrett, the constable of the shingle splitters, had absconded—together with those who were supposedly under his charge. Worse still, nothing had been seen of Constable Richardson who appeared to have run from the brickfields along with Morgan Edwards, a hand in the woodcutter's boat.

With dogged determination Butler and the rank and file of the flank company of the 40th Regiment set about reeling in the escapees. On 14 September John Chadwick and George Lane gave themselves up. They had absconded nine days earlier from a gang on the Gordon River, but not being able to make much progress because of the patrols, which had restricted access to the open ground of the beach, they lit a fire to attract the attention of the guard boat. The following day William Cole and William

White, who had run from the paling splitters' gang, also surrendered. They had crossed Birch's Inlet and the Gordon but, finding their path blocked by soldiers, had returned by the route whence they had come. Reluctant to give themselves up, they somehow survived for 33 days by lurking in the vicinity of the brickfields, before finally surrendering. It was a feat that would not have been possible unless they had been provided with succour in the form of smuggled rations supplied to them by the various gangs who worked in the area.

The evening following Cole's and White's surrender, a strong southerly sprung up. Butler equipped a boat with muffled oars and sent it out to intercept any absconders from the southern shore who might take advantage of the conditions to try to cross to the northern part of the harbour by raft, in an attempt to throw their pursuers off the scent. As the party of soldiers propelled themselves along the shores of Birch's Inlet, their oars wrapped in cloth, they saw a fire on the beach and heard the noise of a group of men at work constructing a catamaran. They landed under the cover of darkness and by morning William Jarrett, Robert Burke and Morgan Edwards were all safely in custody. The raft that they had been working on proved to be an interesting contraption. To his consternation Butler noted that it was held together with a number of small iron staples that must have been made in the blacksmith's shop. He ordered an immediate search and found a supply of the very same article on Henry Griffin, a man whom Butler described as a knave who pretended to be a fool. Griffin was awarded 60 lashes.

But the commandant's more immediate concern was the fate of Constable Richardson—the man who had disappeared at the same time that Morgan Edwards had run. Richardson had been sent to Macquarie Harbour for three years for inattention to duty following the escape of a prisoner from the felony yard of the Hobart Town gaol. Since his arrival at the settlement he had not been charged with any offence and had proved to be a most zealous constable. Butler now wondered whether, rather than attempting to make his escape, the poor man had been left tied up and was suffering somewhere in the bush. He told the runaways that they would get nothing to eat until they let him know where Richardson was. As they were already starving, it was not long before one relented. Morgan Edwards confessed that when Richardson had landed, the constable had walked to the brick shed and ordered the men to prepare a fire while he went to the top of a neighbouring hill. From there he had returned in great haste, having seen Jarrett and Burke lurking in the bush. The constable lit a rag in the brickmakers' hearth and set off for the neighbouring point, but before he could light the signal fire, Morgan Edwards claimed to have 'barbarously' murdered him, pushing his lifeless remains into a deep pool of water. He now offered to point out where the body was and it was duly retrieved by the superintendent who fished it out with the aid of a boat hook.

There appeared to be no solution to the distemper of absconding except the application of increasingly ferocious punishments. Butler did all he could to thrash the urge to escape out of his charges. The first time Robert Hansler attempted to abscond from Macquarie Harbour he ran with Charles Green and Robert Greenfield. After plundering the gang huts at the Gordon River of provisions, clothes and 'in short way every thing they could carry off', the three men eloped in a boat. They were all experienced seamen and despite the stormy weather, they rowed some way down the harbour. Almost certainly their intention was to try and force a passage through the heads; however, a change in the direction of the wind and the approach of the guard boat forced them to take to the scrub. At home on the sea, the three men were also no slouches on land. All had been sent to Macquarie Harbour for absconding. Greenfield had remained at large for three months after he had run from a chain gang. Hansler had escaped from the penal station at Maria Island, crossing the dangerous Mercury Passage to the mainland on an improvised catamaran, and Green had run from Lemon Springs Road Party. Hansler also possessed some knowledge of the remote west coast. He had previously been a hand in a boat that had circumnavigated Van Diemen's Land and been detained for some weeks at the Pieman Heads by bad weather.

When they were apprehended Butler sentenced the three men to a savage mauling on the triangles. He caused them first to receive a hundred lashes for absconding and then when their backs had recovered, a further 100 for stealing the boat and yet another 100 for stealing provisions from the gang—although he, or more likely the settlement surgeon, reduced the last punishment to a mere 36 strokes. The maximum punishment that a magistrate in a penal station was empowered to award was 100 strokes. By breaking the offence up into three charges, Butler effectively increased this to 236. The punishment did nothing, however, to stop Hansler's wild career and he went on to instigate a whole string of further escapes.

Where flogging failed there were always the courts. When Butler secured Morgan Edwards for the murder of Constable Richardson he had him shipped to Hobart Town to stand trial. Despite the fact that Edwards had admitted to the murder while he lay in gaol at Macquarie Harbour, he was acquitted 'owing to some technical niceties', the court disapproving of the manner in which the confession had been starved out of the man. Arthur and Butler were shocked by the decision. Rather than causing Edwards to be shipped back to Macquarie Harbour, they resorted to some legal niceties of their own and had him spirited away to Moreton Bay.

Eight years later Edwards wrote a petition to the governor of New South Wales pointing out his predicament. He had originally been sent to Macquarie Harbour for three years by a magistrates' bench on 'suspicion' of having committed a burglary. Edwards argued that, as he had been acquitted of the 'unfortunate' death of Richardson, his term in a penal station should have ended with expiration of his colonial sentence. Instead it just churned on year after year with no end in sight. When the petition failed to elicit any amelioration in his situation he cut off his fingers in a desperate attempt to avoid ganged labour.

Butler had a special punishment in store for the three young absconders who had made a bid for freedom at the same time as Morgan Edwards had been out in the bush. Shocked that Samuel Bews, Daniel McClean and John Ward should have attempted to escape with so little of their sentences to transportation remaining, he conceived a plan for turning this to his advantage. He wrote to Arthur explaining that, instead of flogging the three absconders, he would send them up to Hobart Town for trial so that they could be 'returned to the Settlement under additional sentence of at least seven years'. He reckoned that such a measure would be sufficient to deter others from engaging 'in such villainy'. On 2 November 1825 the three men were duly placed on trial in the supreme court charged with stealing one boat, value £20, the property of the Crown, and one comforter valued at one shilling, and one jacket valued at ten shillings, the property of the convict coxswain William Simpson Lindon. They were all sentenced to death, but pardoned on condition of transportation for seven years.

From start to finish the case was a sham. Buckley, who had absconded with the three men, was not put on trial because there was no point in doing so. He was already a convict for life and there was no advantage to be had by imposing a further sentence upon him—so instead he was flogged. The boat that Bews, McClean and Ward were said to have stolen had never been in their sole possession—they merely occupied it for the time it took to convey them across the mouth of the Gordon River. Besides, as Butler had already confided to Arthur, the circumstances strongly suggested that the absconders had the tacit, if not active, support, of the ganged prisoners they were supposed to have robbed. Indeed, he punished six of the latter with 75 lashes 'for aiding and abetting the escape' in using 'their utmost efforts' to row the prisoners to the opposite bank of the river. For good measure, the theft of Lindon's jacket and comforter had been added to the supreme court charge—just in case the military jury decided that the escape across the river mouth in the government boat did not constitute a larceny. The trouble was that Lindon was one of the prisoners whom Butler had punished for assisting the escape. How, one might ask, could a man be flogged for aiding and abetting a theft perpetrated on his own person? Either he had been falsely punished, or no robbery had taken place.

Similar trials were to follow. On 18 April 1829, Robert Bourke and William Perring were placed on trial 'for being feloniously at large before the expiration of their sentences and with stealing a boat value £20 the property of the king'. The charge of being feloniously at large was a new offence conjured into being by the eleventh provision of the Transportation of Offenders from Van Diemen's Land Act passed by Arthur and his Executive Council in 1827. In order to ensure that there could be no ambiguity about the terms of the new legislation Arthur instructed Butler to read the crucial sections out to the assembled convicts at Macquarie Harbour. From that point on, any offender sentenced to secondary transportation who subsequently attempted to escape from the place to which they had been transported was liable to suffer death.

Although both men were found guilty, the chaplain who visited Perring in gaol wrote to the executive council to recommend a pardon. The clergyman had been very much taken by Perring's attachment to his wife and children, which had 'produced an uncontrollable desire in him to endeavour to join them'. This, it was claimed, was his sole reason for attempting to escape. Although Arthur was on balance swayed by the argument, the colonial secretary and the chief justice were firmly of the opinion that the man should hang. It was imperative, they insisted, that the full penalty of the law should be carried into effect to preserve the 'safety of the colony' and the 'severity' of a sentence to a penal station. As a result William Perring never got to return to the wife and two children he had left behind in Vauxhall. The sentence to life transportation passed upon him for stripping two sheets of lead from a roof in Billingsgate had already condemned him to a social death. The Executive Council now merely completed the sentence.

The sheer number of absconders provide an indication of the impact that the penal station had on the surrounding region. During the life of the settlement there were at least 150 escape attempts involving 271 separate individuals—or nearly one in four of all those secondarily transported to the place. Many of these tried to bolt on more than one occasion. Charles Curran, for example, attempted to abscond no less than six times, clocking up 550 lashes in punishment before he finally made it clear of the settlement never to return again. A former soldier in the Royals, Curran was rumoured to have made it all the way to England, although John Douglas had written the word 'doubtful' at the end of the report.

It was a word that was in accord with the whole tenor of his list, which was clearly a document calculated to pour scorn on the achievements of runaways. Indeed, it was not really a catalogue of escapes, for it only recorded 112 of the 328 attempts to run that occurred over the life of the settlement. Nor was it a list of those who got clear of the penal station and thus escaped the indignation of being dragged into the commandant's office to stand trial. It could more accurately be termed a list of failed attempts—a catalogue of deaths and disasters designed to maintain the reputation of the settlement as a place from which escape was all but impossible.

The whole exercise appears to have had more impact upon the parliamentarians who questioned John Barnes than it did on the prisoners at Macquarie Harbour. Even the convict department placed little faith in Douglas's list. In March 1831 the Chief Police Magistrate in Hobart Town drew up an alternative record of prisoners who had absconded from the penal settlement and were believed to still be at large. This was subsequently posted in the *Government Gazette* together with a £50 reward for the recapture of the department's lost penal property. The notice included the names of six prisoners whom Douglas had recorded as having 'perished in the woods'. The record he had drawn up, presumably under the instructions of Commandant Butler, was looking more and more tattered as time went by. As a record of the security of the penal station it was about as trustworthy as the account books he had kept while clerk of the Wigton branch of the Bank of Scotland.

The truth was, that far from being a natural prison where desperate men could be securely held, Macquarie Harbour leaked like a sieve. Despite the best efforts of the flank companies of the 48th, 3rd, 40th and 63rd regiments, convicts poured out of its confines. Worse still, many of these succeeded in crossing the miles of broken and rugged terrain that hemmed in the settled districts preventing their westward expansion. It was an unexpected turn of events. While the natural prison proved a barrier to the march of colonisation, it failed to secure the prisoners who had been sent there to labour for the public good. It was as if the logic of Macquarie Harbour had been turned inside out and the whole settlement had started to work in reverse. It was a problem that grew with each ragged runaway who turned up in the settled districts.

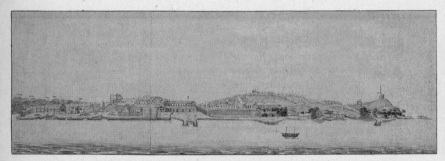

Sketch of Settlement Island, possibly commissioned as evidence for a trial in Hobart Town. (Artist unknown)

9

'Come, O my guilty brethren, come'

Abraham Hood was a Presbyterian—or at least he believed in the tenets of Calvinism. He left the Wesleyan class at Macquarie Harbour because he refused to admit that, as a sinner, he was one of the lowest of the low. As the missionary Reverend William Schofield put it, he withdrew because 'his rigid Calvinism did not harmonise with the probability of falling from grace'. A baker from Dalkeith in Scotland who had previously been employed as a constable in Launceston, Hood like all new arrivals was at first quartered in the penitentiary on Small Island. He remained there until the wrath of one of the other inmates intervened and he had to be shipped to the hospital with a serious wound. The knife he was stabbed with was three inches long. It was just as well that he had been forced to sleep on his side amid the densely packed bodies on the floor. The blanket in which he was wrapped and his arm had shielded him from the full force of the blow. Nevertheless the weapon passed through both, penetrating his side just below the armpit and 'wounding the membrane which invests the lungs'. The assailant had not even bothered to retrieve the weapon—as Butler wrote, the knife was left 'as before' inserted in the wound.

'As before'—the words were rather chilling. Hood was not the first person to have been stabbed in the dark while he lay curled on the Small Island penitentiary floor. A similar attempt had been made the previous year. As with Hood's stabbing, it had proved impossible to discover the identity of the assailant. The small green-timbered room had been crammed with bodies, yet not one of the prisoners locked within its confines professed to have heard a thing. To a man, they claimed that they were completely ignorant of the dreadful events that had taken place. It seemed to Butler impossible to conceal anything in that squalid space. He put every man who had been huddled into the room on trial. Of the 30 men he decided not to punish fourteen, possibly because they lay furthest away from where the attempted murder had taken place and as such were unlikely to have been involved. Of the remainder, he sentenced half to 25 lashes and the rest, who he was sure were the principal instigators of the whole horrid proceeding, to 50 for 'committing, or aiding and abetting in committing a violent outrage'.

Among those Butler flogged was John Ward, the man only recently returned to Macquarie Harbour under a fresh sentence for stealing a gang boat at the mouth of the Gordon and relieving Simpson, the coxswain, of his jacket and comforter. Condemned to serve in the gaol gang, Ward had proved particularly difficult to manage. He had not been long back when he was involved in a violent attempted escape. With six others he had tried to carry off a vessel, but was thwarted by three members of the boat crew who resisted the attempt. When a sergeant from the detachment and several constables joined in the fight, the would-be absconders were overwhelmed. Henceforth Ward openly expressed his contempt for those who acted as petty flunkies.

On one occasion Butler had him sentenced to receive 50 lashes and to serve in irons for 'mocking and insulting' the two constables on Small Island. The commandant became convinced that Ward lay at the heart of much of the villainy perpetrated in the settlement. He detected the hand of the man in all species of robbery, theft and contemptuous and disorderly conduct. In these matters, however, he thought that Ward was too astute to implicate himself and so employed others to execute his little schemes 'whilst he kept himself entirely aloof'. He was like a puppet master of the darkest hue.

Indeed, so much was Butler convinced of Ward's guilt that when Elijah Cooper confessed to the attempted murder of Abraham Hood, the commandant flatly refused to believe him. Cooper claimed that he had planned to murder Hood ever since the two had been in gaol together in Launceston where he had been flogged for some petty offence on Hood's evidence. An agricultural labourer with a speech impediment, Cooper stuttered out his confession. He claimed that he had made a particular point of noting where Hood had lain down and had crawled to the spot on his hands and knees in the dark. When asked where he had got the knife, he told Butler that he had retrieved it from a bag that had hung from a nail in the cookhouse. Yet no one could recollect the bag, let alone confirm that there had been a knife in it. Nor did it appear that Cooper had disturbed anybody during the execution of his supposed crime. In the black of night he claimed to have clambered over a mass of sprawled bodies without waking up a single one of them. In the end Butler decided that it was a ruse. As he explained to the colonial secretary, the prisoners were constantly devising schemes to 'get up to Hobart Town as witnesses or otherwise'.

Men had come forward in the past offering to point out the whereabouts of the decayed remains of past victims murdered in the bush. Invariably these were in some remote location requiring, not just a trip up to Hobart Town, but an excursion into the back blocks of the settled districts. The results were always the same. When push came to shove the prisoner could not recollect the exact location where the bones of the supposed victim could be found and without a body it was pointless to pursue a trial. The man had to be shipped back to Macquarie Harbour after having earned a prolonged break from the rigours of ganged labour.

While Ward remained the chief suspect for the stabbing, he had been joined in more recent months by another man whom Butler regarded with almost equal suspicion. George Lacey was a prisoner possessed of a history likely to gain respect in any penal station. Of the thirteen convicts who had absconded with Matthew Brady, eleven had met their end on the scaffold. Of the two who had been reprieved, George Saxon had voluntarily given himself up. He was also considered to be too young at just twenty. These circumstances were thought sufficient grounds to commute his death sentence to life transportation.

George Lacey's case had been less clear-cut. He claimed, however, that he had been forced to join the escape, an assertion his comrades freely affirmed. It was thus primarily due to the testimony of his executed friends that Lacey's neck was, at least temporarily, spared from a public choking. There were other factors that prompted the decision. Both Saxon and Lacey had been apprehended in the early stages of the outbreak. As more convicts joined Brady and McCabe there was a concern that all would fight to the death if the rebels thought the inevitable consequence of being taken was execution. It was hoped that by reprieving two, others might be induced to surrender. As a strategy it was not a great success.

Having escaped from the gallows Lacey was sent to the penal station at Maria Island off the east coast of Van Diemen's Land. There he caused a great deal of trouble. He refused to consume the meat ration declaring that it was unhealthy. When it was passed by inspection he led a deputation who plonked the stuff down on the commandant's doorstep. He also escaped from the place by crossing the Mercury Passage on a catamaran. In the end it was decided to send him back to Macquarie Harbour. He arrived in late July or early August 1827.

Butler thought that Lacey's character 'was much of the same stamp as Ward's', although he had not been at the settlement long enough 'to afford such repeated proofs of his adroitness'. Nevertheless, the commandant was quite clearly taken aback by the man's effrontery. From the moment of his arrival the place was in a 'perpetual state of agitation' as the man who had escaped with Brady 'supplied a constant stimulus to the bad spirits of the station'.

At eight o'clock on the evening of 17 October 1827 Constable George Rex commenced the rounds of the two barrack rooms on Small Island. Rex was a tall man at five feet eight inches. He claimed to have formerly been a valet to the Duke of Devonshire, a position that would have brought him into contact with the very elite of British society. Following his court martial for desertion Rex was reduced to wearing the coarse grey slops of a felon. As he mustered the Small Island prisoners in for the night, a party rose up and seized him and, despite his size and military training, the former hussar was overpowered and forced to surrender his keys.

Michael Shaughnessy, the hutkeeper, was the next to be secured. He was in the process of bringing in the iron night tub when, like Rex before him, his arms were tied behind his back with strips torn from government issue blankets. A gag made from the same stuff was inserted into his mouth and he was conveyed out of the penitentiary and down the path that led to the waterside. There he was placed on the beach next to Rex. James Cock the cook and Robert Grew the junior constable had already been bound and gagged and placed in the same location. They were soon joined by Henley, who was the other cook, and Clarke, the remaining hutkeeper.

A tall, thin man named McGuire was appointed to stand sentry over the six prisoners while others started to dismantle the penitentiary in search of anything that would float. They took apart the berth that had been erected in the constables' room and broke the doors off their frames. The building was ransacked for shelves and boards and all the materials that were salvaged were carried down the roadway to the shore where they were given to John Williams, who attempted to fashion them into a raft. Williams was a sailor from Runcorn in Cheshire who had been sent to Macquarie Harbour for returning to Britain after being sentenced to transportation. He had escaped from New South Wales and worked a circuitous route home via Van Diemen's Land, Macquarie Island and Batavia before he had been apprehended. He now frantically toiled away in three to four feet of water trying to make something that would float out of the bits and pieces of rubbish that had been used to fit out Small Island.

While Williams worked on the raft, McGuire, Ward and Jenkins re-tied the arms and legs of the men bound on the beach. The bindings were much tighter than they had been before, now making it impossible for the captive men to stand. Shaughnessy and Rex were placed in a nook underneath the small room in the penitentiary, and from where he lay on the ground Shaughnessy could see a large group of prisoners make their way down to the shingle bar to help Williams to launch the catamaran. He heard one of them say 'it would not answer'. He could see the raft sink under the weight of men who tried to clamber on board.

Samuel Measures, a cooper from Leicestershire, came and cut the bindings on Rex's legs and assisted him to his feet. He then led him away. James Cock, who lay bound and gagged on the beach, saw Measures, Kirk and Reid lead Rex into the water. He heard one of them shout 'why don't you keep the bugger down?' He then heard another ask for a knife so that he could 'settle him at once'. Through the mouth of the cave in which he had been placed William Henley had a clear view. In the moonlight he could clearly see Rex being led by Measures and Reid. Fearing the worst, the constable tried to resist, but the two men had hold of his arms and they pulled him along. They stopped level with the entrance of the cave and then turned Rex to face the water. Realising that they wanted him to go in, the constable turned one way and then the other in panic. He looked at Measures and Reid 'full in the face, endeavouring to speak, but could not, being gagged'. They shoved him forward into the water and when he was a little more than knee deep, Measures and Kirk pushed down on his shoulders while Reid pulled him over on his back.

From his place in the nook Shaughnessy later claimed that he had heard the noise of a man being plunged below the surface of the harbour followed by a 'gurgling sound as of water getting into a man's mouth'. For four or five minutes he heard the sound of Rex struggling in the water. Henley saw Reid beckon to his companions on the beach, urging them to join them to help hold the man down, but they all declined. When the three men had finished their unpleasant business they came out of the water leaving Rex's lifeless body floating in the moonlight.

About ten or twelve minutes later Measures walked up to where Shaughnessy lay and, loosening the binding from around his legs, helped him to his feet. He was conveyed to a place just outside of the cookhouse where he found Robert Grew and James Cock. Their hands were untied by Williams and they were told to lie down on the cookhouse floor. As Cock hobbled along on his wooden leg Lacey said to him—'Old man, don't be afraid, we'll not hurt a hair of your head; we have put one tyrant aside on purpose that the Commandant should not flog us. We would rather go to Hobart Town and be hanged than stop here and work in irons.' At first light Cock asked whether he should light a fire as a signal for the guard boat to come over and was told to do so. A sergeant of the 40th Regiment and five privates duly rowed across from Settlement Island. As they eased into the small shoal bay that passed for a boat harbour they found the drowned body of the constable, a man who had formerly been a servant to one of the most fashionable men in London, floating face down with his arms still tied behind his back.

Nothing at first could be seen of the raft that Williams had built. After a quick scan of the harbour it was eventually sighted close to the shore with three men on board. They proved to be Measures, Reid and Kirk. A boat was quickly despatched to pick them up before they could land and escape into the scrub. They made no resistance. The five men who had been bound and gagged on the beach were each brought before the commandant where they told him what had happened. From there they were sent to the office where John Douglas took down their depositions. In all they implicated nine prisoners, including the three absconders who had been the only men to actively participate in the murder of the drowned constable. The accused were all taken from Small Island to the main settlement and housed in the gaol.

The murder rattled the entire station. The sergeant who had discovered the body with its eyes and mouth still open wrote a letter to a friend in Glasgow. It would, he informed him, take a 'quire of paper to give proper detail of the infamous villainy which has taken place here'. 'No man' he continued, 'who has the courage to do his duty can consider himself safe'. Even Rex's funeral turned into a less than solemn occasion. As the body was carried away for burial, James Dalway, a Welsh carpet weaver's apprentice, had the temerity to jeer. He was punished with 50 lashes for 'contemptuous conduct'. Many surmised that the murderers had intended to attack the barracks by landing on Settlement Island at night. Butler even wrote to the colonial secretary expressing his fears that, with so many desperate prisoners in the gaol, they might even yet make an attempt to breakout and overpower the military.

In the circumstances he quickly moved to make an example. As the prisoners were checked into the gaol it was discovered that Ward and Lacey's irons were cut clean through 'with a small saw so fine to be scarcely perceptible'. By now Butler had been informed by the one-legged cook, James Cock, that the sole reason Lacey had offered for drowning Rex was to provide insurance against a flogging. Since he had no power as a magistrate to hear a capital offence the accused could not be punished for murder until they had been tried in a higher court. Nevertheless the commandant sentenced the two men to 75 lashes each for cutting the rings of their irons.

The nine men were placed in the gaol to idle away the hours in the dark until the next brig arrived. It proved to be a long wait. They passed the time in conversation, talking loudly so that they would be heard through the thick cell walls. Private Robert

Baxter, who was standing sentry, could distinctly hear everything they said. One of the men called out to Ward—asking him how he thought things would go. He replied, 'We'll be all hung'. The first man expressed his dismay that the three absconders had not got clear away on the catamaran as 'then there would have been nothing about us'. To this Ward replied, 'I'm sorry we did not put them all out of the way, the same as we did that tyrant, and then there would be none to prosecute'. The conversation then broke off and Lacey was called upon for a song. Despite the flogging he had just received, his demeanour appears to have become somewhat more amenable—he was no longer 'a constant stimulus to bad spirits'. On the contrary he seemed quite resigned to his situation and exhibited a degree of courtesy that belied his former rebellious spirit.

Later that same day he scrawled a note to Butler. 'It is likely' Lacey wrote, that 'the most of us if not all in the course of a few days or weeks … will be consigned to our graves'. In which case, he continued, 'we shall have but a short time to accomplish the great work which we have to undertake in preparation to meet that death which awaits'. He asked Butler if he would 'allow those who are so inclined to books' a Bible and some light so that they could prepare themselves for death. As he concluded, 'There is several amongst us who are belonging to the Church of England and we wish to make the best use of our time. You may depend Sir that is now our intent to conduct ourselves with worthy propriety'. Butler granted the concession. Three weeks later, just before they were removed from the gaol to be put on board the vessel that would carry them up for trial, Lacey wrote to thank the commandant for the indulgences that he had bestowed upon them. These had, he added, 'generally surpassed our expectations when we consider the enormity of the crime for which we are accused'.

The trial was a straight forward affair. The five witnesses that had been placed bound and gagged on the beach ensured that this would be the case. As Ward had put it when they had been in the gaol at Macquarie Harbour, if they had killed them all there might have been some doubt as to the identity of the murderers. Just as when Abraham Hood had been stabbed, the whole party may have wriggled free. Yet the witnesses had been placed on the beach for a reason and they were now brought forward to do their job. They appeared in the witness box one by one to give their damning testimony.

The trial may have been straight forward, but this did not stop it being a sensation. Butler had caused drawings of Small Island and the main settlement to be sent up so that the judge and jury would get some idea of the geography of Macquarie Harbour. The surgeon John Barnes happened to be in town at the time and he was called upon to verify that they were a true likeness of the place where he had served as medical officer.

Later when he was interviewed before a British parliamentary committee Barnes made much of his role in the court proceedings. He claimed that it was only through his evidence that a guilty verdict had been obtained since the other witnesses prevaricated and contradicted each other. He even lied to the committee. He claimed that he had been at Macquarie Harbour at the time of the murder and had examined the body after death. Like the account he gave of Alexander Pearce, it was largely embroidered rubbish; he had not been anywhere near the settlement at the time. He saved the best for last. He claimed that on the conclusion of the trial, Lacey had said to him, 'if it had not been for you, Doctor, we should have pulled through'. According to newspaper accounts, however, the evidence provided by Shaughnessy, Cock, Clarke, Grew and Henley was clear enough to secure a conviction. Indeed Barnes hardly featured in *The Tasmanian*'s report of the case.

The nine accused men appear to have mounted little in the way of a defence. Lacey and Ward seemed more excited by the flogging that they had received on Butler's orders—illegally as they claimed—than the prospect of being sentenced to hang. When the chief justice read out the 'awful sentence' of the law ending with the words 'and may the Lord have mercy on your soul', Lacey replied, 'Amen'. It was almost as if he greeted the verdict with warmth.

The execution followed swiftly. At eight o'clock on the morning of Monday 17 December 1827 the nine men were led to the scaffold. A file of soldiers was arranged outside the gaol wall to control the large crowd that had assembled. Many of the citizens of Hobart Town voluntarily turned out to watch the spectacle. They joined the convicts from the prison barracks who had been assembled under orders and whose numbers considerably swelled the ranks—there were about 600 of them. The crowd nearly filled the entire space in front of the courthouse. Arthur had originally entertained the idea of sending the condemned men back to Macquarie Harbour to swing at the scene of their crime. It would have been hard to find sufficient space to erect a gallows on Small Island, besides the scheme had been tried before with less than satisfactory results.

Three men found guilty of murder had been sent back to Macquarie Harbour to be executed in front of the assembled population of the penal station in February 1825. One of the condemned, Thomas Hudson, had already told Commandant Wright that his sole motive for committing the deed was that 'he was tired of this world' and had fixed upon his grim purpose with a view to 'getting out of it'. A man with a wild and maniacal look, he played the penitent on the scaffold. Not so the other two. Francis Oates and William Allen made the most of the occasion. They kicked their shoes off into the crowd and waved to their fellow prisoners who shouted goodbye. It was said that it had been like 'a parting of friends who were going on a distant journey' rather than that of 'individuals who were about to separate from each other for ever'.

It seemed most unwise to repeat the exercise so a public execution was organised at the usual place in Hobart Town, although this would be far from the view of those condemned to the squalid confines of Small Island. Rather than kicking their shoes into the crowd, the nine accused men went to their deaths singing and praying. They were brought from the gaol in two groups. Ward, Lacey, Measures and Jenkins all professed to be Protestants. They were led out, their arms pinioned, behind Reverend Bedford with whom they had been engaged in earnest prayer since three in the morning. The Wesleyan missionary, William Schofield, had joined them and was deeply affected by the whole process. He described how he felt the power of God as one of the four shouted out in rapture, 'bless God I know I shall go to Heaven angels are waiting for me'. Lacey had prayed particularly fervently and 'his whole soul seemed engaged' as he expressed 'a strong confidence in God'. The remaining five were Roman Catholics and they had prepared for death under the tutelage of Father Conolly. Schofield thought that they were dirty and very gloomy compared to those of the Protestant faith and he was thankful that he had been called by God to the ranks of the Methodists.

It was considered a condemned man's right to say what he wished from the scaffold. It was the job of the clergy, however, to ensure that those who spoke with the halter round their neck played the penitent. Mostly they succeeded, impressing upon them the enormity of their crimes and scaring them witless with visions of eternal damnation. It was commonplace, though, for men of the cloth to assume that convicts had little or no sense of religion and were ignorant of the most fundamental Biblical precepts. This was thought to particularly apply to those in penal stations. Yet there were indications that many among the convicts at Macquarie Harbour were religiously minded.

Literally dozens were tattooed with religious signs and scenes. George Dakin, a pork butcher who boasted that he could 'kill and dress any beast', was inscribed on his right hand with the first half of Proverbs 14. 9, 'fools make a mock at sin'. The tanner John McCarthy was spectacularly marked on his chest with a crucifix depicting 'Our Saviour bleeding on it' additionally adorned with 'an angel with a cup catching the blood'. The distribution of such tattoos suggests that these were not things casually acquired. They were most common among convicts who claimed to be Catholics, and were far less frequently observed on the limbs of Scottish Presbyterians. Only eight per cent of tattooed Scottish convicts arriving in Van Diemen's Land sported a cross or crucifix, compared to 38 per cent of those from Ireland. Calvinist teachings on the sin of idolatry played a role in shaping prisoners' bodies just as they had convinced the convict Abraham Hood that he had not, nor ever would, fall from grace.

When William Watts was sentenced to Macquarie Harbour he took a Bible with him. But he never reached the penal station, being one of the prisoners who piratically seized the *Cyprus* brig. When he was finally recaptured the precious book proved his undoing for it contained a list of family names, the details of which revealed his true identity. It was also inscribed with 'a hymn called the "Thief's Lamentation"', which was written on the inside cover along with other prayers. This was almost certainly a work based on Luke 23, 39–43, the passage which describes how the thief who suffered next to Christ was admitted into heaven. As was the case with slaves, there were many Biblical passages that were likely to appeal directly to convicts.

It was no accident that Arthur had pushed for a Wesleyan to be sent to the penal station. Their message was always likely to have great appeal to convicts. When John Wesley had joined the prisoners in Cardiff gaol in singing a hymn, many had burst into tears. It was no small wonder given the words:

> *Outcasts of men, to you I call*
> *Harlots, and publicans, and thieves!*
> *He spreads his arms to embrace you all;*
> *Sinners alone His grace receives:*
> *No need for him the righteous have;*
> *He came the lost to seek and save.*
>
> *Come, O my guilty brethren, come,*
> *Groaning beneath your load of sin!*
> *His bleeding heart shall make you room,*
> *His open side shall take you in;*
> *He calls you now, invites you home:*
> *Come, O my guilty brethren, come.*

Although the historian John West had written of the prisoners at Macquarie Harbour, 'It was their proverb, that all who entered there, gave up for ever the hope of Heaven', there is little to suggest that this was the case. Indeed, when George Lacey and his fellow prisoners mounted the scaffold it was as though they had deliberately set out to prove the contrary. Young men 'in the very bloom of life', they publicly confessed their sins. With the halter around his neck, Lacey moved forward towards the crowd as far as the length of rope would let him. He warned them of the dangers of drink. 'Depend upon it', he said as he looked over the assembled multitude of gaping countenances turned towards him. There are some of you, he continued, who think of me as an 'out and outer', convict parlance for a man who wanted out and would get out, even if it was via a rope around his neck. It is not, he warned, 'mere bravado that induces me to address you' but to warn that one day we will all meet a God 'whose laws both you and I have broken in so scandalous a manner'.

It was quite a message to deliver to a crowd that consisted of both bonded and free men. 'The time will come' he added 'when you will shudder like me to approach his awful presence'. With that he stepped back to take his place under the beam and they all 'joined with a loud and firm voice in singing a short hymn'. Their caps were then pulled down over their faces and Bedford read the execution prayer, 'he that sheddeth man's blood by man shall his blood be shed', and with that the drop was struck. As Schofield described it, in one moment they were 'before a crowd of spectators, in the next before their judge'. The moment was longer for some than others. One or two died quickly, others were caught struggling in the 'agonies of death', dancing before the crowd.

When Ward had been apprehended by Constable William Jarman on Chelsea Common he had been just seventeen. At the time he had been talking to a friend about a bull bait, that most English of pastimes in which a tethered bull was set upon by dogs especially trained for the business. The task of the dog was to grasp the bull by the fleshy parts of the nose and hold on 'tight as a leech' while the bull bellowed, reared up and lashed out. With its strong underslung jaw and a deeply set nose which allowed the animal to breath while it had the bull's flesh locked in its teeth, the British bulldog was ideal for the purpose. The task of the bull was to catch the dog before it could take hold, flipping it so high into the air with its horns that when it came down it would break its neck. Now it was Ward who was the spectacle. It was his turn to break his neck while the crowd gasped, to be left kicking while the prison barracks' inmates looked on, to have the life choked out of him for the edification of the public.

In the matter of their deaths, however, Ward and Lacey had been far more than passive agents. They had hijacked the stage, leaving Bedford, Conolly and Schofield as mere bit players. Ward had even sent invitations out to several of his 'old friends and acquaintances' so that they might see the manner in which he was turned off. They had, after all, organised the event right from the start. They had put the witnesses bound and gagged on the beach in order to arrange an escape from the hell of Small Island, an escape that would be final.

They might of course have ended things themselves. Suicide was only an option, though, for those who truly did not believe in God. For the religiously minded self-murder was perhaps the worst of all options since the victim had no time to repent and would therefore condemn their soul to eternal damnation with certainty. That was no escape at all. By drowning Constable George Rex, by immersing him below the cold waters of Macquarie Harbour, by ensuring that there were others there to see what had passed, the nine men had arranged their own deaths. The state had obliged by supplying them with Bibles, candles and clergymen from no fewer than three denominations. The ultimate sanction that Arthur possessed had been corrupted and used for an altogether unintended purpose. There was no way of stopping what had passed, of changing course so that Ward and Lacey could be prevented from using the state to terminate their terms to penal labour. It was as though the nine men had cut out a brig from under the noses of the convict department and one and all, prisoners, public, clergy and colonial officials, had been forced to watch them sail away.

Phillip's Island with the commandant's boat in the foreground. The crew are sporting straw boaters made from the experimental crop of wheat. (Thomas Lempriere)

10

And in duty bound will ever pray

On 20 November 1827 the sentence to transportation that had been passed on John Douglas by the Court of Justiciary in Edinburgh expired. From that day forth he was once more a free man. Three days later, when he had finished celebrating, he took the liberty of writing to Butler asking the commandant to represent his situation to the lieutenant governor. Now he was free, Douglas wished to be paid a free man's wage. In order to promote his case he emphasised the extent to which his duties had increased. These were now, he explained, '50 fold' greater than they had been at the time the penal station had first formed, yet the salary he was paid had remained the same, a shilling per day. It was not a lot of money, even after rations, grog, lamp oil and a roof and bed were thrown in. Indeed, it had taken him over a year and a half to pay back the £28.10 he owed to Lucas. As a result he was hardly better off now than when he had come back to Macquarie Harbour to resume the situation of confidential clerk to the commandant. Butler duly wrote to the colonial secretary enclosing Douglas's application for a salary increase and politely requesting that it be forwarded to Arthur together with the commandant's favourable recommendation.

Petitions were elaborate things, embellished with gothic capitals and elegant flourishes that curved across the paper directing the eye to their obsequious words. Each petition writer offered to exchange faithful loyalty for the particular indulgence he sought. As documents, they often ended with the formal phrase 'and in duty bound will ever pray'—a deferential expression of gratitude offered for whatever favour the petition writer anticipated. They were designed to be handed up from one person to another, collecting recommendations en route until they reached their intended destination. Each set of hands through which the document passed became part of the transaction. They endorsed the contents of the application and stood guarantor for the character of the petition writer. Petitions worked because they bound the writer within a chain of authority—in short, they were mechanisms for strengthening hierarchical ties.

Butler's letter praising Douglas's exemplary conduct, intelligence and attention to method was sent on the same brig that conveyed Lacey, Ward and the other prisoners accused of murdering Rex to Hobart Town to stand trial. It had been rather an unusual voyage. Together with the murderers placed double-ironed in the hold were two witnesses who had been called for the defence. Old acquaintances of Ward, the two men played no substantial role in the trial. It seems that they had been called merely as a favour since the trip to Hobart Town would provide them with several weeks' relief from ganged labour. This was considered a holiday, even if some of the time would be spent buffeted around in the hold of the *Prince Leopold*. Somewhere else on board, room had to be found to quarter the five witnesses for the prosecution—the men who had been placed bound and gagged on the beach. It was necessary to prevent all contact between them and the accused.

A few days after the trial the five witnesses wrote two petitions of their own. Their situation was desperate. They were stowed on board the brig *Prince Leopold* on the point of being returned to Macquarie Harbour. They addressed the first missive to the master of the vessel begging pardon for taking the liberty of bothering him, but pleading for him to intervene on their behalf. As the officer into whose charge they had been placed, they asked him to represent their case to the lieutenant governor pointing out the dangers of their situation. Macquarie Harbour, they warned, was a place full of 'such characters' who would do them a 'great injury', possibly even 'terminate' their existence. The nine 'unhappy men' who had been sentenced to death as a result of their testimony had plenty of companions who would not think twice about wreaking revenge.

The second petition was addressed directly to the lieutenant governor. They humbly prayed that his excellency would be 'pleased to command that they be removed to some other penal settlement', wherever 'his Excellency may think fit'—anywhere was preferable to Macquarie Harbour. Arthur, as it turns out, had already decided that Henley and Clarke should remain in Hobart Town and that only Grew, Shaughnessy and Cock would be returned. He now revisited the decision, deciding to send Robert Grew to Maria Island.

In early January 1828, Shaughnessy and Cock arrived back at the settlement. Again they put pen to paper, this time addressing the petition to the attorney general. They pointed out the 'awkward manner' in which they were situated. They told him of their fear that they would at the 'first favourable opportunity fall a sacrifice to the causeless rage of some wicked and malicious person'. The whole murder trial must have been a particularly difficult business for Shaughnessy. He knew two of the accused men well, having worked as a stockman with them at Weasalls Plains before all three had been fingered for giving succour to Brady and McCabe.

Cock pressed his case no less vigorously. A former soldier in the 14th Regiment, he wrote once more to the lieutenant governor. In so doing he made an extraordinary claim. He informed Arthur that while he had willingly testified in court, it 'of course' meant that henceforth he would 'be considered as a man not to be trusted amongst the major part of the people in the colony'. He may as well have told Arthur that the moral authority of the Crown was no more than paper-thin. Outside the colonial elite who rode on horses and ate strawberries, Cock implied that the rule of law counted for little. There was another moral order percolating below the surface of polite society, a code of conduct that may not have been propped up by courts and legal opinion but one which was invested with the weight of popular consent.

Prior to the *Prince Leopold* sailing to Hobart Town one of the members of the settlement boat crew had slipped a memorial of an altogether different nature into the hands of a sailor. Lucas, who was supervising the loading of the vessel, saw the clandestine transaction and confiscated the piece of paper, handing it over to Butler who read it with incredulity. The letter was a character reference addressed to Thomas Williams, a boot and shoemaker in Brisbane Street, Hobart Town. It had been written by Richard Biggs who was employed as schoolmaster to teach those among the convicts who could not read or write. Biggs had been sentenced to transportation for receiving £645 stolen by his younger brother. He had given the money to his girlfriend who had sewn the notes into a feather bolster before spending the morning lying next to him in bed sipping gin laced with peppermint. He now put pen to paper to aid his friend Robert Grew, the Small Island constable whose evidence in the Rex murder trial had proved crucial.

The letter set out to explain that Grew had no choice in the matter of the trial. He had to come to Hobart Town 'as an evidence'. Since he had been placed bound and gagged on the beach he could hardly deny what he had seen. Besides, he had been informed by Ward and Lacey that it was their desire that he should do so. He was not, in other words, really appearing at the bequest of the prosecution—an act that would otherwise be 'directly opposite to his inclination'. He had merely been given an opportunity of a 'slant' to Hobart Town, like the two witnesses called up for the defence. Biggs was worried, however, that others were bound to mistake Grew's motives and 'immediately blame if not condemn him'. He requested that Williams, a man whose 'word will be taken in the case', would go to the trouble to represent the truth of the matter to his friends. This would ensure that Grew's actions would be seen 'in the proper light' and he would not be suspected of having done anything that was inconsistent with 'his general character'.

Brisbane Street was not the most salubrious of addresses. It lay towards the back of the town where there were few shops or other businesses. Nevertheless, Bent's *Almanack* of 1829 carried an entry for Thomas Williams' shoemaking establishment. The place was still there in 1831, where the street number was given as ten. The letter that Biggs had written suggested that there were men and women at the other end of the social scale from Arthur to whom the petitioner's prayers might also be addressed and that it was important to do so if a man was to keep his reputation. It was perhaps a reminder, if a reminder was needed, that those who had been transported made up by far the largest component of colonial society. If a man wished to avoid being ostracised he had to obey colonial etiquette, lower-order style. Several old Macquarie Harbour hands found themselves in precarious positions when later called to account for their actions. Benjamin Riley, a zealous constable who often went armed in order to help the military track down absconders, was said to be hated by the wider convict population. Gottfried Hanskie, who put his experience in three European armies to good effect rounding up runaways, was subsequently attacked in the prison barracks by one of those he had captured at the Pieman Heads. When John Smith was serving time in the chain gang at St Peter's Pass he was forced to abscond. He tried to seek protection in the superintendent of convict's office in Hobart Town where, as he explained, he had run on account of 'the ill usage he received from the men in consequence of his having been an overseer at Macquarie Harbour'.

Four other prisoners at Macquarie Harbour signed the petition written in support of Robert Grew. They were persons who, as Biggs put it, were known to Thomas Williams and could vouch for the truth of the letter. It was to be a painful experience for all. Thomas Lawton, the sailor who had attempted to smuggle the letter on board the *Prince Leopold*, was punished with 100 lashes. Richard Biggs was awarded 75 strokes for having the audacity to write the missive, and the four prisoners who had affixed their names to the bottom of the ill-fated note were all given 50. Robert Grew was also punished. The order to send him to Maria Island was rescinded and the man was promptly returned to Macquarie Harbour. There were further consequences that had more lasting impacts than the cutting strokes of the lash. One of those who had been induced to sign the memorial was a young carver and gilder named John Knight who for a while had been employed in the settlement shipyard. He was a prisoner who was certainly no novice when it came to the business of petition writing.

Knight's journey to Macquarie Harbour had started in a typical enough fashion. Richard Elsam had been walking along Temple Bar near Chancery Lane when he felt a tug at his watch. He immediately put his hand to his fob but found that his seal and key had been cut off the ribbon. Turning swiftly he collared Knight, manhandling the lad into a shop doorway. The young apprentice protested his innocence. He said that he was the son of a gentlewoman and denied taking the seal, he had merely been attempting to make his way through the press. By now a small crowd had assembled. A patrolman made a search of the area, retrieving a knife that had been discarded close to the shop doorway. The seal, key and cut ribbon were found close by. Knight was put on trial the very next day; Old Bailey proceedings were often indecently rushed and it was not unusual for the accused to be given little time to prepare a defence. Despite his age—he was described as just fifteen—he was sentenced to transportation for life. The long sentence was largely due to the nature of the offence. The fashion of sporting handkerchiefs and watch ribbons in prominent places provided easy pickings and harsh sentences became commonplace in an attempt to protect the sartorial elegance of the London gent.

Transported to New South Wales on the *Recovery*, Knight was apprenticed at first in the dockyard in Sydney. He remained working in the carpenters' shop there for four years before he attempted to secrete himself on board a vessel in the harbour. When he was recaptured he was awarded 100 lashes and banished to Port Macquarie, New South Wales, for the remainder of his sentence. Imagining his case to be 'wholly desperate' he eloped once more and after the most severe trials was taken and sent as punishment to Macquarie Harbour. While labouring there in a timber rolling gang, 'exposed to every misery' to which that settlement was prone, he witnessed the murder of Constable George Craggs.

On 13 December 1824 Craggs was stabbed by an absconder named Thomas Peacock. By the standards of the age, Craggs was a giant. A farmer's labourer from County Durham he stood six foot one and a half inches in his bare feet. Sent to Macquarie Harbour for seven years for stealing twenty bottles of wine from the colonial surgeon's house, he was first employed as a watchman and then as a constable. Despite his size, however, he could not stop the five foot four and a half inch Peacock from sticking a knife into his stomach in a desperate attempt to wriggle free from his grasp. Despite the gash in his side, Craggs maintained his grip until help arrived. The wounded constable and the apprehended absconder were both loaded into a boat for the return voyage to Settlement Island. During the passage Craggs bled to death. Rather than expressing dismay Peacock rejoiced, exclaiming that 'he should now die happy since he had caused his death'. Although Peacock was shipped to Hobart Town to stand trial for the crime, the whole proceedings had to be put on hold when he announced that he wished to subpoena two prisoners to give evidence in his defence. Word had to be delivered to the penal station to send the witnesses up, one of whom was John Knight.

Later Knight was to claim that while he was waiting for the trial to recommence Arthur had spoken to him during one of his 'periodical visitations of the gaol'. While Knight did not spell out exactly what passed between the two he implied that he had been persuaded to change his testimony as a result of various inducements held out to him. These included the promise that he would be 'liberated at the prorogation of the Supreme Court then sitting'. Despite having been subpoenaed to Hobart Town as an evidence for the defence, he was careful to emphasise that Peacock had been found guilty and executed. It is difficult to conclude that he did not play a part in ensuring that the noose was tightened around the man's neck.

Whatever the facts of the matter, Knight was shipped back to Macquarie Harbour after the completion of the trial. He now embarked on a fresh campaign designed to secure relief from penal servitude. He first wrote a petition to 'His Excellency Ralph Dorling Esqr.'—it was an unfortunate spelling error, although he made a better job of Darling's title. He assured the 'Captain General & Governor in Chief New South Wales' that he had been a mere lad, aged just thirteen, when he had cut the ribbon that secured Richard Elsam's seal and watch. He promised that in future his conduct would be better and he pleaded for some relief to the 'interminable nature of my sentence', hoping that Darling would not leave him 'doomed to never ending misery'.

It is not immediately clear how Knight got the petition out of the penal station. It certainly does not appear to have gone by any official route. Darling sent it on to Hobart Town and from there it was sent back to Macquarie Harbour for Commandant Butler's comment. By now Knight had sent another petition addressed, perhaps more appropriately, to Lieutenant Governor Arthur. As well as attempting to prick Arthur's conscience over the matter of the shady transaction in the gaol, Knight again pressed the issue of his youth. On his arrival in New South Wales, he claimed, 'he had not attained his fourteenth year, and his subsequent misconduct was entirely owing to his extreme youth and inexperience; a repetition of which reflection and more mature years' would effectually prevent. Perhaps not surprisingly, Arthur professed not to remember the case. He was, however, impressed when he read Butler's report of Knight's progress as an apprentice shipwright. The commandant reported that Knight had proved 'smart and useful' and his name had not appeared in the 'black, or trial books of the settlement' since his arrival.

Arthur now saw a role for penal stations that he had not previously envisaged. He scrawled a memo on Butler's letter: 'I remember some time since to have had a report that there were some very idle disorderly boys whom it was difficult to manage.' All this was true. Settlers were loath to take on the services of youths who had no particular skills to recommend them as they were reluctant to pay training costs when there was no guarantee that they would reap any long-term return. As a result there were many young lads who cluttered the barracks in Hobart Town where they remained a nuisance.

Arthur now conceived a plan to send them to Macquarie Harbour where they could be instructed in trades 'by which means they may hereafter become useful'. He later expanded the scheme to Maria Island and in 1834 caused a purpose-built settlement for juvenile offenders to be constructed at Point Puer on the Tasman Peninsula. As for Knight, he wrote 'Let him be informed that, if he goes well as a ship-carpenter for 12 months longer he shall be suffered to return to Hobart'. Thus it was that the shipwright almost secured relief from his penal suffering. His attempt to intervene on Grew's behalf, however, proved costly and the intercepted letter put paid to any notion that he would achieve any form of early release from the penal station.

It is tempting to conclude that Knight was induced to affix his name to the Grew petition in order to effect some rehabilitation of his own reputation in anticipation of a return to Hobart Town. If Grew's character had been tarnished by the evidence he had given in court, the same is likely to have been true of Knight. If so, then he acted prematurely. As he had found to his cost, the petition writing process was not without its pitfalls and at times it could do more harm than good. Promises of good conduct were dangerous if they were not backed up with favourable reports. As Butler wrote, the men who signed the letter were 'not of the most unexceptional character'. The 50 lashes that Knight was forced to endure stood testimony to this less than ringing endorsement.

Past conduct certainly mattered when it came to the evaluation of the petition writer's pleas. The fate of the five witnesses who had been bound and gagged and placed on the beach by Lacey and his confederates was proof of this. Arthur had little difficulty in permitting two, Henley and Clarke, to remain in Hobart Town. Clarke had been sent to Macquarie Harbour for receiving four pieces of timber, property of the government. While Henley's crime was more serious—he had stolen £75 in promissory notes and a significant amount of clothing from a house in Elizabeth Street—he had already been at the settlement for a number of years. Robert Grew, on the other hand, had been despatched to Macquarie Harbour for making away with a serious haul. He had broken into a dwelling house and made off with £715 in silver coin and promissory notes, the property of a soldier in the 40th Regiment. Considering that the theft of a mere 40 shillings was sufficient to make the offence capital he was lucky to have been sentenced to just seven years' transportation. Arthur's decision to send him to Maria Island was thus a significant concession. It was also one that suggested that the crimes committed by Shaughnessy and Cock were particularly henious.

Shaughnessy had been an associate of Matthew Brady. At least he had been named as such by his former master, George Farquharson, in a sixteen-page petition that the latter had written to Arthur in a futile attempt to save his neck. The word of a gentleman, even one who had been strung up from the gallows, carried no small weight, especially when those he had accused were alleged to have succoured revolt. On the face of things, Cock presented much less of a threat. He was, if anything, an object of pity. He had lost his leg on the surgeon's table in 1815 when he had been wounded during the taking of the French colony of Guadeloupe. Sentenced to seven years' transportation he had maintained himself in Hobart Town by running a disorderly house.

It may well have been there that he had plotted with two friends, Thomas Bird and Joseph Bond Clark, to enter into an elaborate fraud. It was claimed that the three men would frequently retire to a room with pen, ink and some paper. Despite the fact that all three were still under sentence they dabbled in various business enterprises. Clark had entered into a stockholding agreement with a man named John York. He now claimed to have used his equity in the business to lever £500 paid over in the form of ten promissory notes. The notes, effectively amounting to IOUs, were witnessed by Cock and Bird and a free man named William Fraser. This was a common way of transacting business in a colony where money was in short supply. But it was a system that was open to abuse.

To the consternation of those who tried to redeem them York refused to honour payment, claiming that the ten pieces of paper were forgeries. It did not take long to round up the culprits. The notes had all been made out in favour of Clark and he certainly appeared to have been the chief beneficiary. While he had struggled to pay for his lodgings prior to their circulation, he had subsequently appeared about town dressed, not 'meanly' as before, but in the manner of a merchant. For the short time it took the paperwork trail to unravel he must have cut quite a figure. As Cock, Bird and Fraser had witnessed the notes they were dragged into the growing scandal. From the start the case was taken seriously. Measures needed to be put in place to deal with the miscreants in order to restore shaken business confidence. As Fraser was a free man he could not be subjected to summary justice. A suitable example could be made of the three convicts, however, and they were put on trial before a magistrates' bench. While Fraser's case was bound over to be heard in the supreme court, Cock, Bird and Clark were sentenced to receive 100 lashes and to be transported to Macquarie Harbour for four years.

By the time they arrived at the penal station in January 1824 legal questions were being asked about the case. Since the supreme court was empowered to employ the maximum force of the law it was likely, indeed even probable, that Fraser would receive a more severe sentence. While he would escape a flogging he might well be sentenced to hang for the offence. The anomaly needed to be addressed, but this would be difficult unless the magistrates' bench ruling that had been applied to his three convict accomplices could be overturned. The attorney general was consulted on the matter. He declared the lower court ruling to be null and void on the grounds that the bench did not have the power to try such a serious matter. It had been, in his words, 'an incompetent authority'. As a result the three prisoners were brought up from Macquarie Harbour to take their place in the dock with William Fraser. As they later claimed this was a breach of the principle that no subject should be tried twice for the same crime. As might have been anticipated the court sentenced all four to death, although they were subsequently reprieved on condition of life transportation. Fraser protested, having been advised that no legislative act had been 'passed to punish the crime of forgery in these colonies'. He also pleaded that he had been 'long incarcerated' and 'prayed his discharge'. The prayer succeeded and he was pardoned and returned to Hobart Town after spending only a short time at Macquarie Harbour.

It appears, however, that Fraser's accusation carried legal weight. Although in later years all confessed to have, at best, a hazy recollection of the matter, it is clear from the sheriff's calendar that the sentence for at least three of the accused was rescinded. The record showed that Fraser, Bird and Cock were all unconditionally pardoned. For some reason the same provision was not extended to Clark, although this was probably a clerical oversight. The nub of the matter was that not only had the three convicts been tried twice for the same offence but there were serious questions about the validity of both trials. From beginning to end the affair was a mess.

It was a problem that Arthur inherited. He arrived in Van Diemen's Land on 22 May 1824, a month before the supreme court trial, but after the decision to embark on this legally problematic course of action had been taken. His administration did little to clear up the matter. No word was sent to Macquarie Harbour to inform Bird and Cock that their colonial sentence to life imprisonment had been rescinded and for years they remained on the penal station books as convicts for life. This was perhaps as good a way as any of sweeping the whole matter under the carpet. It was certainly in keeping with the way that Arthur used Macquarie Harbour as a place where convicts could be detained irrespective of court rulings. If challenged, he could always fall back on the argument that, as lieutenant governor, he had the right to detain a prisoner anywhere within the bounds of the colony that he might decide was right and fitting. Macquarie Harbour was a convenient colonial cupboard where skeletons could be kept securely out of sight and perhaps, more importantly, out of mind.

The affair, however, did not go away. Although ignorant of the full scale of the miscarriage of justice that had been perpetrated upon them the three prisoners doggedly pursued their case. As they argued, 'it is a thing unknown in the whole code of British Laws, to punish a man twice for the same offence'. It was a particularly emotive issue, especially since the notion that a man could be flogged and sentenced to death for the same crime was regarded as a gross abuse of authority. This is why Ward and Lacey had kicked up such a fuss during their trial. They argued that the moment they had been taken on a capital charge Butler had no authority to flog them. They said as much to Cock to allay his fears after he had watched Rex drown: 'Old man don't be afraid…we have put one tyrant aside on purpose that the Commandant should not flog us. We would rather go to Hobart Town and be hanged then stop here and work in irons.'

A similar case later caused Arthur's administration a great deal of trouble. In 1834 a runaway named Greenwood was apprehended on the New Town race course. In the ensuing struggle a convict constable was 'cut and maimed' and the absconder was duly sentenced to receive 100 lashes by the magistrates Spode and Mason. They also committed him to trial. Found guilty, he was sentenced to death and, despite protests, the sentence was carried into effect. Indeed, so promptly did the execution follow the trial that it was said that 'the man's back had not healed from the effect of the lash'. As the *Van Diemen's Land Annual* put it, in 'this manner was the poor wretched creature deprived of his life'. The execution was looked upon as 'a disgrace to the colony'. *The Colonist* described the whole affair as a 'refinement on torture' and *The Tasmanian* called it an exercise in the 'execrable Machiavelian doctrine "that all means are justifiable to obtain a desired purpose"'. The case certainly provided ammunition for Arthur's many enemies. It was widely publicised in colonial newspapers and pamphlets and accounts of the affair were still in circulation as late as the 1870s, more than twenty years after the last transport vessel had docked.

Cock's dilemma was that each time he wrote to Arthur to point out the injustices of his case, the more reluctant the lieutenant governor became to intervene on his behalf. Although both the original magistrates' hearing and the controversial re-trial had occurred in Sorell's period of office, he could not answer the prayer of the one-legged cook without admitting serious fault on behalf of the chief justice and the previous attorney general. The more Cock pressed the issue the more of an embarrassment it became. In part this was because Cock and his friends Clark and Bird did not ask for some favour that could be traded for a promise of future good behaviour. Instead they demanded justice. They wanted the second sentence that had been passed upon them struck off. They were, of course, ignorant of the fact that that is precisely what had occurred but the decision had been concealed from them. The four years to which Cock had been sentenced to a penal station expired on 11 October 1827, just six days before, bound and gagged, he was forced to become an involuntary witness to murder. His original sentence to transportation would expire in March 1828. Despite this he had been forced to return to a penal station where he faced the daily possibility of retaliation from the many friends of Ward and Lacey.

Cock had already represented his case to Captain Butler but the commandant was powerless to act since the former soldier and his co-accused were entered in the settlement books as transportees for life. As he counted down the last days of his original sentence to transportation, James Cock and his two friends embarked on an extraordinary campaign. They wrote first to Arthur and the current attorney general and, when these letters failed to get a response, to the barrister Joseph Tice Gellibrand, the ill-starred attorney general who had authorised their second trial in 1824. It was all to no avail. Their prayers did not even receive so much as an acknowledgment.

Fed up with being rebuffed they embarked upon a more audacious course of action. In May 1828 somewhere in the confines of Settlement Island the three men caused a new petition to be drawn up. This time it was made out to the 'Honourable the House of Commons in Parliament Assembled'. They outlined their cause in detail. They explained that they had written to the lieutenant governor and the chief justice 'praying for consideration of their case, but have never received any answer'. They pointed out that in the intervening time two of them had become free 'by the expiration of their original sentences', but were still detained in a penal station. 'Being friendless', they explained that they had decided to submit their 'unfortunate and unprecedented case to this honourable House, confiding in the justice and proverbial humanity of British laws'.

They did not stop at this however. They addressed a covering letter to Joseph Hume Esquire, the member of parliament for Aberdeen and a noted campaigner against flogging. They begged his pardon for intruding upon his time but explained that they had been induced to do so by a knowledge of his 'generous and disinterested feelings in the cause of liberty and the punishment of oppression'. Both letter and petition were handed to Butler who was asked to forward them to the colonial secretary so that he might submit the communication to London with the regular mails.

Apparently they were never received. The colonial secretary denied ever seeing the letter and its accompanying 'humble prayer'. Arthur professed his ignorance of the whole matter. No trace of the documents could be found in any of the files, it was as though they had disappeared into thin air. Oddly, the colonial government decided to act on the matter in the same month that the petition was supposed to have been delivered into their hands. Having done nothing for years—the men had received no correspondence on the issue since at least June 1825—the executive council suddenly decided to discuss the case on 19 May 1828. Seven days later instructions were sent to Butler ordering him to send up Cock, Bird and Clark on the next vessel. Conveyed to Hobart Town on the *Cyprus* they were placed in the prison barracks while Arthur and his council debated the case. For three further months nothing happened and then a notice appeared in the *Hobart Town Gazette*. James Cock and Joseph Clark were free. Their certificates had been prepared and were waiting at the office. Bird, who had originally been sentenced to fourteen years' transportation, was informed that he would be freed in March 1835. He was now no longer a prisoner for life although nothing could be done to peel the 100 lashes off his back.

This should have laid the matter to rest but in fact it did nothing of the sort. Clark was summoned back to the office by the chief constable to be told that a mistake had been made and his certificate had been issued in error. He was ordered to hand it over there and then. Clark later described it as forcible robbery. As he had been the chief beneficiary of the fraud the executive council decided not to exercise any more mercy beyond consenting to remove him from the confines of Macquarie Harbour. Not being able to find any record to the contrary the colonial government insisted that the life sentence passed on him in 1824 was still in force.

Arthur might have thought that this was the end of the affair but in December he received very unpleasant news. As the lieutenant governor already knew, despite the formidable terrain that surrounded the settlement, the penal station had proved an ineffectual means of thwarting the machinations of runaways. Now it transpired that other goods were smuggled out of the station. From time to time parcels of tobacco were intercepted and once a box containing the remains of 'two stuffed native cats' was sent up to Hobart Town, although when it arrived the contents proved quite rotten. Now it transpired that something else had made its way out of the settlement which threatened to produce a greater stink. Cock, Bird and Clark had sent a copy of the letter they had addressed to Joseph Hume. This time, conscious of the failure of their previous petitions to extract any form of official response, they added a postscript, which read: 'We have sent a letter similar to this and the documents accompanying it through the medium of the Commandant, but as we have reason to apprehend that they may not reach your hands through the official channel we have taken the liberty of sending this privately.'

It was never fully explained how the letter found its way across half the oceans of the world to the office of the member for Aberdeen. Presumably it had been smuggled out of Macquarie Harbour in the same way that Thomas Lawton had attempted to pass the memorial in favour of Robert Grew to a seaman on board the *Prince Leopold*. It was probably directed in the first instance to someone in Hobart Town known to be sympathetic to their cause with instructions to place the parcel on a vessel bound for the port of London.

There were other radical members of parliament to whom the three men could have chosen to write but Joseph Hume was a particularly good choice. He was a shareholder in the Australian Agricultural Company and had developed a reputation for being a 'post-box for colonial complaints'. Not only did he have an interest in Australian issues, but he had also already crossed swords with George Arthur when he had spoken out in the House of Commons against his conduct as superintendent in Honduras. Unlike the colonial administration, Hume wrote back to the men promising that an inquiry would be instituted. He now wanted to know why he had not received the copy of the petition that Cock, Bird and Clark claimed they had sent by official channels. If the original had ever been placed in the by now weighty bundle of papers relating to the affair in the colonial secretary's office, it was removed and Arthur denied ever having seen it. All that can be said on this matter is that the timing of Clark, Bird and Cock's removal from Macquarie Harbour strongly suggests that it had in fact been received. Hume now wrote to assure the three men that he had 'called the attention of the Government to the possibility of any Governor or Commandant daring to withhold any Petition sent to Parliament'. To Arthur's chagrin it was now the conduct of his administration that was the subject of official scrutiny and not the prisoners under his charge; the eye of the paperwork panoptican had turned.

The lieutenant governor was furious. He wrote to Sir George Murray, the secretary of state for the colonies, complaining that corresponding with convicts was 'little calculated to promote the submission of these depraved characters to the constituted authorities, or to make them feel the disgrace and ignominy of being transported!' But the fact of the matter was that Clark was now considerably emboldened and redoubled his attempts to seek his freedom. The former hatter's apprentice from Great Oakley in Essex wrote once more to Joseph Hume. He now talked openly of his many friends 'at home'. He even threatened to write to the Lord Chancellor describing his case as the worst abuse of the 'law of England' since 'the reign of King James the 1st'. He now took to signing his petitions 'your Excellency's obedient and devoted servant, in all things where in the liberty of the subject is not infringed'. Now in Hobart Town, Clark took his case directly to the lieutenant governor who met with him in his office on three or four occasions. Arthur confessed that he could hardly forget the experience for he had the misfortune to hear 'every part of his story over and over' exercising, in the process 'no small degree of forbearance—for a more wicked, impudent man I never met with'. Yet what Arthur thought of Clark was now irrelevant.

In March 1830 the lieutenant governor was ordered by the secretary of state for the colonies to issue a full pardon. By now he had received unequivocal advice that Clark's second trial had been illegal. To Arthur's great annoyance even this did not placate the man who continued to write demanding some compensation for unjust deprivation of liberty. To this Arthur flatly refused to consent but the damage had been done. In an attempt to ensure that no further embarrassments occurred he wrote to Captain Briggs, Butler's replacement as commandant at Macquarie Harbour, instructing him that it was 'of the utmost importance that all letters of complaint should be without delay submitted for his consideration'. As a result a number of other prisoners were removed from the station, it being discovered that their terms of transportation had in fact expired.

In one of his many letters Clark had assured the colonial secretary that he would be sorry to cause any further 'unpleasant-ness' with any of the authorities in this colony. By this stage, however, unpleasantness had been caused aplenty. Joseph Hume in particular had Arthur firmly in his sights. When the lieutenant governor tried to cover up the Greenwood affair it was Hume who got wind of it and prodded the colonial office into action. He must have been struck by the similarity between this case and the complaint that he had received from Cock, Bird and Clark, both of which involved men who were sentenced to be flogged and then executed. As Butler had done when the same allegation was raised against him by Ward and Lacey, Arthur argued that the two punishments were awarded for different charges. Greenwood had been sentenced to 100 lashes for absconding and to death for attempting to murder the constable who had apprehended him. As a defence it failed to assure the lieutenant governor's growing number of critics, among whom Joseph Hume could most certainly be numbered. He became one of a body of radical members of parliament who pressed for Arthur's recall.

Even when Arthur was back in London the issue dogged him. When the House of Commons debated the practice of military flogging, the *Cornwall Chronicle* reported that the 'name of Colonel Arthur was, as might be expected, roughly handled'. He was charged with having illegally flogged a soldier when he was in Honduras. Although the secretary of war refused to instigate a committee of inquiry, this did little to placate the colonial press. As the *Chronicle* chose to put it, Arthur 'was not likely to lose the gratification of lacerating the carcase of a menial, who had offended him because the punishment was illegal. No!, No, he would "CHANCE IT!"—for what probability was there of a common soldier gaining satisfaction for injury done him by his commanding officer?' One might add common felon and, as if to make the same point, the paper published a cartoon depicting a convict flogged with a hundred lashes before being taken up the hill to be hanged.

Although he was never compensated for the 32 months that he was held a prisoner illegally or for suffering a 'punishment on his bare back which nearly cost him his life', Clark secured his freedom via the storm he created with his pen. It took him some time but he blew his man down. By the time Clark had succeeded in hounding Arthur into granting his freedom the lieutenant governor had begun to entertain serious doubts about the wisdom of maintaining Macquarie Harbour as a penal station. Given the trouble the place had caused him, this was perhaps no wonder.

Watercolour of Billardiera longiflora *showing the reproductive organs split open with a scalpel to aid classification. (William Buelow Gould)*

11

Under the rose

Two evenings each week John Douglas left his quarters and walked the short distance to the old penitentiary where he assisted the Reverend William Schofield at work in the school. There were several classes. The first and the most basic taught the rudiments of the alphabet to pupils who were mostly old men. Others were taught by Schofield to read the Testaments, while Richard Biggs, the schoolmaster, conducted lessons in spelling and writing. Douglas took the most advanced class. The former bank clerk instructed his charges in the art of bookkeeping, a talent which he had once used to his advantage against the Bank of Scotland. As the whale oil spluttered in the lamps he sharpened his pen, mixed a little ink from the powder supplied in paper wraps from the commissariat, and ruled out neat lines on a foolscap page.

In the evenings Schofield did not work in the school with Douglas, he busied himself with a diary in which he recorded much about the daily life of the settlement and much more about his own inner turmoil. The chaplain was in his mid-thirties and had been posted to Van Diemen's Land by the London Missionary Society to preach the good news to the outcasts of civilisation. When he arrived in Sydney he was warned of the horrors of Macquarie Harbour by a fellow Wesleyan. The Reverend Mansfield had told him that if he had been instructed to go he would have refused, risking suspension rather than taking up the position.

Forewarned, Schofield asked Arthur if he might be sent to Maria Island, but the lieutenant governor's response proved rather bruising. Over the course of breakfast at Government House the Wesleyan was brow beaten into accepting the posting. As he later confessed he left the meeting harbouring 'some very painful feelings'. It is thus not surprising that it was with some foreboding that he set off on the journey to the penal station. As he and his wife Martha boarded the vessel that would take them beyond the gates of hell he had to remind himself that it was God's bidding that he should be called to rescue souls in this lowest sink of the Empire and he steeled himself for the task ahead.

There were many times when the missionary's faith was tested. At first it seemed as though he was surrounded with overwhelming wickedness in this place where a man might murder another simply because he was tired of life. He felt, as he confessed, like David with his sling and five stones about to confront Goliath. He thought the whole place a 'moral desert'. It was all far removed from what might conventionally be considered as missionary work. Something of his disappointment can be detected in his correspondence with George Augustus Robinson, the self-proclaimed saviour of the Aboriginal peoples of Van Diemen's Land. In comparison to convicts, Schofield exclaimed that here was a 'noble race' of 'poor destitute creatures' who were deserving of conversion and salvation. By contrast, when the missionary sat in John Mayo's cell, a man who had been driven to murder because he could no longer bear to live without tobacco, he felt unable to pray with him. It was a dreadful thing to admit, but he had little empathy for the souls he had been sent to save.

His sense of isolation was heightened by the antics of the other officers. He had watched with dismay as his neighbour, Dr Garrett, drank himself half to death, appearing dishevelled at his door to tell the sick 'to go to Hell & be damned'. When Garrett had been invited to Ensign Stubbeman's quarters the evening had degenerated into a drunken brawl. The surgeon had broken a table and smashed a tumbler. When he hit Stubbeman across the face the ensign drew his sword, but Garrett retaliated by lashing out with his stick and the two men exchanged blows.

The tension between the civil and military officers had been exacerbated by the airs and graces affected by Butler's replacement as commandant, Captain James Briggs. Shortly after he had arrived at the settlement in July 1829 Briggs had insisted that the civil officers should sit behind the military at divine service. As a result many among the former took umbrage and refused to attend. As Schofield remarked, it was ridiculous to be so particular about rank in a place of worship. He thought the whole affair 'as bad as caste among the Heathens'.

Things soon got worse. The chaplain delivered a sermon that included the words 'Not many win, not many noble are called', a standard Wesleyan pitch, but Briggs took it all as a personal insult and henceforth he withdrew from the 'means of grace'. Thereafter, relations between the commandant and Schofield remained 'cold'. The rest of the rank and file of the 63rd Regiment seemed equally unreceptive to the message of Christ's Gospel and Schofield confided that preaching to them was like 'plowing in the rocks'.

He consoled himself by training a choir, assembling sixteen men and two boys for the purpose, some of whom possessed excellent voices. The convict sailor James Porter, for example, was noted for his fine tone and he was sometimes called to the commandant's house to entertain dinner guests with songs of the sea. The sound of the choir, Schofield confided to his parents, was quite delightful, although on occasions it was drowned out by the wind which battered the boards of the shipwright's shed that served as a makeshift chapel. Sometimes the winter gales blew so hard that Schofield had to keep his voice at full stretch to make himself heard. But on days when the weather was calm he reported with delight that a 'death like stillness' descended on the ranks of his captive congregation and as he started to pray he could 'sometimes hear a few say amen'.

It was the evening class, however, that gave him the most cause for joy. He saw the weekly service as an opportunity to increase recruits and he railed from his makeshift pulpit against those who had not availed themselves of the opportunity to read and write. They were, he maintained, no better than the brutes of creation, mere beasts who lacked the necessary faculties to improve their lot. The school provided him with an opportunity to work on the minds of prisoners, to expose them to the glories of the Gospel and to cause them to reflect on the precarious condition of their souls. At first the commissariat officer, Thomas Lempriere, agreed to help but was disappointed with Schofield's insistence that evening classes should commence and conclude with the singing of hymns. Lempriere was convinced that this would prove counterproductive, giving the impression that the school was a religious institution and inevitably lead to a decline in numbers. Schofield disagreed. To him the whole point of the class was that it should serve as a mechanism for bringing the fallen to God.

As the school grew so too did the number of prisoners who professed their new-found faith. Schofield was careful to police his religious converts. He insisted that each should admit their guilt, acknowledging their inferiority in a process that differed little from Captain Briggs's insistence that the etiquette of rank should always be observed. To reinforce the message the chaplain commanded that each 'continue to evidence their desire for salvation' by 'rendering obedience to the powers that be—Honor to whom Honor—Fear to whom Fear'. The message was inescapable. In the penal world officially sanctioned salvation could only be extended to the servile. He reinforced the message by demanding that converts inform on those who erred through the 'commission of sin, or omission of duty' on penalty of being summarily dismissed from his little flock.

It is perhaps little surprise that the commandant approved of these rules, adding that he thought them 'well calculated to reform the habits and improve the morals'. It was no accident that the majority of convicts that Schofield considered genuine converts already occupied positions of trust, such men were used to exercising submission. It was certainly the case that the missionary demanded their respect. When John Thompson messed up the lines on his slate and attempted to turn Schofield into an object of ridicule the chaplain had no qualms about charging him. The miscreant was awarded 25 lashes and banished to the living hell of Small Island.

While Schofield was at pains to point out what was expected of those who wished to conform to the path of righteousness, toeing the line had added attractions. The chaplain often wrote memorials in favour of the members of his little congregation and many were released early. Among the first to be brought up were William Phillips and George Holloway. Impressed by Schofield's account of the reforming power of religion, Arthur ordered them to be assigned to Government House where they could be shown off to visitors. They were living proof that it was possible to reform the very worst of the worst. Such were the rewards of the penitent thief Arthurian style.

It was not necessary to sign up to Schofield's rules in order to secure an early release from the penal station, although this certainly helped. Class participation brought its rewards. In the first year and a half of the operation of the school, 90 Macquarie Harbour convicts attended in one capacity or another. Of those, nineteen did not stay the course and a further four either died or absconded. Over one in four, however, were removed to Hobart Town. It was a significant success rate and there were any number of prisoners who would put up with Schofield's hymns in order to improve their chances of securing a passage on the outward bound brig past Liberty Point and out of the gates of hell.

Schofield was aware of the dangers of being duped. From the outset he thought that the majority who attended divine service did so in order to introduce themselves to his notice in the hope he would provide for their welfare from 'a temporal point of view'. Further, he wrote in his diary, almost as a reminder to himself, 'which I cannot conscientiously do without an unequivocal proof of a change of heart and life'. As he later admitted, 'In this place a minister must be as wise as a serpent and as harmless as a dove, there is so much deception that it is difficult to say who is sincere'.

Yet, he saw in the slow transformation of the penal station evidence of the reforming power of the school. It was as if he and his small band of acolytes had succeeded in tempering the ardent spirits of the convict population. Throughout the course of 1829 the number of lashes doled out by commandants Butler and Briggs declined. On 2 January 1830 the last two prisoners in the chain gang had their irons struck off by the blacksmith. The next day was a Sunday and for the first time the dull clink of shackles could not be heard as the prisoners assembled for the service in the makeshift chapel. As Schofield marvelled, it was a thing 'never known at Macquarie Harbour'. Others agreed that a remarkable transformation had taken place. In one of his more lucid moments Garrett confided that the place was a paradise compared to when he had first served there as colonial assistant surgeon four years ago. Relatively speaking there were now few thefts, quarrels or fights and the conduct of the prisoners could generally be described as 'praiseworthy'. Schofield concluded that there could be 'no doubt of the great utility of a preached Gospel in this place'.

Even Small Island was slowly abandoned as a place of punishment. By June 1832 there were only nine prisoners left on the windswept rock. The following year all were removed and the place was instead employed as a makeshift barracks for those among the Peternidic and other west-coast peoples who had agreed to accompany George Augustus Robinson to Flinders Island. After the completion of the new penitentiary in April 1828 it became possible to house a far greater proportion of the convict population on Settlement Island. Although the surgeon's belief in anti-contagionism ensured that the new building was exposed to the force of the wind, it was in other ways designed with comfort in mind. Each of the three rooms was heated by a fireplace and the completed building sported carved columns and ornamental lintels decorated with flowers and diamonds.

The settlement had changed in other ways too. When opportunities arose the standard ration was augmented with fish. The boat crew at the heads caught large numbers of cod, ling, salmon and trumpeter. The officers also dined on wombat, wallaby, swan and echidna. The latter was a particular favourite and stuffed with sage and onion and roasted it was said to have 'all the flavour and taste of goose'. The scurvy that had loosened Neil Douglas's teeth had become a rare occurrence by the early 1830s. The production of potatoes from Phillip's Island, supplemented by those supplied by the pilot, did much to hold the condition at bay.

The officers' gardens, which had been liberally fertilised with nightsoil and scratched over by chickens, proved surprisingly productive. Many in the nineteenth century were enthusiastic about the value of excrement. The journalist Henry Mayhew waxed lyrical about the stuff and in the 1860s it was estimated by one scholar that, if profitably utilised, the value of London's sewage would be 'equal to the local taxation of England, Ireland and Scotland'. The waste of the penal settlement was certainly turned to good account in Schofield's garden. The chaplain reported that his little vegetable plot produced 'cauliflowers, shallots, onions, carrots, beans, turnips, cabbages, peas, red beetroot, lettuces, potatoes, cape-goose berries, red currants, parsley, balm, thyme and sage'. While the diversity of plants grown in the government gardens was not as great, they too now produced parsley, carrots and onions for the use of the hospital. According to Lempriere the vegetables grown on the island 'were of a quality and size that would not have disgraced the stalls of Covent Garden'. The stinking waste that collected in the penitentiary night tubs was clearly good stuff.

If the produce of their gardens protected the officers from scurvy, it unwittingly exposed them to other dangers. Diarrhoeal diseases remained a constant problem, especially as they seemed just as prevalent among the free officers as the prisoners. The Reverend Schofield was struck down several times by what he referred to as 'dysentery'. Sometimes he was forced to his bed for up to two weeks despite the administration of Epsom salts and other purgatives. While successive doctors blamed the condition on the sudden and violent changes in temperature that could plunge the settlement from hot to cold, it is far more likely that it was the vegetables from the clergyman's liberally fertilised garden that were responsible for the spread of infection.

Despite all this the trend in mortality was distinctly downwards. Over the life of the settlement the annual convict death rate from all causes was 33 per 1000 per year. Many of these deaths were occasioned by accidents, especially drownings, or were the result of other violent acts. The figure for deaths from medical causes was thirteen per 1000, the same as for soldiers stationed in barracks in the British Isles in the 1830s, a group with a similar age and gender structure. Yet this masked considerable differences over the life of the settlement. The average death rate per 1000 for medical causes for the first three years of the settlement was 23. By contrast, for the three years from 1829 to 1831 it was just seven per 1000. This in itself is at odds with the reputation of the settlement as a place that was calculated to produce suffering.

There is evidence that the workload undertaken by convicts at the settlement declined over time. The proportion of prisoners subjected to ganged labour steadily reduced. By October 1829 it stood at just 31 per cent of the convict population. There were now prisoners at the station who were employed in the most unlikely positions, as bookbinders, turners, broom makers and stockkeepers. There were ten pairs of sawyers alone and eighteen shipwrights, carpenters and coopers who worked in the shed that doubled on Sundays as a chapel. The place now bristled with artisans of all descriptions. This had profound implications for the management of the penal station. While the number of mechanics had increased, the demand for ganged labour had reduced. The reclamation of Settlement Island had been completed so there was now no longer any need for prisoners to dredge the floor of the harbour to provide material for landfill. In the past much of this work had been completed by the chain gang. Now there were not only fewer prisoners in irons but there was less in terms of physically demanding labour for them to perform.

Gangs were a key mechanism for delivering punishment. Each gang was driven at work by an overseer who was tasked with making sure that the rate of production was maintained. It was his job to ensure that anyone who slackened off the pace was put on trial. As the rate of ganged labour decreased the complexity of the tasks undertaken by the convict population increased. The most visible sign of this was the output from the shipyard. In 1829 alone, the mechanics working there completed the *Tamar* brig and finished a number of other vessels including a schooner, two sloops, two cutters, two launches and at least three whaleboats. In the same year they received orders to start work on two schooners and twelve smaller vessels. Output for the shipyard in that year was over 300 tons.

Shipbuilding was always an important undertaking but as time progressed the penal station's slipyards became more productive. Of the vessels of 25 tons or over constructed at Macquarie Harbour, four were completed before January 1829 and eleven after that date. The largest, a 250-ton copper-bottomed whaler, was sold in 1831 by public auction. Many of the other craft were purpose-built to suit the needs of the colony. Sloops were constructed along the same lines as those that operated in the River Tyne, and were used in running stores from Hobart Town to New Norfolk. Fore- and aft-rigged, they were designed to lay close to the wind, a valuable attribute when operating in the close confines of a river estuary.

The settlement shipwrights also experimented with new timbers in order, as Butler put it, to determine their 'comparative values'. Many of the brigs were adapted to ease the difficulties presented by the bar at the head of the harbour. When the *Cyprus* was rebuilt, for example, she was equipped with a false keel while the *Tamar* was designed to draw only eight feet and two inches of water when fully laden. The shipwrights took great pride in their work, chalking the names of each completed vessel on the beams of the shed in which they worked.

But ships were not all that the settlement produced. Mechanics turned out large amounts of furniture and house fittings, including panel doors, architraves and sash windows for the orphan school, writing tables and a nest of pigeon holes for the government clerks, ward tables for the hospital and mess fittings for the military barracks. The carpenters' and blacksmiths' shops manufactured other objects—water buckets, turned wooden bowls for the Hulk Chain Gang, wheelbarrows, iron-hooped mess kids, ships' oars and wharf piles, as well as treenails by the tens of thousands. By March 1831, the ordnance storekeeper in Hobart Town wrote to complain about the lack of space in the engineering store. A recent inventory had revealed that there were 64 sash windows, 32 door frames, 500 water buckets and 850 wooden bowls in the store, all supplied from Macquarie Harbour. It 'would be advisable' he thought 'to discontinue the manufacture of these articles for the present'.

The cost of maintaining Macquarie Harbour was the subject of much discussion. The *Hobart Town Almanac* for the year 1831 calculated that the output of the station was some £4600, the combined value of the timber shipped from the settlement plus the output of the shipyard, carpenters' and shoemakers' shops. When this was offset against the station's running costs, estimated to be in the order of £8000, it was claimed the settlement made a net loss of £3400. While it was perhaps remarkable that a place of secondary punishment should contribute monies to offset over half of its running costs, the calculation was absurdly crude. As the colonial historian John West pointed out, the number of prisoners sent to the place for punishment who returned as 'skilful mechanics' should have been factored into the equation. The real problem, however, was that the more productive the place became the more difficult it was to ensure that it remained a place of terror where convicts would dread to be sent.

In order to ensure that shipwrights, carpenters and blacksmiths remained productive it was necessary to reward them for their endeavours rather than to drive them to work by threatening to strip the skin off their backs. Thus the reformation in the prisoners' habits which Schofield attributed to the power of the Gospel could more plausibly be explained by the cold hard logic of economics. It was a process that had originated inside the confines of the lumberyard rather than being directed from above. As the prisoners mastered the trades crucial for the running of the settlement they slowly took control of the place. For example, Butler had ordered the construction of a 'substantial and burdensome vessel' which subsequently became known as 'the keel'. This strange craft was employed to carry the 'immensely heavy logs' required in the construction of wharfs, jetties, fences and public buildings. It was an essential piece of equipment since eucalypts do not float. It was also the sole practical means of conveying stone, lime and bricks to Settlement Island.

The only person who was skilled in the business of navigating 'the keel' was John Vickers, a seaman from London who 'displayed great industry and activity' in performing this duty 'as well as skill in the management' of this peculiar vessel. As the end of Vickers' sentence of seven years to Macquarie Harbour approached, Butler ruminated upon the consequences of losing his services.

He was a man, the commandant confessed, that he was most reluctant to part with as 'from his strength, and active habits', he would be most difficult to replace. In other respects, Vickers was hardly a model prisoner. Before his elevation to keel attendant he had clocked up 527 lashes and spent a year in irons. Yet Butler now had no choice but to supply him with every indulgence he wished in order to elicit his co-operation in training a replacement.

As life in the settlement improved Macquarie Harbour became the subject of a growing number of artistic endeavours. A prisoner by the name of Charles Henry Theodore Costantini was particularly handy with a box of watercolours. Costantini had trained in Paris as a medical student before being convicted of forgery and banished to New South Wales for life. When his master's child was bitten by a snake he was credited with saving the infant's life and was supplied with a pardon as a reward. Not long after he returned to England, though, he was reconvicted for stealing two £5 notes and shipped to Van Diemen's Land for seven years. Because he had been transported before Arthur ordered him to be despatched to Macquarie Harbour where he was put to work in the hospital as a medical assistant. When Butler heard that the Frenchman had a talent for painting he wrote to the lieutenant governor requesting that paper, pencils, brushes and colours be sent down by the next brig. Arthur approved, eager to gain a more 'accurate knowledge of the station and its environs'.

Thomas Lempriere, the settlement commissariat officer, also fancied himself as something of an artist and between them the two painted a number of views of Settlement Island and the surrounding landscape. Other watercolours were completed by William Buelow Gould, a former decorator from the Spode pottery in Staffordshire who arrived at Macquarie Harbour as a prisoner in September 1832. Gould was assigned to Garrett's replacement as settlement surgeon, Dr William de Little, and together they explored the bays and inlets and shores of the harbour, equipped with notebook, colours, pencils and other instruments of scientific enquiry. They caught fish in a seine net and Gould meticulously recorded the features of each new species they encountered. They also travelled in search of plants, retrieving specimens as they went so that their likeness could be recorded. Gould's detailed watercolours show the fruit split open to reveal the seeds and the details of the stamen to assist in the identification of each genus.

In the settlement's later years excursions seem to have become quite the thing. Schofield recalled a trip that he took with his wife Martha and Dr Garrett to the King River. Rowed there and back by a seven-man boat crew, the party had feasted on black swans before sleeping out under the stars. The chaplain wrote to his aunt and uncle in Bradford telling them of his plans to take Martha up the Gordon River which he described as 'serpentine in form' and 'most beautiful'. It was as if the whole settlement had succumbed to some mysterious outbreak of Stockholm syndrome. In contrast to the gloomy tones in which Macquarie Harbour and its surroundings had formerly been characterised the settlement officers now displayed an empathy with the mountains and rivers that ringed the penal station, holding it captive.

The watercolours and drawings of Settlement Island stand testimony to the pride invested in a place that had been so comprehensively reshaped by human endeavour. Each artist sought to convey the verdant green of the gardens, the neatly ordered windbreaks and the sinuous curves of the latest vessel assembled by the shipwrights from ancient timbers cut from the surrounding forests. In 1830 Butler sent Arthur another view of the settlement by Costantini and he recommended the artist 'as a claimant for the indulgence of removal'. It was by now a familiar refrain. The case of convict after convict was presented before the lieutenant governor, not merely because the man's sentence was about to expire or because of their good conduct but on account of the service they had rendered the station. Thus, Charles Hackett was described as 'a useful and expeditious carpenter', John Brady as a good gardener who understood the laying out of grounds and walks and how to keep them in order, and the bricklayer William Bull as a man who had demonstrated 'zeal and propriety' in the construction of various buildings at the settlement.

Incentives were now so liberally bestowed at Macquarie Harbour that it was said that the place no longer held any terror. Prisoners there, it was rumoured, received 'tea, sugar, tobacco, and rum daily'. These articles were certainly in circulation. Seven gallons of spirits were distributed among the prisoners on New Year's Day and on other occasions convicts were punished, not for smoking, but for taking inadequate care of tobacco entrusted into their care.

When Captain Briggs was replaced as commandant by Major Pery Baylee in December 1832, the settlement regime became even more relaxed. Baylee had been born in Limerick and had a reputation for being a jovial fellow. As one convict said, when he took charge 'all was joy beaming in every countenance'. It was alleged that during his regime government boots were routinely supplied to convict artisans as an incentive and that hundreds of pounds of English leather were in private hands. Souvenirs were certainly distributed to visitors to the settlement. Richard Pell, one of the boatmen, manufactured beautiful carved walking sticks from pieces of dogwood and other prisoners prepared stuffed specimens of the local fauna for supply to scientifically minded gentlemen or attempted to sell them swan skins. Many now owned their own property. Constable Bradshaw, for example, had a new brown cloth jacket, two waistcoats (one made of blue cloth and the other of Marseilles, a heavy cotton fabric with a raised pattern) and a red woollen shirt and comforter. John Vickers the keel attendant also owned a jacket, and the signalman kept his savings, £1.0.6, in a sewing bag stashed in his hut.

Slowly it must have dawned on everyone that Macquarie Harbour was no longer really a penal station. When the Quakers Backhouse and Walker visited in 1832 they were pleasantly surprised to find that the settlement was nowhere near as bad as its reputation had led them to believe. This would not have come as news to Arthur. As early as 1826 he had started to express reservations about the place and had contemplated abandoning it in favour of a station that presented fewer opportunities for absconding. He wrote to the under secretary at the colonial office to explain that as the limits of the settled districts expanded the barrier between the colonists and the 'wretched criminals' consigned to the penal station would inevitably decrease, making escape easier. There were other disadvantages too. The incessant winds, the bar across the harbour, the lack of water and the restricted size of Settlement Island all served to restrict the capacity of the penal station to deliver punishment to large numbers of prisoners. Yet it was apparent that as the convict population of the colony grew further capacity would be required to punish those who fell foul of the law.

At first Arthur favoured King Island as the site for an alternative station. Isolated in the western Bass Strait escape would have certainly been more difficult. He was concerned, however, that the 'softness' of the climate and the 'natural beauty' of the place would render it unfit as a site of secondary punishment. Such miscreants, he insisted, must necessarily be subjected to the 'very last degree of misery consistent with humanity'. Nevertheless he organised for a party to go to Bass Strait to accurately survey the island. The expedition did not go entirely according to plan. The surveyor was assaulted by one of his boat crew while attempting to chart the coastline—the man was shipped to Macquarie Harbour for five years as punishment—and although several bays were discovered on the leeward side of the island, the best of these was described as 'very open' and the bottom as 'foul'. It was also difficult to identify what type of labour the convicts could do to produce sufficient benefits to offset the running costs of an island penal establishment. In all, the whole scheme was abandoned. Given the regularity with which ships were subsequently lost on the coast of King Island it was probably a wise decision.

The lieutenant governor contemplated doing away with penal stations altogether. He considered that it might be possible to expand the number of chain gangs so that convicts could be sentenced to physically demanding labour within the confines of the settled district without posing a threat to the colonists. The scheme had the advantage that it would dramatically reduce the costs of supply, eliminating the need to despatch colonial vessels into dangerous storm ravaged waters. It would also result in the construction of roads, causeways and other public utilities.

Accordingly he authorised the formation of a sturdy gang to commence work on building a causeway over the Derwent at Bridgewater. From 1830 onwards hundreds of convicts were worked in irons, hacking rock out of a quarry face and wheeling barrows to the water's edge. As each load was tipped into the soft mud it promptly sank. It was the most soul-destroying labour—ton after ton of rock disappeared in to the tidal flats. The displaced mud and sand formed banks on either side as the causeway inched forward. It took six years to complete 1200 yards and for a further decade convict gangs laboured on tidal defences and repairs in an effort to make the whole project serviceable. While the work was demanding, the chains that were supposed to hold the prisoners in place proved less secure than Arthur might have hoped.

Leg irons were effective up to a point. They certainly curbed the rate of absconding. Prisoners in chain gangs were nine times less likely to run than those working on the roads out of irons. In order to be practical they had to be light—they weighed around three pounds a pair. It was possible to double-iron a prisoner or forge heavier chains but this significantly retarded the pace of work and hence increased the operating costs of the gang. But as many prisoners demonstrated irons could be worked loose. They could be smashed on a rock to distort them into an oval that could be worked backwards and forwards until the ankle and heel were cleared and, at the cost of some skin, the ring could be slipped off the foot. The bald fact was that prisoners in leg irons were still twice as likely to run away as assigned convicts, a reminder that it was poor conditions that drove absconding rates. Where prisoners were driven to work no amount of physical restraints or natural obstacles would prevent some among their number from getting away. In fact the absconding rate from chain gangs was higher than it was from penal stations.

Arthur convened a committee to examine the issue. Although this recommended that Maria Island be abandoned it was of the opinion that it was 'absolutely necessary for the perfect control and punishment of convicts of the very worst description' that at least one penal station be maintained. Apart from other considerations this solved the problem of where to send those audacious prisoners who still contrived to escape even after chains had been riveted to their legs.

Arthur now turned his attention to converting the timber cutting station that had recently been established at Stewart's Bay on the Tasman Peninsula into an alternative place of hard labour and confinement for secondary offenders. The settlement, which he renamed Port Arthur, had originally been conceived as a replacement for the government sawing establishment at Birch's Bay in the D'Entrecasteaux Channel. From the start, however, Arthur used it as a place of probation for convicts transferred from Maria Island and Macquarie Harbour. While he was conscious that any mitigation of a sentence to secondary transportation 'should be exercised with the greatest discretion', by employing Port Arthur as an intermediate station for prisoners recommended for indulgence it was possible to free up space to punish others. The policy had an added advantage; it enabled the government to benefit from the skills that prisoners had acquired at Settlement Island. In April 1831, for example, former convicts from Macquarie Harbour staffed the hospital at Port Arthur as well as the shipyards and carpenters' and blacksmiths' shops. They were also prominent among the settlement boat crews and saw teams.

As the inadequacies of substituting chain gang labour at Bridgewater for a sentence to a penal station became apparent, Port Arthur was adapted into a place of secondary punishment. By 1832 it had been reclassified as a penal station, although the colonial office in London was not informed of the change until two years later.

The new station helped solve a number of dilemmas. It was much closer to Hobart Town, eliminating the difficulties of supply that had plagued Macquarie Harbour. Fresh water was abundant. There was also enough land to increase the capacity if needed, which was certainly not possible in the confined space of Settlement Island. By December 1835 the convict population at Port Arthur had climbed to 1104, or roughly twice the numbers it was possible to detain at Macquarie Harbour and Maria Island combined. In a station of this size economies of scale made it possible to subject a greater number of prisoners to the rigours of ganged management as a smaller proportion were required to help maintain the settlement (a ratio of one ganged prisoner for every non-ganged, compared to less than one to two at Macquarie Harbour). The place was also hard to escape from. While it was not an island it may as well have been. Linked to the rest of the colony via two narrow isthmuses at Eaglehawk and East Bay necks, all land-based attempts to escape could be channelled to a point where they could be intercepted. What is more, Arthur now had a station that was geographically close enough to be efficiently managed from Hobart Town.

As preparations were made to abandon Macquarie Harbour the population of the settlement was steadily reduced. It was with some irritation that Arthur agreed to prolong the life of the station so that the brig *Frederick* could be finished. When the vessel was eventually launched hardly anybody remained save a military detachment and a small band of convict mechanics and seamen. It was now that James Porter used the voice he had previously put to good affect in Schofield's choir to distract the guard. The song that Porter sung to the unsuspecting soldiers was a lament to the impoverished conditions that had accompanied the end of the Napoleonic Wars:

> *The money is with-drawn and our trade is diminishing,*
> *For mechanics are wandering without shoes or hose,*
> *Come stir up the wars and our trade will be flourishing,*
> *This grand conversation was under the rose.*

While he was still in full voice the signal was hammered out on the deck for the convicts to rise up and seize the vessel. Porter and nine others sailed her away to the coast of South America in a repeat of the *Cyprus* affair.

The phrase 'under the rose' meant something said or plotted in secret, the rose being sacred to Harpocrates, the Greek god of silence. For this reason the rooms of taverns were sometimes decorated with roses to indicate that what was said in their confines should not be made public. The plan to seize the *Frederick* had been plotted in secret for weeks. Some of those involved had even taken clandestine lessons in navigation from William Philips, a Cornish fisherman who had been sent to the penal station after a plot to take the *Argyle* transport had been betrayed. The plan to take the *Frederick* remained, like so much that had been plotted at Macquarie Harbour, 'under the rose'. Porter and his fellow absconders now joined the long list of prisoners who had successfully conspired to leave the penal station by surreptitious means. As they pulled away he confessed he could not express his feelings, his heart expanded in his chest; it was the happiest moment of his life.

Not all were so pleased to see the back of Macquarie Harbour. John Douglas had been at the settlement right from the start and had spent the greater part of ten years in the place. He knew the seasons, having kept a meteorological journal in which he recorded the temperature and rainfall. He 'took pleasure', as the commissariat officer recalled, in such things and now he was unsure about the prospect of leaving. He confided in Schofield that it had been his wish 'for some time past to remain unnoticed and unknown'. Now he was free he had no great desire to return to Wigton where he had sullied the good name of his father. He was 44 years old and had seen 'quite enough of the bustling scenes of this life' to fear what lay ahead.

He plotted an alternative future. Sarah Simmons, the doctor's assigned servant, had caught his eye. He flattered himself that his 'connection' with the young woman might turn to their 'mutual benefit'. He constructed a plan to stay on at the settlement, to move into the commandant's house with its great cabin shaped parlour. There they could live by tilling the soil and raising chickens and pigs, safe in the knowledge that they would be lords of all they could survey. In short, they would escape by staying put. As a plan it was crushed on the floor of the doctor's kitchen while Douglas lay ill in bed. It was there that Sarah Simmons entertained Benjamin Laws until five in the morning. The news of her infidelity was broken to the sickly clerk by his friends, anxious to protect him from the beguiling charms of the woman with whom he had fallen in love but whom they suspected was merely intent on using him to extract some mitigation of her sentence. With that Douglas was condemned to scratch out a living with the sharpened nib of his quill until the eyes in his head failed him and his aching limbs gave out.

The death of the station had been the product of many things but most could be traced to the work of the prisoners themselves. It was they who had undermined the defences of the place, using whispered words to fill in the blank sections on the surveyor's map. When the level of punishment had been increased in an attempt to beat them into submission they had taken the beatings and still run. Even the gallows, that ultimate state sanction, had been turned into a method of escaping penal retribution. When the laws of the colony had been changed, or distorted, in order to increase the power of the state, this too had been challenged by resort to petitions smuggled out to a higher legal authority. In the end the only way of making the place work had been to seek the compliance of the convict population, striking off their irons and increasing their levels of incentive until the terrors of the place had been reduced to the point when it no longer functioned as a penal station proper.

Macquarie Harbour had been undermined from within as comprehensively as the plaster walls of the gaol had been covered in graffiti. There among the numerous images of hanged men and other sundry 'drop-scenes' could be found the words—'Daniel O'Connell, The Man of the People'. The Irish politician who had championed Catholic emancipation, O'Connell was commonly known as 'the Liberator' and was a noted critic of the Australian penal establishments. With an eye on New South Wales and Van Diemen's Land he once wrote that 'unless the Governors of our distant colonies were kept under proper control, there was no extent of despotism which they would not practise'. At Macquarie Harbour, however, that check had come in the end as much from within as without. It was thus a fitting end to the place that the last vessel to be built there, the *Frederick*, had been cut away by her self-liberating crew. Now abandoned the former penal station was left to the mercy of the natural defences once seen as vital to maintaining the security of the station.

In 1836, after twelve years in the post, Arthur was finally recalled by the British government. His replacement, John Franklin, had made quite a name for himself as a polar explorer. An extract from his 'Narrative of a Journey to the Polar Sea' had appeared in the *Hobart Town Gazette* in March 1824 describing his battles with the humble mosquito. Notwithstanding wood smoke and the flashing of gunpowder, Franklin's party had been plagued by vast swarms of the insects. Although they had fumigated their tents to the point of suffocation the army of winged assailants had penetrated their blankets, goring the party and staining their clothes with blood. Despite the experience the naval captain's enthusiasm for fresh adventures remained undaunted. When the

British government decided to abolish convict assignment and replace it with probation, Franklin saw an opportunity to once more don the mantle of explorer.

The planned changes to the transportation system were sweeping. Convicts ceased to be sent to New South Wales and all those landed in Van Diemen's Land were from now on to be subjected to a term of probationary labour in a gang before they could be hired out at cheap rates to settlers. The new regulations were designed to ensure that the punishment of transportation would fit the crime, the period of probation being fixed by the severity of the sentence that had been imposed on each prisoner by the courts in Britain and Ireland. It fell to Franklin to superintend the introduction of the new system. Faced with the responsibility of establishing a string of probation stations and the possibility that the colony would now receive a substantial number of secondarily convicted felons from New South Wales, he conceived of an audacious plan.

He instructed the surveyor, James Calder, to cut a track to Macquarie Harbour. Once completed, Franklin proposed to follow in Calder's footsteps accompanied by his wife, Lady Jane, and a retinue of assistants sufficient to carry the couple's considerable baggage. Their aim would be to 'examine into the nature of the country' between the settled districts and the site of the former penal station so that Franklin 'might judge the fitness of employing a large body of convicts to establish a land-communication between them'. He also hoped that it might prove possible to open up the intervening country to 'enterprising settlers'. Once a road had been cut to the west he planned to re-open Macquarie Harbour as a place of secondary punishment, supplied this time via ox cart from the interior rather than a perilous passage by sea.

The scheme was ludicrous in the extreme. As Calder set out
he knew that there was little chance of roads, probation stations
and settlements springing up in his wake. As he struggled on in
the knowledge that the only party likely to avail themselves of
his crude track was that commanded by the Franklins, he plunged
ahead like a 'rhinoceros' blazing a trail up slopes far too steep to
take a road and through deep marshes thick with leeches. In the
event, it took the Franklins much longer to hack their way
through to Macquarie Harbour than they had anticipated. When
he saw first hand the nature of the country that he had proposed
to open up with a stroke of a pencil across a map, Sir John
realised that it was a hopeless task. He had already abandoned
the scheme by the time they reached the site of the former penal
station and saw the extent to which the little outpost had been
overrun by the untrammelled commons that surrounded it.

Settlement Island was a wreck. The 'super-luxuriant pruriency'
of the Macquarie Harbour vine had enabled the plant's sinuous
creepers to penetrate the officers' quarters, violating the space
inside. The barracks was sadly weatherworn and the commandant's
house with its imposing circular front was 'in a tottering condition'.
The fences that had once stamped the mark of property over
the clipped slopes of the little island now competed with a mass
of native trees and shrubs 'interlaced in one inextricable tangle'
that 'rendered every garden a nearly impracticable wilderness'.
The signal hill where formerly the ensign had fluttered was
clothed with 'a thick and impervious screen' formed by the
'umbrageous many-armed shrubs and creepers'.

The European plants had also broken out of their carefully
tilled quarters and clover, mint, potatoes and other vegetables
and fruit trees now 'blent together in rank profusion'. It was a
process aided by the loads of excrement and lime with which
the slopes had been so painstakingly fertilised. Everything was

now so matted together that the fruit were difficult to attain and were 'insipid in flavour and reproduction'. Fuelled by the faeces of the former inmates, it had taken just nine years for the whole place to go to seed. In the thick of it all was the sweet briar 'luxuriant in the extreme, its hips and thorns, far exceeding in magnitude' any Franklin and his party had elsewhere beheld. In spring it would bloom, covering with roses the spaces where schemes 'subversive of the system of discipline' had once been hatched. Soon the great mass of vegetation would join forces with the wind and pull down fences, walls and roofs leaving little but bricks and stones.

The following year, Franklin was recalled and 'the imbicile [*sic*] reign of the Polar explorer' came to an end. The task of introducing probation would have been beyond the most able administrator, the whole idea had been muddle-headed in the extreme and Franklin now returned to his real passion. At 59 he set out on an expedition to locate the Northwest Passage. It was said that he was so anxious to rehabilitate his name that he would 'die of disappointment if he were not allowed to go'.

The reprieve proved to be temporary. When the *Erebus* became caught in pack ice off the coast of King William's Island in the summer of 1847 every man of the 129-member expedition disappeared into the polar wastes. It was not until seven years later that the first news of their fate was revealed to an incredulous public. After conducting interviews with the local Inuit, Dr John Rae of the Hudson Bay Company concluded that, 'From the mutilated state of many of the bodies and the contents of the kettles, it is evident that our wretched Countrymen had been driven to the last dread resource—cannibalism'. The publication of Rae's findings in the *Illustrated London News* caused a sensation. The author, Charles Dickens, was particularly shocked and attempted to mount a defence of Franklin's reputation. He could not believe that a gentleman would resort to such bestial lengths in order to prolong his own life. But as a young Irish absconder had said 30 years earlier on a remote beach at the mouth of the King River: 'No man can tell what he will do when driven by hunger'.

I hope and trust you'll understand
Its truth that I record;
I hope each hand of Pluto's band
May meet a just reward.

John Thompson, aged 22,
prisoner, Macquarie Harbour penal station

Acknowledgements

This book could not have been written without the help of many generous people. The task of piecing together the lives of over 1200 individuals from sources scattered through many archives was aided by Elinor Morrisby, Luke Clarke and Ian Duffield. Thanks are also due to Brad Manera and Darren Clifford who supplied information on the operation of the Georgian army, Peter Brown for organising the chemical analysis of samples and Linden Scholes who helped with the painful task of data coding. Simon Barnard drew the maps and provided much more in the way of encouragement and moral support. I must also acknowledge the work of Ian Brand who, before his untimely death in 1990, transcribed a great deal of the surviving Macquarie Harbour correspondence. I am grateful to Fiona Preston, Department of Primary Industry and Water Library, for letting me have access to this material. Thanks are also due to the staff at the Archives Office of Tasmania, the State Library Tasmania, the Tasmanian

Museum and Art Gallery, the Queen Victoria Museum and Art Gallery, the Mitchell Library, the State Record Office of New South Wales, the British National Archives and the Scottish Record Office. The difficult task of deciding which of the many Macquarie Harbour stories to include, and which to leave out, was aided by Belinda Lee and Alison Alexander. Together with Katherine Scholes they were kind enough to proof drafts of this book, a task for which I am much indebted. I would also like to thank Luke Badcock, Cassandra Pybus and Ian Duffield who generously commented on earlier versions. Together with Marcus Rediker they have been a constant source of encouragement. A great deal of fieldwork went into this book; work that would have been impossible without the assistance of World Heritage Cruises, the Parks and Wildlife Service and the Round Earth Company. I would like in particular to thank Sarah, Troy and Guy Grining and Richard and Kathi Davey. It has been a wonderful experience to walk the ground of Macquarie Harbour with Richard and to talk with him about the remarkable history of the penal station. This book had its genesis in those conversations. I hope that it retains a little of his passion. Finally I must thank my wife, Clare, whose sound counsel has done so much to shape this book. She has been a constant source of support and inspiration.

Conversion table

1 inch	2.5 centimetres
1 foot	0.3 metres
1 yard	0.9 metres
1 fathom	1.8 metres
1 mile	1.6 kilometres
1 acre	0.4 hectares
£1 (one pound)	$2.2
1s (one shilling)	11 cents
1d (one penny)	0.9 cents
1 gallon	4.5 litres
1 bushel	35 litres
1 ounce	28 grams
1 pound	450 grams
1 ton	1016 kilograms

Notes

The following references refer only to quotations employed in the text. A full set of references and other supporting materials can be found at http://iccs.arts.utas.edu.au/hellsgates.html

Abbreviations

AOT, Archives Office of Tasmania
DL, Dixson Library
HRA, Historical Records of Australia
ML, Mitchell Library
NA, National Archive
SRO, Scottish Record Office
SRNSW, State Record Office New South Wales

PAGE vi: Artist unknown, detail of 'View of the Heads of Macquarie Harbour', State Library New South Wales, V6b/Mac H/3a.

PAGE xi: Reports and other papers relating to a visit to the Australian colonies and South Africa, 1832–1840, by J. Backhouse and G. W. Walker, ML. B706.

Notes

1 'Pluto's land'

PAGE xii Detail of 'Chart of Van Diemen's Land' by Thomas Scott (1824), Allport Library and Museum of Fine Arts, State Library of Tasmania.

PAGE 1 *Pluto's land*: Reports and other papers relating to a visit to the Australian colonies and South Africa, 1832–1840, by J. Backhouse and G. W. Walker, ML. B706.

PAGE 2 *Sacred to the genius of torture*: J. West, *The History of Tasmania*, Angus and Robertson, London, 1981, p. 395.

PAGE 3 *As dreary and as inhospitable*: M. Hordern, *King of the Australian Coast: The Work of Phillip Parker King in the* Mermaid *and* Bathurst *1817–1822*, Melbourne University Press, Carlton, 2002, p. 150.

PAGE 4 *This wood is of a fine white yellow*: G. Kerr and H. McDermott, *The Huon Pine Story: A History of Harvest and Use of a Unique Timber*, Mainsail, Portland, Victoria, 2000, p. 2.

PAGE 5 *Escape from thence*: Governor Macquarie to Secretary of State, 16 May 1818, *HRA*, ser. I, vol. IX, pp. 795–6.

PAGE 7 *Closely covered heavy timber*: Hobart Town Gazette, 9 February 1822.

2 Voyage through the gates of hell

PAGE 8: Thomas Lempriere, 'Grummet Island off Sarah Island', Allport Library and Museum of Fine Arts, AUTAS001124063025.

PAGE 10 *Broke and wore out*: Captain Bateman to Port Officer, 28 May, 1829, AOT, CSO1/359/8229.

PAGE 10 *Shivered the top mast*: Hobart Town Gazette, 11 November 1826.

PAGE 13 *The one on one side*: J. Backhouse, *A Narrative of a Visit to the Australian Colonies*, Hamilton Adams, London, 1843, pp. 36–7.

PAGE 14 *European Cable*: List of articles required for moorings at Macquarie Harbour, 20 August 1822, SRNSW, CSO 6053 4/1756, pp. 152–5.

PAGE 14 *I am at all times exposed*: J. Lucas to Colonial Secretary, 10 March 1829, AOT, CSO1/384/8681.

PAGE 15 *Rocks, hills and sands*: John Popjoy per *Larkins* to NSW and *Admiral Cockburn* to VDL, SRNSW, bound indents, and AOT, CSO/1/416/9354.

PAGE 16 *All who entered*: J. Backhouse, *Narrative of a Visit to the Australian Colonies*, Hamilton Adams, London, 1843 p. 45.

PAGE 16 *Rocks, caves, lakes*: The quote is from *Paradise Lost*, book ii, 11, 620 ff. J. West, *The History of Tasmania*, p. 397.

PAGE 17 *Centre of calculation*: S. Ryan, *The Cartographic Eye: How Explorers Saw Australia*, Cambridge University Press, Cambridge, 1996, p. 176.

PAGE 18 *A large number*: James Kelly's account of the discovery of Macquarie Harbour, 28 December 1815, AOT, LCJ1881/75.

PAGE 20 *Almost daily*: Commandant to Colonial Secretary, 10 January 1824, AOT, CSO1/134/3235.

PAGE 21 *The appearance*: T. J. Lempriere, *Penal Settlements of Van Diemen's Land*, Royal Society of Tasmania, Launceston, 1954, p. 26.

PAGE 24 *The surf often broke*: ibid., p. 30.

PAGE 25 *A kind of hasty pudding*: ibid., p. 47.

PAGE 26 *Fresh water sailors*: Commandant to Colonial Secretary, 24 June 1827, AOT, CSO1/242/5863.

PAGE 26 *A pistol shot*: Memoranda by Convict Davis, DL, MS, Q168.

PAGE 27 *Highly dangerous:* Commandant to Colonial Secretary, 24 January 1828, AOT, CSO1/237/5735.

PAGE 28 *Or 6 inches*: Memoranda by Convict Davis.

PAGE 32 *To be sold*: Papers delivered by John Barnes Esq., and referred to in the Evidence of 12 February 1838, *British Parliamentary Papers*, 1837–1838 (669) XXII.

PAGE 32 *Foulness and general bad quality*: Mr J. Hobbs, Boat Voyage round Tasmania in 1824, 28 March 1824, CJ 1881/75; and Lieutenant Governor Sorell to George Arthur, HRA, ser. III, vol. IV, p. 151.

PAGE 33 *Attempting an unnatural offence*: AOT, Con 31/1, 6 December 1823 and 16 November 1829.

PAGE 33 *Upwards of six feet*: T. Lempriere, *Penal Settlements*, p. 27.

PAGE 34 *An abrupt bank*: ibid., p. 44.

PAGE 35 *A dreadful thing*: Commandant to Colonial Secretary, 26 January 1829, AOT, CSO1/1/327/8493.

PAGE 36: Thomas Lempriere, 'Soldier's Island & part of Farm Bay from the settlement farm, Macquarie Harbour', Allport Library and Museum of Fine Arts, AUTAS001124062829.

PAGE 37 *A strong gang*: Commandant to Colonial Secretary, 16 February 1824, AOT, CSO1/134/3236.

PAGE 37 *A bush block*: Expenditure since 7 July 1824, AOT, CSO1/104/2498.

PAGE 37 *From the nature*: Journal of George Washington Walker, 7 June 1832, ML, B727.

PAGE 37 *Up to their knees*: Journal of the Reverend William Schofield, 6 June 1831, ML, A428.

PAGE 38 *A strong gang*: Commandant to Colonial Secretary, 10 January 1824, AOT, CSO1/134/3235.

PAGE 38 *Iniquity was carrying on:* Memoranda by Convict Davis.

PAGE 39 *Strong chain*: Commandant to Colonial Secretary, 16 February 1824, AOT, CSO1/134/3236.

PAGE 39 *Such accidents*: T. Lempriere, *Penal Settlements*, p. 39.

PAGE 40 *Wet and stormy*: Regulations for the employment and control of Prisoners under sentence at Macquarie Harbour, 6 July 1824, *HRA*, ser. III, vol. V, p. 633.

PAGE 40 *Once on shore*: T. Lempriere, *Penal Settlements*, pp. 47–8.

PAGE 40 *Bleak and exposed*: The Report of a Visit to Macquarie Harbour, Van Diemen's Land by James Backhouse and George W. Walker', ML, B706; and Journal of George Washington Walker, 6 June 1832, ML B727.

PAGE 41 *It was a most*: Memoranda by Convict Davis.

3   The 'crimes' of the damned

PAGE 42: Thomas Lempriere, 'Philips Island from the N. W. extremity to the overseer's hut, Macquarie Harbour', Allport Library and Museum of Fine Arts, AUTAS001124063116.

PAGE 49 *Outrage*: W. Beatty, *Early Australia with Shame Remembered*, Cassell, London, 1962, p. 79.

PAGE 49 *For making away*: AOT, Con 31/29, 18 March 1829.

PAGE 49 *Not only of the gang*: *Colonial Times*, 23 March 1827.

PAGE 50 *We feel no small*: *Hobart Town Gazette*, 3 February 1827.

PAGE 51 *Waiting up*: P. Tardiff, *Notorious Strumpets and Dangerous Girls*, Angus and Robertson, Sydney, 1990, p. 355–6.

PAGE 53 *She had her mizzen*: Court-martial proceedings against Gottfried Hanske and Christoph Beulter, Private Soldiers in the 2nd Light Battalion King's German Legion, 13 September 1810, NA, WO/71/222.

PAGE 53 *Mermaid, kangaroo, snake*: AOT, Con 31/13 and CSO 43, p. 55 and papers relating to the *Lady East*, ML, Tas Papers, 21.

4 The law of the sea (as applied on land)

PAGE 60: Thomas Bock, 'Sketches of Tasmanian Bushrangers', State Library New South Wales, f.26 Alexander Pearce executed for the Murder of a Man named Cox at Macquarie Harbour, DL, PX 5 [a933028h].

PAGE 62 *Law of the sea*: P. Collins, *Hell's Gates: The Terrible Journey of Alexander Pearce Van Diemen's Land Cannibal*, Hardie Grant, South Yarra, 2002, pp. 136–8.

PAGE 63 *Been placed by fortune*: D. Sprod, *Alexander Pearce of Macquarie Harbour: Convict, Bushranger, Cannibal*, Cat and Fiddle, Hobart, 1977, p. 28.

PAGE 63 *The flesh of Traviss*: Sprod, *Alexander Pearce*, p. 29.

PAGE 64 *One had been killed*: *Hobart Town Gazette*, 16 November 1822.

PAGE 65 *A man was then appointed*: Memoranda by Convict Davis.

PAGE 66 *Fifty times worse*: Beatty, *Early Australia*, pp. 79–83.

PAGE 66 *A great portion*: Commandant to Colonial Secretary, 18 August 1829, AOT, Con 85/1.

PAGE 67 *Cool, deliberate and premeditated*: *Hobart Town Courier*, 7 March 1829.

PAGE 68 *Subject to ungovernable*: ibid.

PAGE 68 *Transported as a felon*: Court Martial proceedings against John Salmon, Private Marine 56th Company, 12 December 1822, NA, ADM 1/5465.

PAGE 68 *Abusing his master*: AOT, Con 31/38.

PAGE 69 *It was found*: *Hobart Town Gazette*, 25 June 1824.

PAGE 70 *No man can tell*: ibid.

PAGE 70 *Glanced in fearfulness*: ibid.

PAGE 71 *For the sole purpose*: Sprod, *Alexander Pearce*, p. 128.

PAGE 71 *The most delicious*: Evidence 12 February 1838, *British Parliamentary Papers*, 1837–8 (669) XXII.

PAGE 72 *Selling unwholesome*: Sprod, *Alexander Pearce*, pp. 97–118.

PAGE 72 *Vampire legends*: *Hobart Town Gazette*, 25 June 1824.

PAGE 72 *Opened the vein*: J. Polidori, 'The Vampyre' in E.F. Bleiler, ed., *Three Gothic Novels*, Dover, New York, 1966, p. 274.

PAGE 73 *Unblessed of man*: G. Mackaness ed., *Narrative of Overland Journey by Sir John and Lady Franklin and Party from Hobart Town to Macquarie Harbour 1842 by David Burn*, Australian Historical Monographs, Sydney, 1955, pp. 7 and 33.

PAGE 73 *Vlad the Impaler*: R. Tannahill, *Flesh and Blood: A History of the Cannibal Complex*, Abacus, London, 1996, pp. 146–7.

PAGE 73 *I have seen the same*: M. Clarke, *For the Term of his Natural Life*, Australian Print Group, Bellerive, 1988, pp. 64 and 209–13.

PAGE 74 *Canot [sic] paliate*: Memoranda by Convict Davis.

5 The law of the lash

PAGE 76: Thomas Bock, 'Sketches of Tasmanian Bushrangers', State Library New South Wales, f.17 James MacKenney, DL, PX 5 [a933020].

PAGE 79 *A formidable instrument*: Evidence of 12 February 1838, *British Parliamentary Papers*, 1837–1838, (669) XXII.

PAGE 80 *Picture frame*: Reports and other papers by Backhouse and Walker, ML, B706.

PAGE 80 *Back like of Bullocks*: Memoranda by Convict Davis. Tow is a small bundle of flax.

PAGE 81 *Altering a note of hand*: AOT, Con 31/23, 21 September 1822.

PAGE 83 *You say that Bonyparty*: E. P. Thompson, *The Making of the English Working Class*, Penguin Books, Harmondsworth, 1981, pp. 330–1.

PAGE 86 *Strong athletic men*: *Hobart Town Gazette*, 1 April 1826.

PAGE 86 *In order to deprive*: AOT, Con 31/29, 22 November 1822.

PAGE 88 *In those days*: D. Graves, ed., *Merry Hearts Make Light Days: The War of 1812 Journal of Lieutenant John Le Couteur, 164th Foot*, Robin Brass Studio, Toronto, 1993, pp. 52–3.

PAGE 88 *Undaunted spirit!*: *Hobart Town Gazette*, 28 May 1824.

PAGE 89 In *the Army's view*: R. Hughes, *The Fatal Shore: A History of the Transportation of Convicts to Australia 1787–1868*, Pan Books, London, 1988, p. 378.

PAGE 90 *The most inhuman*: Memoranda by Convict Davis.

PAGE 92 *Would go home*: ibid.

PAGE 93 *A perfect master*: ibid.

PAGE 93 *And placed it under*: ibid.

PAGE 95 *Are known by the company*: J. A. Amato, *On Foot: A History of Walking*, New York University Press, New York, 2004, p. 4.

PAGE 95 *Being of the opinion*: AOT, Con 31/42.

PAGE 96 *Hawking stuffed animals*: P. Blom, *To Have and to Hold: An Intimate History of Collectors and Collecting*, Penguin, London, 2002, pp. 23, 88–90.

PAGE 97 *The cock it crows*: P. Stanley, *For Fear of Pain: British Surgery 1790–1850*, Rodopi, Amsterdam, 2003, p. 32.

PAGE 98 *Various other testimonials*: Colonial Surgeon Scott to Lieutenant Governor Sorell, 29 July 1822, AOT, CSO1/95/2267.

PAGE 101 *At court all the day*: M. Nicholls, ed., *The Diary of the Reverend Robert Knopwood, 1803–1838*, Tasmanian Historical Research Association, Hobart, 1977, p. 459.

PAGE 102 *Imputed crime*: Henry Crockett to Colonel George Arthur, 5 November 1825, AOT, CSO/1/290/6960.

PAGE 102 *Disgusting, yet dangerous*: The memorial of Joshua Eynon Drabble, 10 September 1822 and 30 June 1825, AOT, CSO1/162/3884.

PAGE 103 *I feel it due*: Henry Crockett to James Scott Esq., 7 October 1825, AOT, CSO1/95/2267.

PAGE 103 *I cannot report*: Henry Crockett to Lieutenant Governor Arthur, 10 October 1825, AOT, CSO1/95/2267.

PAGE 104 *At the time*: Henry Crockett to Lieutenant Governor Arthur, February 1826, AOT, CSO1/95/2267.

PAGE 104 *Mr Crockett*: Sprod, *Alexander Pearce*, pp. 128–9.

PAGE 106 *A hard blow*: Court martial proceedings against John Flynn, alias John Foror, alias Keefe a Marine, 14 March 1820, NA, ADM 1/5462.

PAGE 107 *A great liar*: Return of male and female prisoners and their respective sentences at Macquarie Harbour for the quarter ending 30th September 1825, DL, Add 568.

PAGE 107 *Upbraiding*: AOT, Con 31/19, 18 May 1827.

PAGE 108 *Raising false reports*: AOT, Con 31/13, 5 November 1822.

6   Fifteen acres

PAGE 112: Artist unknown, detail of 'N. W. View of Macquarie Harbour V. D. L.' State Library New South Wales, V6B/MACH/1.

PAGE 113 *As many as the schooner*: Memoranda by Convict Davis.

PAGE 114 *The extreme inclemency*: George Arthur to Thomas Brisbane, 30 September 1825, SRNSW, CSO4/6974.1, pp. 41–5.

PAGE 114 *Extremely well educated*: Captain Robinson to Lieutenant Governor Arthur, AOT, CSO1/271/6541.

PAGE 114 *A free man*: Commandant's Clerk to John Douglas, 17 August 1824, AOT, CSO1/104/2498.

PAGE 114 *The relative distances*: Superintendent to Commandant, 5 August 1824, AOT, CSO1/104/2498.

PAGE 116 *I was once*: *Hobart Town Gazette*, 10 December 1824.

Notes

PAGE 117 *All flesh is as grass!*: Warton to Lieutenant Governor Arthur, no date, AOT, CSO1/271/6541.

PAGE 117 *Midnight revelries*: Warton to Lieutenant Governor Arthur, 11 August 1824, AOT, CSO1/104/2498.

PAGE 117 *Disordered*: Commandant's Clerk to John Douglas, 17 August 1824, AOT, CSO1/104/2498.

PAGE 118 *In regret*: Warton to his parents, 30 July 1824, AOT, CSO1/271/6541.

PAGE 118 *I am induced*: Warton to Lieutenant Governor 31 July 1824, AOT, CSO1/271/6541.

PAGE 119 *Strong, capacious and airy*: Lempriere, *Penal Settlements*, p. 28.

PAGE 121 *4 to 6 inches*: Commandant to Lieutenant Governor, 22 July 1825, AOT, CSO1/ 226/5517.

PAGE 122 *Jumbled together*: Commandant to Lieutenant Governor, 31 December 1825, AOT, CSO12/227/5528.

PAGE 122 *Frequently in the course*: Commandant to Colonial Secretary, 20 June 1825, AOT, CSO1/226/5498.

PAGE 122 *Give a damn*: James Robinson, AOT, Con 31/34; 23 February 1830.

PAGE 122 *An impression*: Benjamin Horton AOT, Con 31/18: and Benjamin Bowers Con 31/1; both 5 February 1825.

PAGE 126 *At this inclement*: Commandant to Colonial Secretary, 31 July 1824, AOT, CSO1/134/3236.

PAGE 127 *Opening cavities*: Lieutenant Governor to Commandant, 16 June 1824, HRA ser. III, vol. V, p. 631.

PAGE 127 *At all hours*: Commandant to Colonial Secretary, 21 June 1825, AOT, CSO1/2/10.

PAGE 131 *A landscape of rich*: Mackaness, *Narrative of Overland Journey*, p. 43.

PAGE 131 *An insult to him*: Commandant's Clerk to John Douglas, 17 August 1824, AOT, CSO1/104/2498.

PAGE 132 *Nothing else but*: S. Miller, *Conversation: A History of a Declining Art*, Yale, New Haven, 2006, p. 86.

PAGE 132 *Low estate*: A. G. L. Shaw, *Sir George Arthur*, Melbourne University Press, Carlton, 1980, pp. 23–5.

PAGE 133 *A convict dog*: Commandant's Clerk to John Douglas, 17 August 1824, AOT, CSO1/104/2498.

PAGE 135 *Dagger of slander*: Deposition of Superintendent, 12 August 1824, AOT, CSO1/104/2498.

PAGE 135 *Such damned scoundrels*: Warton to Lieutenant Governor, 14 August, AOT, CSO1/104/2498.

PAGE 135 *Gentleman*: Register of Deaths, AOT, RGD 35, 820/1845.

PAGE 136 *Absenting himself*: Con 31/9, 1 April 1824.

PAGE 136 *The men did not*: Memoranda by Convict Davis.

PAGE 136 *Better footing*: Lieutenant Governor to Under Secretary of State, 4 September 1826, AOT, GO 33/1/870.

7   The mills of empire

PAGE 138: Thomas Lempriere, 'New Sawpits, Macquarie Harbour', Allport Library and Museum of Fine Arts, AUTAS001124062894.

PAGE 139 *On a salt diet*: Neil Douglas to Colonial Secretary, 20 June 1825, AOT, CSO1/226/5503.

PAGE 141 *Urged the others*: Commandant to Lieutenant Governor, 9 June 1825, AOT, CSO1/8/124.

PAGE 143 *Impeding the work*: Robert Greenfield, AOT, Con 31/15, 2 May 1827 and 2 September 1829.

PAGE 146 *Servitude*: A. Atkinson, 'The free-born Englishman transported: convict rights as a measure of eighteenth-century empire', *Past and Present*, vol. 144, 1994, pp. 109–10.

PAGE 150 *A numerous tribe*: E. Curr, *An Account of the Colony of Van Diemen's Land Principally Designed for the Use of Emigrants*, Platypus Publications, Hobart, 1967, pp. 14–5.

PAGE 152 *If no immigrant*: *Colonial Times*, 18 September 1829.

PAGE 153 *Still tongue*: C. M. H. Clark, *Select Documents in Australian History 1788–1850*, vol. 1, Angus and Robertson, London, 1977, p. 131.

PAGE 154 *These should be bound*: *The Times*, 17 July 1823 and 9 September 1826.

PAGE 155 *Except that the master*: P. Ratcliff, *The Usefulness of John West: Dissent and Difference in the Australian Colonies*, Albernian Press, Launceston, 2003, p. 359.

PAGE 160 *Such as weavers*: T. Butler, 'Report on Macquarie Harbour', *British Parliamentary Papers*, XII (1837–1838), Appendix (F), no. 26.

PAGE 160 *Which independent of*: ibid.

8   Mr Douglas's list

PAGE 164: W. B. Gould, 'Mountain Trout', Gould's sketchbook of fishes, Allport Library and Museum of Fine Arts, AUTAS001124072786.

PAGE 166 *No event of my life*: John Douglas to Colonial Secretary, 12 March 1825, CSO1/193/4568.

Notes

PAGE 168 *Never accomplished*: *Hobart Town Gazette*, 16 April 1824.

PAGE 168 *There were constantly*: Sprod, *Alexander Pearce*, pp. 138–50.

PAGE 170 *It was impossible to give*: J. Fawcett, ed., 'Unlawful Return From Transportation, 1843', <www.hotkey.net.au/~jwilliams4/d6.htm> [12 January 2007].

PAGE 171 *Still more reckless*: Reports and other papers relating to a visit to the Australian colonies and south Africa, 1832–1840 by J. Backhouse and G. W. Walker, DL, B706, vol 1, p. 268.

PAGE 171 *Supposed to have died*: Charles Love, AOT, Con 14/2 and Con 31/28.

PAGE 172 *Extremely wet*: Commandant to Colonial Secretary, 25 April 1827, AOT, CSO1/102/2454.

PAGE 173 *Mutinous conduct*: Punishment Records of Newcastle Penal Settlement, SRNSW, CSO 6019 4/3864, p. 61.

PAGE 174 *The most exhausted*: *Hobart Town Gazette*, 26 November 1824.

PAGE 175 *Very fine grass*: T. Kent, Statement of his Escape from Macquarie Harbour, DL, MSQ 571.

PAGE 175 *The Pieman*: Sprod, *Alexander Pearce*, pp. 106–18.

PAGE 177 *The impropriety of sending*: Commandant to Lieutenant Governor, 12 September 1831, AOT, Con 85.

PAGE 177 *Never fail to talk*: Commandant to Colonial Secretary, 25 April 1827, AOT, CSO1/103/2475.

PAGE 179 *Perfectly rotted*: Commandant to Colonial Secretary, 24 February 1827, AOT, CSO1/60/1253.

PAGE 180 *Fires spread along*: Kent, Statement of his Escape.

PAGE 181 *An easy conquest*: Commandant to Colonial Secretary, 24 February 1827, AOT, CSO1/60/1253.

PAGE 181 *Said that the Buffs*: N. J. B. Plomley, ed., *Friendly Mission: The Tasmanian Journals and Papers of George Augustus Robinson 1829–1834*, Tasmanian Historical Research Association, Hobart, 1966, p. 756.

PAGE 182 *Pristine region*: K. Windschuttle, *The Fabrication of Aboriginal History*, vol. 1, Macleay Press, Sydney, 2002, p. 370.

PAGE 182 *Did all they could*: Plomley, *Friendly Mission*, p. 770.

PAGE 182 *Regardless of the extent*: *Hobart Town Gazette*, 12 July 1823 and 9 April 1824.

PAGE 183 *He declared*: Commandant to Lieutenant Governor, 25 October 1824, AOT, CSO1/134/3246.

PAGE 184 *Of a moderate*: Memoranda by Convict Davis.

PAGE 185 *Spread terror*: Attorney General to Lieutenant Governor, 2 January 1826, *HRA*, ser. III, vol. V, p. 289.

PAGE 186 *Heard two shots*: E. Fitzsyonds, ed., *Brady: Van Diemen's Land 1824–1827*, Sullivan's Cove, Hobart, 1979, pp. 107–9.

PAGE 187 *Render themselves formidable*: Commandant to Colonial Secretary, 10 February 1826, AOT, CSO1/243/5883.

PAGE 187 *Sacrifice of private property*: Memoranda by Convict Davis.

PAGE 188 *Keep the buggers down*: William Swallow, Surrey Winter Assizes, December 1830, NA, HO 17/59 KP18.

PAGE 188 *Throw down a kettle*: *The Colonial Times*, 4 September 1829.

PAGE 191 *A principal promoter*: *Hobart Town Gazette*, 29 October 1825.

PAGE 191 *A good workman*: return of male and female prisoners and their respective sentences at Macquarie harbour for the quarter ending 30 September 1825, DL, ADD568.

PAGE 192 *Trouble and anxiety*: Commandant to Lieutenant Governor, 24 September 1825, AOT, CSO1/226/5514.

PAGE 194 *Barbarously*: Commandant to Lieutenant Governor, 18 September 1825, AOT, CSO1/226/5513.

PAGE 196 *Unfortunate death*: T. O'Connor, 'Power and Punishment: The Limits of Resistance at the Moreton Bay Penal Settlement, 1824–42, BA (hons) thesis, University of Queensland, 1994, p. 24.

PAGE 196 *Returned to the Settlement*: Commandant to Lieutenant Governor, 19 September 1825, AOT, CSO1/226/5514.

PAGE 197 *For aiding and abetting*: Owen Lenaghan, AOT, Con 31/27; Robert Wright, Con 31/45; Gilderoy Lee, Con 31/27; John Calicot, Con 31/6; and William Simpson Lindon, Con 31/27; all 3 September 1825.

PAGE 197 *For being feloniously*: Criminal Trials, 1829, *HRA*, vol. III, no. IX, pp. 998–9.

PAGE 198 *Safety of the colony*: Executive Council Minutes, 9 July 1829, AOT, EC/4/1.

9 'Come, O my guilty brethren, come'

PAGE 202: Artist unknown, 'S. W. View of Macquarie Harbour V. D. L.', State Library New South Wales, V6B/Mac H/3b.

PAGE 203 *His rigid Calvinism*: Journal of the Reverend William Schofield, 6 February 1829, ML, A428.

PAGE 204 *Wounding the membrane*: Assistant Colonial Surgeon to Commandant and Commandant to Colonial Secretary, 1 October 1827, AOT, CSO1/199/4742.

PAGE 204 *Committing, or aiding*: See, for example, John Ward per *Dromedary*, AOT, CON 31/45, 22 June 1826.

PAGE 205 *Whilst he kept*: Commandant to Colonial Secretary, 7 September 1827, AOT, CSO1/216/5188.

PAGE 206 *Get up to Hobart Town*: Commandant to Colonial Secretary, 1 October 1827, AOT, CSO1/199/4741.

PAGE 207 *To afford such*: Commandant to Colonial Secretary, 7 January 1828, AOT, CSO1/216/5188.

PAGE 209 *Why don't you keep*: *The Tasmanian*, 14 December 1827.

PAGE 210 *Old man*: ibid.

PAGE 211 *Quire of paper*: *Glasgow Herald*, 1 August 1828.

PAGE 211 *Contemptuous conduct*: AOT, Con 31/9, 19 October 1827.

PAGE 211 *With a small saw*: Commandant to Colonial Secretary, 7 January 1828, AOT, CSO1/216/5188.

PAGE 212 *We'll be all hung*: *The Tasmanian*, 14 December 1827.

PAGE 212 *It is likely*: George Lacey to Commandant, 23 October 1827, AOT, CSO1/215/5188.

PAGE 212 *Generally surpassed*: ibid.

PAGE 213 *If it had not*: Evidence of 12 February 1838, *British Parliamentary Papers*, 1837–1838, (669) XXII.

PAGE 214 *And may the Lord*: *The Tasmanian*, 14 December 1827.

PAGE 214 He was tired: Evidence of 12 February 1838, *British Parliamentary Papers*, 1837–1838, (669) XXII.

PAGE 215 *Bless God*: Journal of Reverend William Schofield, 12 December 1827, DL, A428.

PAGE 216 *Kill and dress*: AOT, Con 23/1.

PAGE 216 *Our Saviour bleeding*: Con 23/1.

PAGE 216 *A hymn called*: *The Times*, 23 September 1830.

PAGE 217 *Outcasts of men*: Thompson, *The Making of the English Working Class*, p. 40.

PAGE 217 *It was their proverb*: West, *The History of Tasmania*, p. 397.

PAGE 218 *Mere bravado*: Journal of Reverend William Schofield, 17 December 1827.

10 And in duty bound will ever pray

PAGE 220: Thomas Lempriere, 'Philips Island (from Point Dingy) Macquarie Harbour', Allport Library and Museum of Fine Arts, AUTAS001124062977.

PAGE 221 *50 fold*: John Douglas to Commandant, 26 November 1827, AOT, CSO1/216/5208.

PAGE 223 *Such characters*: William Clarke, Robert Grew, William Henley, James Cock and Michael Shaughnessy to Lieutenant Governor, 12 December 1827, AOT, CSO1/216/5188.

PAGE 224 *Be considered as a man*: James Cock and Michael Shaughnessy to Attorney General, 8 January 1828; and James Cock to Lieutenant Governor Arthur, 3 October 1828, CSO1/235/5661.

PAGE 225 *Directly opposite*: Richard Biggs to John Williams, November 1827, CSO1/237/5728.

PAGE 226 *The ill usage*: John Smith Con 31/38, 10 December 1829.

PAGE 228 *He should now die*: *Hobart Town Gazette*, 3 September 1825.

PAGE 228 *Periodical visitations*: John Knight to Lieutenant Governor, 20 April 1827, AOT, CSO1/58/1230.

PAGE 229 *His Excellency*: John Knight to Governor in Chief, New South Wales, 30 October 1826, AOT, CSO1/58/1230.

PAGE 230 *Smart and useful*: Commandant to Colonial Secretary, 12 May 1827, AOT, CSO1/58/1230.

PAGE 230 *I remember*: ibid.

PAGE 230 *By which means*: ibid.

PAGE 233 *An incompetent*: Petition of Joseph Bond Clark, Thomas Bird and James Cock to the Honourable the House of Commons in Parliament Assembled, *HRA* ser. III, vol. VIII, p. 620.

PAGE 233 *Passed to punish*: ibid., p. 621.

PAGE 235 *It is a thing*: Case of Joseph Clark, James Cock and Thomas Bird, *HRA*, ser. III, VIII, p. 623.

PAGE 235 *Old man*: *The Tasmanian*, 14 December 1827.

PAGE 235 *The man's back*: J. Ross, *The Hobart Town Almanack and Van Diemen's Land Annual for 1836*, Hobart Town, pp. 180–1.

PAGE 235 *A disgrace*: *The Colonist and Van Diemen's Land Commercial and Agricultural Advertiser*, 22 April 1838.

PAGE 235 *Execrable Machiavelian*: *Cornwall Chronicle*, 9 September 1837.

PAGE 237 *Praying for consideration*: Petition of Joseph Bond Clark, Thomas Bird and James Cock to the Honourable the House of Commons in Parliament Assembled, *HRA*, ser. III, vol. VIII, p. 620.

PAGE 237 *Generous and disinterested*: Joseph Clark, Thomas Bird and James Cock to Joseph Hume MP, *HRA*, ser. III, vol. VIII, p. 618.

PAGE 239 *Two stuffed*: The Statements of Robert Collins and Thomas M'Guire, 15 June 1832, ML, Tas Papers 35.

PAGE 239 *We have sent*: Joseph Clark, Thomas Bird and James Cock to Joseph Hume MP, *HRA*, ser. III, vol. VIII, p. 619.

PAGE 239 *A post-box*: J. J. Eddy, *Britain and the Australian Colonies 1818–1831: The Techniques of Government*, Oxford University Press, Clarendon, 1969, pp. 48, 57–9.

PAGE 240 *Called the attention*: Mr Hume to Joseph Clark and Others, 15 December 1828, *HRA*, ser. III, vol. VIII, p. 627.

PAGE 240 *Little calculated*: Lieutenant Governor to Colonial Secretary, 12 September 1829, *HRA*, ser. III, vol. VIII, p. 611.

PAGE 240 *The reign of King James*: J. B. Clark to Lieutenant Governor, 14 July 1829, AOT, CSO1/234/5661.

PAGE 241 *Every part*: Lieutenant Governor to Colonial Secretary, 18 August 1830, *HRA*, ser. III, vol. IX, p. 423.

PAGE 241 *Of the utmost*: Principal Superintendent to Colonial Secretary, 11 May 1830, AOT, CSO1/456/10164.

PAGE 241 *Unpleasantness*: J. B. Clark to Lieutenant Governor, 28 February 1832, AOT, CSO1/234/5661.

PAGE 242 *Name of Colonel Arthur*: *Cornwall Chronicle*, 9 September 1837.

PAGE 242 *Punishment on his bare*: J. B. Clark to Colonial Secretary, 28 February and 3 May 1832, AOT, CSO1/234/5661.

11 Under the rose

PAGE 244: W. B. Gould, Billardiera longiflora, Queen Victoria Museum and Art Gallery, CR 19, 1958-75-4-009.

PAGE 246 *Some very painful*: Journal of the Reverend Schofield, 31 October 1827.

PAGE 246 *Moral desert*: Chaplain to Commandant, no date, AOT, CSO1/209/4957.

PAGE 247 *Noble race*: Plomley, *Friendly Mission*, p. 83.

PAGE 247 *To go to Hell*: Journal of the Reverend Schofield, 22 April 1831.

PAGE 247 *As bad as caste*: Journal of the Reverend Schofield, 6 September 1829.

PAGE 247 *Not many win*: Chaplain to Reverend Carvossa, 12 September 1829; Letter Book of the Reverend William Schofield, ML, B862.

PAGE 248 *Plowing in the rocks*: Journal of the Reverend Schofield, 26 September 1830.

PAGE 248 *Death like*: Schofield to his Parents, 20 January 1831, Letter Book of the Reverend William Schofield ML, B862.

PAGE 249 *Continue to evidence*: Chaplain to Commandant, no date, AOT, CSO1/209/4957.

PAGE 249 *Well calculated*: Commandant to Chaplain, 29 November 1828, AOT, CSO1/209/4957.

PAGE 250 *A temporal*: Journal of the Reverend Schofield, 1 June and 17 July 1828.

PAGE 251 *Never known*: *ibid.*, 3 January 1830.

PAGE 252 *All the flavour*: Lempriere, *The Penal Settlements*, p. 44.

PAGE 252 *Equal to the*: S. Johnson, *The Ghost Map*, Allen Lane, London, 2006, pp. 115–16.

PAGE 252 *Cauliflowers*: Schofield to Mr and Mrs Corson, 20 January 1831, Letter Book of the Reverend William Schofield, ML, B862.

PAGE 255 *Comparative values*: Commandant to Colonial Secretary, 24 February 1827, AOT, CSO1/60/1251.

PAGE 255 *Would be advisable*: Ordnance Storekeeper to Colonial Secretary, 7 March 1831, AOT, CSO1/463/10294.

PAGE 256 *Skilful mechanics*: West, *The History of Tasmania*, p. 424.

PAGE 256 *Substantial and burdensome*: Commandant to Colonial Secretary, 17 September 1827, AOT, CSO1/110/2699.

PAGE 257 *From his strength*: Commandant to Colonial Secretary, 23 August 1828, AOT, CSO1/290/6988.

PAGE 257 *Accurate knowledge*: Commandant to Aide-de-Camp Lieutenant Frankland, 11 January 1828, AOT, CSO1/234/5663.

PAGE 258 *Serpentine in form*: Schofield to Mr and Mrs Corson, 20 January 1831, Letter Book of the Reverend William Schofield, ML, B862.

PAGE 259 *As a claimant*: Commandant to Colonial Secretary, 16 August 1830, Con 85.

PAGE 259 *A useful*: Commandant to Colonial Secretary, 29 April 1829, AOT, CSO1/397/8998 and 9 May 1829, CSO1/372/8497.

PAGE 259 *Tea, sugar, tobacco*: Colonial Secretary to Commandant, 27 January 1830, CSO/43.

PAGE 259 *All was joy*: R. Davey, ed., *The Travails of Jimmy Porter: A Memoir*, Round Earth Company, Strahan, 2003, p. 35.

PAGE 261 *Very last degree*: Lieutenant Governor to Under Secretary of State, 4 September 1826, AOT, GO 33/1/870.

PAGE 262 *Absolutely necessary*: Executive Council Minutes, EC4/1, 6 February 1832.

PAGE 263 *Should be exercised*: *ibid.*, 15 September 1830.

PAGE 264 *The money is with–drawn*: Bodleian Library, Ballads Catalogue: Firth c. 16(95) <bodley24.bodley.ox.ac.uk/cgi-bin/acwwweng/ballads>

Notes

PAGE 265 *For some time past*: John Douglas to Reverend Schofield, 20 March 1832, DL, MSQ 643.

PAGE 267 *Daniel O'Connell*: Mackaness, *Narrative of the Overland*, p. 43.

PAGE 267 *Unless the Governors*: Eddy, *Britain and the Australian Colonies*, pp. 58–9, 77–8.

PAGE 268 *Examine into the nature*: J. Franklin, *Narrative of Some Passages in the History of Van Diemen's Land, During the Last Three Years of Sir John Franklin's Administration of its Government*, Platypus, Hobart, 1967, p. 40.

PAGE 269 *Rhinoceros*: C. J. Binks, *Explorers of Western Tasmania*, Taswegia, Devonport, 1989, pp. 150–8.

PAGE 270 *Insipid in flavour*: Mackaness, *Narrative of the Overland*, pp. 42–3.

PAGE 270 *The imbicile [sic] reign*: *Van Diemen's Land Chronicle*, 24 January 1842.

PAGE 270 *From the mutilated*: As quoted in O. Beattie and J. Geiger, *Frozen in Time: Unlocking the Secrets of the Doomed 1845 Artic Expedition*, Plume, New York, 1990, p. 60.

PAGE 271 *No man can tell*: *Hobart Town Gazette*, 25 June 1824.

PAGE 271 *I hope and trust*: Reports and other papers by J. Backhouse and G.W. Walker, ML, B706.

Bibliography

Primary Sources

State Library of Tasmania

Settlement order book (Macquarie Harbour), commencing 22 October 1825, ending 10 July 1829, TL.Q_365.643

Archives Office of Tasmania

Alphabetical register of male convicts, CON 23
Assignment lists and associated papers, CON 13
Colonial Secretary's Office Correspondence Files 1824–36, CSO1
Conduct records of male convicts arriving in the assignment period, CON 31
Conduct records of male convicts arriving in the assignment period, supplementary volumes, CON 32
Description list of male convicts, CON 18
Draft and Duplicate Copies of Annual Official, Financial and Statistical Reports, AOT, CSO/50

Executive Council Minutes EC/4

Indents of male convicts, CON 14

J. Hobbs, Boat Voyage Round Tasmania in 1824, 28 March 1824, LCJ 1881/75.

James Kelly's account of the discovery of Macquarie Harbour, 28 December, 1815, LCJ 1881/75

Macquarie Harbour Letter Book, CSO 43

Macquarie Harbour Letter Book, CON 85/1

Miscellaneous Indents MM 33 Series

Outward despatches GO 33

Register of Births, Deaths and Marriages, RGD 34, 35, 36

Register of prisoners tried in criminal cases SC 41/1 and 41/2

Statistical Returns of Van Diemen's Land 1824–39 (Hobart, 1839)

Statistics of Tasmania 1804–1854 (Hobart, 1856)

Tasmanian Statutes 1826–1959 (Hobart, 1959)

State Record Office, New South Wales

Bound indents for transport vessels arriving in New South Wales

Colonial Secretary's Office correspondence files, vols x820, 2665, 6009, 6015, 6019, 6023, 6053, 6974

Muster rolls for transport vessels arriving in New South Wales

Mitchell Library

Alphabetical Return of Prisoners who have absconded from Macquarie Harbour, DL, B706

Annex and Journal of George Washington Walker, 6 June 1832, DL, B727

Chaplain's letter book, Macquarie Harbour, DL, B862

George Town Police Court Record Book 1820–1825, 27 October 1821, Spencer 165

Journal of George Washington Walker, DL, B727

Journal of the Rev. William Schofield, DL, A428

List of casualties at Macquarie Harbour, DL, Add 281

List of Prisoners Murdered at Macquarie Harbour, and Return of prisoners in George Town awaiting transportation to Macquarie Harbour, DL, Add 281

Memoranda by Convict Davis Servant to Mr Foster, Superintendent of Convicts, Norfolk Island—1843—Relating principally to Macquarie Harbour, DL, MS, Q168

Montagu to Spode, 23 March 1829, DL, Add 569

The Muster Master: A Chapter of Colonial History by an Old Van Diemonian (1874), AM 15 D/2

Reports and other papers relating to a visit to the Australian colonies and South Africa, 1832–1840 by J. Backhouse & G. W. Walker, DL, B706

Return of male and female prisoners and their respective sentences at Macquarie Harbour for the quarter ending 30th September 1825, DL, Add 568

Statements of Robert Collins and Thomas M'Guire, 15 June 1832, Mitchell, Tas Papers 35

Thomas Kent, Statement of his Escape from Macquarie Harbour, DL, MSQ 571

National Archive

Muster of convicts arriving in Van Diemen's Land in the period 1816–21, HO/10/43

Muster of convicts in Van Diemen's Land December 1823, HO/10/45

Muster of convicts in Van Diemen's Land December 1825, HO/10/46

Muster of convicts in Van Diemen's Land December 1830, HO/10/47

Muster of convicts in Van Diemen's Land December 1832, HO/10/48

Muster of convicts in Van Diemen's Land December 1833, HO/10/49

Muster of convicts in Van Diemen's Land December 1835, HO/10/50

Papers relating to Courts Martials (Army), WO/71 series

Papers relating to Courts Martials (Navy), Adm 1 series

Petitions for Mercy, HO 17/59

Quarterly muster of Convicts at Macquarie Harbour penal station 31 March 1829, CO 280/20

Register of Courts Martials, WO/92

Scottish Record Office

Precognitions for criminal trials AD14/20

Newspapers

The Colonial Times
The Colonist and Van Diemen's Land Commercial and Agricultural Advertiser
The Connaught Journal
Cornwall Chronicle
Glasgow Herald
Hobart Town Courier
Hobart Town Gazette
The Tasmanian
The Times

Printed sources

Amato, J. A., *On Foot: A History of Walking*, New York University Press, New York, 2004

Armstrong, J. C., 'The slaves, 1652–1795' in R. Elphinck and H. Giliomee, eds, *The Shaping of South African Society, 1652–1820*, Longman, London, 1979

Atkinson, A., 'The free-born Englishman transported: convict rights as a measure of eighteenth-century empire', *Past and Present*, vol. 144, 1994, pp. 109–10

——*The Europeans in Australia: A History, Vol 1*, Oxford University Press, Oxford, 1998

——*The Europeans in Australia: A History, Vol 2*, Oxford University Press, Oxford, 2004

Backhouse, J., *A Narrative of a Visit to the Australian Colonies*, Hamilton Adams, London, 1843

Bairstow, D., *A Million Pounds, A Million Acres: The Pioneer Settlement of the Australian Agricultural Company*, Damaris Bairstow, Cremorne, 2003

Batchen, G., *Forget Me Not: Photography and Remembrance*, Van Gogh Museum, Amsterdam, 2004

Beattie, O. and Geiger, J., *Frozen in Time: Unlocking the Secrets of the Doomed 1845 Arctic Expedition*, Plume, New York, 1990

Beatty, W., *Early Australia with Shame Remembered*, Cassell, London, 1962

Bent, A., *Tasmanian Almanack for the Year of Our Lord 1829*, Bent, Hobart Town, 1829

Binks, C. J., *Explorers of Western Tasmania*, Taswegia, Devonport, 1982

Blom, *To Have and to Hold: An Intimate History of Collectors and Collecting*, Penguin, London, 2002

Bowler, P. J., *Evolution: The History of an Idea*, University of California Press, Berkeley, 1989

Brand, I., *Escape from Port Arthur*, Jason, West Moonah, 1978

——*Penal Peninsula: Port Arthur and Its Outstations 1827–1898*, Regal, Launceston, 1978

——*Sarah Island: An Account of the Penal Settlements of Sarah Island, Tasmania, from 1822 to 1833 and 1846 to 1847*, Regal, Launceston, 1990

British Parliamentary Papers, *Report from the Select Committee on Transportation, Minutes of Evidence etc.*, 1837 (518) XIX

——*Report from the Select Committee on Transportation, Minutes of Evidence etc.*, 1837–1838 (669) XXII

Burroughs, P., 'Crime and punishment in the British Army, 1815–1870', *English Historical Review*, vol. 100, no. 396, 1985, pp. 545–71

Chapman, P and Jetson, T., *Historical Records of Australia, Resumed Series III, Vol. VII (1828)*, Australian Government, Canberra, 1997

——*Historical Records of Australia, Resumed Series III, Vol. VIII (1829)*, Melbourne University Press, Carlton, 2003

——*Historical Records of Australia, Resumed Series III, Vol. IX (1830)*, Melbourne University Press, Carlton, 2006

Chesterman, M., 'Criminal trial juries in Australia: from penal colonies to a federal democracy', *Law and Contemporary Problems*, vol. 62, no. 2, 1999, pp. 69–102

Clark, C. M. H., *Select Documents in Australian History 1788–1850*, vol. 1, Angus & Robertson, London, 1997

Clarke, L., 'Lost to all Humanity'?: suicide, religion and murder pacts in convict Van Diemen's Land, BA (hons) thesis, University of Tasmania, 2002

Clarke, M., *For the Term of his Natural Life*, Australian Print Group, Bellerive, 1988

Collins, P., *Hell's Gates: The Terrible Journey of Alexander Pearce, Van Diemen's Land Cannibal*, Hardie Grant, South Yarra, 2002

Connell, R. W. and Irving, T. H., *Class Structure in Australian History*, Longman, Melbourne, 1982

Connor, J., *The Australian Frontier Wars 1788–1838*, University of New South Wales Press, Sydney, 2002

Corbin, A., *The Foul and the Fragrant: Odour and the Social Imagination*, Papermac, London, 1996

Bibliography

Crais, C., *White Supremacy and Black Resistance in Pre-Industrial South Africa*, Cambridge University Press, Cambridge, 1992

Curr, E., *An Account of the Colony of Van Diemen's Land Principally Designed for the Use of Emigrants*, Platypus Publications, Hobart, 1967

Curtin, P., *Death by Migration: Europe's Encounter with the Tropical World in the Nineteenth Century*, Cambridge University Press, Cambridge, 1989

Davey R. I., ed., *The Travails of Jimmy Porter: A Memoir 1802–1842*, Round Earth Company, Strahan, 2003

Davis, R. P., *The Tasmanian Gallows: A Study of Capital Punishment*, Cat and Fiddle Press, Hobart, 1974

Derby, G., *William Buelow Gould*, Copperfield, Sydney, 1980

Dixon, J., *Narrative of a Voyage to New South Wales and Van Diemen's Land*, Melanie Publications, Hobart, 1984

Domar, E., 'The causes of slavery or serfdom: a hypothesis', *Journal of Economic History*, vol. 13, 1970, pp. 18–32

Duffield, I., 'The life and death of "Black" John Goff: aspects of the black convict contribution to resistance patterns during the transportation era in eastern Australia', *Australian Journal of Politics and History*, vol. 33, no. 1, 1987, pp. 30–44

——'Daylight on convict lived experience: the history of a pious negro servant', *Tasmanian Historical Studies*, vol. 6, no. 2, 1999, pp. 29–62

Duly, L. C., '"Hottentots to Hobart and Sydney": The Cape supreme court's use of transportation, 1828–38', *Australian Journal of Politics and History*, vol. 25, 1979, pp. 39–50

Druett, J., *Rough Medicine: Surgeons at Sea in the Age of Sail*, Routledge, New York, 2001

Dyster, B., 'Public employment and assignment to private masters, 1788–1821, in S. Nicholas ed., *Convict Workers: Reinterpreting Australia's Past*, Cambridge University Press, Cambridge, 1988, pp. 127–51.

Eddy, J. J., *Britain and the Australian Colonies 1818–1831: The Techniques of Government*, Oxford University Press, Clarendon, 1969

Ekirch, A. R., *Bound for America: The Transportation of British Convicts to the Colonies, 1718–1775*, Clarendon, Oxford, 1990

Emsley, C., *Crime and Society in England 1750–1900*, Longman, London, 1991

Evans, G. W., *A Geographical, Historical and Topographical Description of Van Diemen's Land with Important Hints to Emigrants*, London, 1822

Evans, R. and Thorpe, W., 'Commanding men: masculinities and the convict system', *Journal of Australian Studies*, vol. 56, 1998, pp. 17–34

Finlay, V., *Colour: Travels through the Paintbox*, Sceptre, London, 2002

Firth, F., *In Memorian: A Biographical Sketch of the Late Rev. William Schofield*, Sydney, 1878

Fitzsymonds, E., ed., *Mortmain*, Sullivan's Cove, Hobart, 1979

——*Brady: Van Diemen's Land 1824–1827*, Sullivan's Cove, Hobart, 1979

Flanagan, R., *Gould's Book of Fish: A Novel in 12 Fish*, Pan Macmillan, Sydney, 2001

Fleig, D., *The History of Fighting Dogs*, Neptune City, Neptune, 1996

Fletcher, B., *Landed Enterprise and Penal Society*, Sydney University Press, Sydney, 1976

Fletcher, I., *Badajoz 1812*, Osprey, Botley, 1999

Foucault, M., *Discipline and Punish: The Birth of the Prison*, Vintage, New York, 1995

——*The Order of Things: An Archaeology of the Human Sciences*, Routledge, London, 2002

Foulkes, N., *Scandalous Society: Passion and Celebrity in the Nineteenth Century*, Abacus, London, 2003

Gatrell, V. A. C., *The Hanging Tree: Execution and the English People, 1770–1868*, Oxford University Press, Clarendon, 1994

Goodwin, T., *A Descriptive Account of Van Diemen's Island*, London, 1821

Graves, D., ed., *Merry Hearts Make Light Days: The War of 1812 Journal of Lieutenant John Le Couteur, 164th Foot*, Robin Brass Studio, Toronto, 1993

Griffiths, T., *Hunters and Collectors: The Antiquarian Imagination in Australia*, Cambridge University Press, Cambridge, 1996

Grose, F., *The 1811 Dictionary of the Vulgar Tongue: Buckish Slang, University Wit and Pickpocket Eloquence*, Senate, London, 1994

Hay, D., 'Crime and justice in eighteenth- and nineteenth-century England', *Crime and Justice*, vol. 2, 1980, pp. 64–5

Haynes, R., 'From habitat to wilderness: Tasmania's role in the politicising of place' in D. Trigger and G. Griffiths, eds, *Disputed Territories: Land, Culture and Identity in Settler Societies*, Hong Kong University Press, Hong Kong, 2003, pp. 81–107

Higman, B. W., *Slave Populations of the British Caribbean 1807–1834*, University of the West Indies Press, Jamaica, 1995

Hirst, J., *Convict Society and Its Enemies*, Allen & Unwin, Sydney, 1993

Hirst, W., *Great Escapes by Convicts in Colonial Australia*, Kangaroo Press, Roseville, 1999

Hordern, M., *King of the Australian Coast: The Work of Phillip Parker King in the Mermaid and Bathurst 1817–1822*, Melbourne University Press, Carlton, 2002

Bibliography

Howard, M. R., 'Walcheren, 1809: A Medical Catastrophe', *British Medical Journal*, vol. 319, 1999, pp. 1642–5

Hudson, R., *Hudson's English History: A Compendium*, Weidenfeld & Nicolson, London, 2005

Hughes, R., *The Fatal Shore: A History of the Transportation of Convicts to Australia 1787–1868*, Pan Books, London, 1988

Jeffrey, C., *Geographical and Descriptive Delineations of the Island of Van Diemen's Land*, London, 1820

Johnson, J., *The Ghost Map*, Allen Lane, London, 2006

Johnston, A., 'The 'little empire of Wybalenna': becoming colonial in Australia, *Journal of Australian Studies*, vol. 81, 2004, pp. 17–31

Karskens, G., *The Rocks: Life in Early Sydney*, Melbourne University Press, Melbourne, 1997

Kercher, B., 'Perish or prosper: the law and convict transportation in the British Empire, 1700–1850', *Law and History Review*, vol. 21, no. 3, 2003, pp. 568–72

Kerr, G. and McDermott, H., *The Huon Pine Story: A History of Harvest and Use of a Unique Timber*, Mainsail, Portland, Victoria, 2000

Kingdom, W., *An Abstract of all the Most Useful Information Relative to the United States of America, and the British Colonies of Canada, The Cape of Good Hope, New South Wales, and Van Diemen's Land*, London, 1820

Laugesen, A., 'The politics of language in convict Australia, 1788–1850', *Journal of Australian Colonial History*, vol. 4, no. 1, 2002, pp. 17–40

——*Convict Words: Language in Early Colonial Australia*, Oxford University Press, Melbourne, 2002

Last, P.R., Scott, E. O. G. and Talbot, F. H., *Fishes of Tasmania*, Tasmanian Fisheries Development Board, Hobart, 1983

Linebaugh, P., *The London Hanged: Crime and Civil Society in the Eighteenth Century*, Verso, London, 2003

Lempriere, T. J., *Penal Settlements of Van Diemen's Land*, Royal Society of Tasmania, Launceston, 1954

Leslie, E., 'The ownership of a plank: David Harrison and the wreck of the *Peggy*' in J. S. Cummins, ed., *Cannibals: Shocking True Tales of the Last Taboo on Land and Sea*, Lyons, Guildford, 2001, pp. 45–55

Logan, W. B., *Oak: The Frame of Civilization*, Norton & Company, New York, 2005

Loone, M., 'Why Run? A Comparative Study of Convict Runaways in Van Diemen's Land 1833–34', BA (hons) thesis, University of Tasmania, 2004

MacDonald, H., *Human Remains: Episodes in Human Dissection*, Melbourne University Press, Carlton, 2005

MacFie, P. and Hargraves, N., 'The Empire's First Stolen Generation: The First Intake at Point Puer, 1834–39', *Tasmanian Historical Studies*, vol. 6, no. 2, 1999, pp. 129–54

MacFie, P., 'Government sawing establishments in Van Diemens Land, 1817–1832', *Australia's Ever Changing Forests*, vol. 5, 2002, pp. 105–31

McGillivery, A. R., 'Convict settlers, seaman's greens, and imperial designs at Port Jackson: a maritime perspective of British settler agriculture', *Agricultural History*, vol. 78, no. 3, 2004, pp. 261–88

Mackaness G. ed., *Narrative of Overland Journey by Sir John and Lady Franklin and Party from Hobart Town to Macquarie Harbour 1842 by David Burn*, Australian Historical Monographs, Sydney, 1955

McKay, A., 'The assignment system of convict labour in Van Diemen's Land, 1824–1842', M.A. Thesis, University of Tasmania, 1959

McLachlan, I., *Place of Punishment: Port Macquarie 1818–1832*, Hale & Iremonger, Sydney, 1988

Marsh, R., *Seven Years of My Life*, Buffalo, Faxon and Stevens, 1847

Maxwell-Stewart, H. and Duffield, I., 'Beyond Hell's Gates: religion at Macquarie Harbour penal station, *Tasmanian Historical Studies*, vol. 5, no. 2, 1997, pp. 83–99

——'Skin deep devotions: religious tattoos and convict transportation to Australia, *Written on the Body: The Tattoo In European and American History*, Reaktion, London, 2000, pp. 118–35

Maxwell-Stewart, H. and Hindmarsh, B., '"This is the Bird that Never Flew": William Stewart, Major Donald MacLeod and the *Launceston Advertiser*', *Journal of Australian Colonial History*, vol. 2, no. 1, 2000, pp. 1–28

Maxwell-Stewart, H., '"Penal Labour" and Sarah Island: life at Macquarie Harbour', in I. Duffield and J. Bradley, eds, *Representing Convicts: New Perspectives on Convict Forced Labour Migration*, Leicester University Press, London, 1997, pp. 142–62

——'The search for the invisible man' in L. Frost and H. Maxwell-Stewart, eds, *Chain Letters: Narrating Convict Lives*, Melbourne University Press, Carlton, 2001, pp. 49–63

——'Land of sorrow, land of honey: aspects of the life of Judah Solomon' in P. Elias and A. Elias, eds, *A Few from Afar: Jewish Lives in Tasmania from 1804*, Hobart Hebrew Congregation, Hobart, 2003, pp. 13–20

Bibliography

——'The Life and Death of James Thomas', *Tasmanian Historical Studies*, vol. 10, 2005, pp. 55–64

Maynard, M., *Fashioned from Penury: Dress as Cultural Practice in Colonial Australia*, Cambridge University Press, Cambridge, 1994

Melville, H., *Moby Dick*, Penguin, London, 1986

Miller, S., *Conversation: A History of a Declining Art*, Yale, New Haven, 2006

Morgan, S., *Land Settlement in Early Tasmania: Creating an Antipodean England*, Cambridge University Press, Cambridge, 1992

Nicholas, S., 'The Convict Labour Market', in S. Nicholas, ed., *Convict Workers: Reinterpreting Australia's Past*, Cambridge University Press, Cambridge, 1988, pp. 111–26

——'The Organisation of Public Work' in S. Nicholas, ed., *Convict Workers: Reinterpreting Australia's Past*, Cambridge University Press, Cambridge, 1988, pp. 152–66

Nicholls, M., ed., *The Diary of the Reverend Robert Knopwood, 1803–38*, Tasmanian Historical Research Association, Hobart, 1977

Oats, W., *Backhouse and Walker: A Quaker View of the Australian Colonies 1832–38*, Blubber Head Press, Hobart, 1981

O'Connor, T., 'Power and punishment: the limits of resistance at the Moreton Bay penal settlement, 1824–42, BA (hons) thesis, University of Queensland, 1994

——'Buckley's chance: freedom and hope at the penal settlements of Newcastle and Moreton Bay', *Tasmanian Historical Studies*, vol. 6, no. 2, 1999, pp. 115–28

Ó Gráda, C., *Ireland: A New Economic History 1780–1939*, Clarendon Press, Oxford, 1994

Philbrick, N., *In The Heart of the Sea: The Tragedy of the Whaleship Essex*, Viking, London, 2000

Pike, D., ed., *Australian Dictionary of Biography*, vols 1 and 2, Melbourne University Press, Carlton, 1966

Plomely, N. J. B., ed., *Friendly Mission—The Tasmanian Journals and Papers of George Augustus Robinson, 1829–34*, Tasmanian Historical Research Association, Hobart, 1966

Polidori, J., 'The Vampyre' in E. F. Bleiler, ed., *Three Gothic Novels*, Dover, New York, 1966, pp. 255–83

Porter, R., *Disease, Medicine and Society in England, 1550–1860*, Macmillan, Houndmills, 1987

——*Flesh in the Age of Reason*, Allen Lane, London, 2003

Pybus, C. and Maxwell-Stewart, H., *American Citizens, British Slaves: Yankee Political Prisoners in an Australian Penal Colony 1839–1850*, Melbourne University Press, Melbourne, 2002

Pybus, C., *Black Founders: The Unknown Story of Australia's First Black Settlers*, University of New South Wales Press, Sydney, 2006

Raboteau, A. J., *Slave Religion: The 'Invisible Institution' in the Antebellum South*, Oxford University Press, Oxford, 1976

Ratcliff, P., *The Usefulness of John West: Dissent and Difference in the Australian Colonies*, Albernian Press, Launceston, 2003

Rediker, M., *Between the Devil and the Deep Blue Sea*, Cambridge University Press, Cambridge, 1987

Reid, S., 'Purchase of position in the Napoleonic Wars', *Living History*, 2 November 1999, <http://www.livinghistory.co.uk/1800-1900/articles/xw_127.html>

Ritchie, J., *The Evidence to the Bigge Reports: New Wales Under Governor Macquarie, Vol 2*, Heinemann, Melbourne, 1971

Robbins, W. M., 'Spatial Escape and the Hyde Park Barracks', *Journal of Australian Colonial History*, vol. 7, 2005, pp. 81–96

Roberts, D., '"A sort of inland Norfolk Island'? Isolation, coercion and resistance on the Wellington Valley convict station, 1823–26', *Journal of Australian Colonial History*, vol. 2, no. 1, 2000, pp. 50–72

Rogers, N. A. M., *The Wooden World: An Anatomy of the Georgian Navy*, Fontana, Glasgow, 1990

Ross, J., *The Van Diemen's Land Anniversary and Hobart Town Almanack for the Year 1831*, James Ross, Hobart Town, 1831

——*The Hobart Town Almanack and Van Diemen's Land Annual for 1836*, Ross, Hobart Town, 1836

Ryan, L., *The Aboriginal Tasmanians*, Allen & Unwin, Sydney, 1996

Ryan, S., *The Cartographic Eye: How Explorers Saw Australia*, Cambridge University Press, Cambridge, 1996

Sargent, C., *The Colonial Garrison 1817–1824: The 48th Foot, the Northamptonshire Regiment in the colony of New South Wales*, TCS Publications, Canberra, 1996

Schaffer, I., 'The forgotten women convicts of Macquarie Harbour, 1821–1826', *Tasmanian Ancestry*, vol. 18, no. 2, 1997, pp. 94–8

Shakespeare, N., *In Tasmania*, Knopf, Sydney, 2004

Sharma, S., *Landscape and Memory*, Harper Perennial, London, 2004

Shaw, A. G. L., *Sir George Arthur Bart., 1784–1854: Superintendent of British Honduras, Lieutenant-Governor of Van Diemen's Land and of*

Bibliography

Upper Canada, Governor of the Bombay Presidency, Melbourne University Press, Carlton, 1980

Shayt, D. H., 'Stairway to redemption: America's encounter with the British prison treadmill', *Technology and Culture*, vol. 30, no. 4, 1989, pp. 908–38

Silver, L.R., *The Battle of Vinegar Hill: Australia's Irish Rebellion*, Watermark Press, Sydney, 2002

Simpson, A. W. B., *Cannibalism and the Common Law*, University of Chicago Press, Chicago, 1984

Solomon, R. J., *Urbanisation: The Evolution of An Australian Capital*, Angus & Robertson, Sydney, 1976

Sontag, S., *Regarding the Pain of Others*, Penguin, London, 2004

Sprod, D., *Alexander Pearce of Macquarie Harbour: Convict, Bushranger, Cannibal*, Cat and Fiddle Press, Hobart, 1977

Stanley, P., *For Fear of Pain: British Surgery 1790–1850*, Rodopi, Amsterdam, 2003

Sturgis, J., ed., *A Boy in the Peninsular War: The Services, Adventures and Experiences of Robert Blakeney*, John Murray, London, 1899

Sturma, M., *Vice in a Vicious Society: Crime and Convicts in Mid-Nineteenth Century New South Wales*, Queensland University Press, St Lucia, 1983

Tannahill, R., *Flesh and Blood: A History of the Cannibal Complex*, Abacus, London, 1996

Tardiff, P., *Notorious Strumpets and Dangerous Girls*, Angus & Robertson, Sydney, 1990

Thompson, E. P., *The Making of the English Working Class*, Penguin Books, Harmondsworth, 1981

Turnbull, P., '"Rare work amongst the Professors": the capture of indigenous skulls within phrenological knowledge in early colonial Australia' in B. Creed and J. Hoorn, eds, *Body Trade: Captivity, Cannibalism and Colonialism in the Pacific*, Routledge, New York, 2001, pp. 3–23

Watson, F., ed., *Historical Records of Australia*, Series I, vol. IX, Australian Government, Sydney, 1914–25

——*Historical Records of Australia*, Series III, vols II, IV, V, VI, Australian Government, Sydney, 1914–25

Wentworth, W. C., *A Statistical, Historical, and Political Description of the Colony of New South Wales, and its Dependent Settlements on Van Diemen's Land*, London, 1819

Wesley, C., *The Journal of Charles Wesley*, London, 1849

West, J., *The History of Tasmania*, Angus & Robertson, London, 1981

Western, J. R., 'Roman Catholics holding military commissions in 1798', *The English Historical Review*, vol. 70, no. 276, 1955, pp. 428–32

Windschuttle, K., *The Fabrication of Aboriginal History*, vol. 1, Macleay Press, Sydney, 2002

Websites

Bodleian Library, Ballads Catalogue: Firth c. 16(95), <http://bodley24. bodley.ox.ac.uk/cgi-bin/acwwweng/ballads>

Fawcett, J., ed., 'Unlawful Return From Transportation, 1843', 2002, <http://www.hotkey.net.au/~jwilliams4/d6.htm>

Maxwell-Stewart, H., ed., Memoranda by Convict Davis Servant to Mr Foster, Superintendent of Convicts, Norfolk Island, 1843—Relating principally to Macquarie Harbour, <http://iccs.arts.utas.edu.au/ narratives/davis1.html>

Petrow, S., and Kercher, B., eds, Decisions of the Nineteenth Century Tasmanian Superior Courts, Division of Law, Macquarie University, School of History and Classics, University of Tasmania, <http://www. law.mq.edu.au/sctas>

Preston, F., ed., 'Ian Brand's Macquarie Harbour Historical Research', Department of Primary Industry and Water, <http://dpiw.tas.gov.au/ library/Brand/Front%20page.html>

The Proceedings of the Old Bailey, London 1674 to 1834, <http://www. oldbaileyonline.org>

Index

Index